Defending the Ypres Front
1914–1918

Jan Vancoillie (born 1976) is a Belgian military historian. His interest in the First World War began developing when spending his childhood holidays with his grandparents, who farmed the ground where Polderhoek Château once stood. He studied modern history in Kortrijk and Leuven, with a MA thesis on Geluveld during the Great War. His specialty is the German Army of 1914–1918 and German military cemeteries. Jan works as an independent historian and battlefield guide.

Kristof Blieck (born 1976) is a teacher who has worked for over ten years as an educational officer at the Memorial Museum Passchendaele 1917. He is a passionate First World War enthusiast, with a particular interest in the daily life of the soldiers, on the Western Front in particular, during 1914–1918. He is heavily involved in living history projects and organizes First World War events in Belgium.

Defending the Ypres Front 1914–1918

Trenches, Shelters and Bunkers of the German Army

Jan Vancoillie and Kristof Blieck

Pen & Sword
MILITARY

First published in Great Britain in 2018 by
Pen & Sword Military
An imprint of
Pen & Sword Books Ltd
47 Church Street
Barnsley
South Yorkshire
S70 2AS

Copyright © Memorial Museum Passchendaele 1917, 2018

ISBN 978 1 52670 746 8

The right of Jan Vancoillie and Kristof Blieck to be identified as Authors of this
work has been asserted by them in accordance with the Copyright, Designs and
Patents Act 1988.

A CIP catalogue record for this book is
available from the British Library.

Typeset by Aura Technology and Software Services, India
Printed and bound in India by Replika Press Pvt. Ltd.

Pen & Sword Books Limited incorporates the imprints of Atlas, Archaeology,
Aviation, Discovery, Family History, Fiction, History, Maritime, Military,
Military Classics, Politics, Select, Transport, True Crime, Air World,
Frontline Publishing, Leo Cooper, Remember When, Seaforth Publishing,
The Praetorian Press, Wharncliffe Local History, Wharncliffe Transport,
Wharncliffe True Crime and White Owl.

For a complete list of Pen & Sword titles please contact
PEN & SWORD BOOKS LIMITED
47 Church Street, Barnsley, South Yorkshire, S70 2AS, England
E-mail: enquiries@pen-and-sword.co.uk
Website: www.pen-and-sword.co.uk

Contents

List of Maps   vii

Preface   ix

Foreword by the Authors   xi

Foreword by Nigel Cave, Editor of the English Edition   xiii

Introduction   The Origins of the Front Line in Flanders   xvi

Chapter 1   The Development of the Defences of the Ypres Front   1

Chapter 2   Defence by Concrete   59

Chapter 3   Who did the Building?   143

Chapter 4   Defence materials: Origin and Transportation.   207

Tours Section   239

Conclusion   277

Glossary of some German Terms   281

Bibliography   284

Index   290

To the landowners and farmers who have preserved vestiges of the Great War over the decades and made them accessible to the public; such physical reminders of this conflict make a most important contribution to the understanding of the war in Flanders to the battlefield visitor and enhance the memory of the men of 1914–1918.

List of Maps

1. Relief map of the Ypres area.   xviii–xix
2. Trench map (late 1916): German defence lines (in blue) east of Ypres.   17
3. Trench map (end 1916): German defence lines (in blue)
   northeast of Ypres and west of Zonnebeke.   20–1
4. Trench map (December 1916): German defence lines (in blue)
   between Wytschaete and the Ypres-Comines Canal.   22–3
5. Trench map showing the Flandern I Stellung in
   Divisional Sector Zonnebeke in June 1917.   120–1
6. Trench map showing the Flandern I Stellung in the
   Divisional Sectors Passendale and Langemark in June 1917.   122
7. An overview area map, covering the front from the North Sea
   to just south of Lille, showing different positions and switch
   lines as they existed or were planned in late June 1917.   127
8. Overview map, from the summer of 1917, of the positions and
   switches to the east and northeast of Ypres, extending from the front line
   to the Flandern III Stellung.   130–1
9. Trench map of the Flandern III Stellung (later renamed Flandern I Stellung),
   dated October–November 1917 in the Divisional Sectors Roeselare and Passendale. 134–5
10. Overview map showing all the important command posts of
    the Flandern I Stellung between Roeselare and Ledegem.   136
11. Overview map of the finished and planned positions and switches as they
    stood in July 1917, showing the planned Flandern IV Stellung and
    Flandern V Stellung.   138
12. An overview map of the (new) Flandern II Stellung near
    Ardooie (the location of a Pionier Park), north east of Roeselare,
    indicating the sites of the planned bunkers.   141
13. A company sketch map showing locations of deep dugouts between
    Westrozebeke and Passendale, late August 1917.   149
14. Overview map of an area north of Ledegem, from late 1917,
    showing the bunkers under construction by 3rd Landwehr Pionier
    Kompagnie des XIII Armeekorps.   154–5

15. Sector Zwarteleen (note Hill 60 on the left edge of the map),
occupied by Infanterie Regiment 126 from 23 November to 21 December 1914.   160

16. Sector Groenenburg (Shrewsbury Forest to the British), as occupied by
Infanterie Regiment 126 from 26 December 1914 to 20 February 1915.   162

17. Sector Doppelhöhe 60 (Mount Sorrel), as occupied by Infanterie Regiment
126 from 4 May to 24 June 1915.   166

18. A map of Sector Hooge, as occupied by Infanterie Regiment 126 from
26 September to 28 December 1915.   169

19. A map of Infanterie Regiment 163's sector (17th Reserve Division)
during the winter of 1916-1917.   176

20. Sector Wieltje, as occupied by Infanterie Regiment 161
(185th Infanterie Division) in early 1917.   181

21. Sketch map of the hutted camp near Vijfwegen built by
2nd Kompagnie Armierungs Bataillon 131.   191

Tour Mapping

22. Outline location map of Tour Stops.   239

23. Trench map showing the Bois de Wytschaete area
(28 SW2 Edition 5A 1 April 1917). The location of Dietrich is
indicated by a blue star.   241

24. Pedestrian access route to Mineshaft Dietrich.   241

25. Trench map extract showing the Bayernwald/Bois Quarante area.   245

26. Location map of Bayernwald trenches and bunkers.   245

27. Trench map showing the Zandvoorde Command Post.   249

28. A trench map extract showing the Cryer Farm Bunker.   251

29. A trench map extract showing the area now occupied by the
Tyne Cot Cemetery and Memorial.   258

30. Regimental Sector of Reserve Infanterie Regiment 28
(185th Infanterie Division) in early 1917.   262

31. Trench map extract showing the location of Kaserne Herzog Albrecht 2.   263

32. Trench map extract showing the Broenbeek area in August 1917.   265

33. A modern map of the area of the gun turret emplacement south of
Houthulst Forest.   267

34. A modern map of the area north of Ledegem, showing the locations of
the bunkers of the Flandern I Stellung.   270

Maps 22, 24, 26, 33 and 34 © OpenStreetMap contributors.

Preface

After the Second Battle of Ypres came to a close in May 1915, the front line in the Salient had moved ever closer to Ypres. Zonnebeke and Passendale were now in the German rear area. The following period of two years is a relatively 'quiet' period on the Flanders Front. The phrase 'All Quiet on the Ypres Front' (like the novel by Erich Maria Remarque), captures basically the war year of 1916 in the Salient (with the notable exception of the first weeks of June). German army reports hardly mention worrying developments here as the great offensives took place in France (around Verdun and on the Somme). Because of territorial gains in 1915 as a consequence of the Second Battle of Ypres and the relative peace at the front, the German soldiers of the Sanitäts Kompagnien (stretcher bearer companies) could gather in the dead who had been left between the lines of late 1914 and early 1915, and bury them in concentration cemeteries. For example, two new German cemeteries were created at the cross roads of Broodseinde (Zonnebeke). Many solitary field graves, which were difficult to maintain and threatened to be lost, were exhumed and the remains taken to concentration cemeteries.

Although offensive military operations during 1916 in Flanders were limited, the area around Zonnebeke was buzzing with building activity. The Germans started developing in late 1916, based on the lessons learnt at Verdun and the Somme, a complete defence network in depth. Offensive thoughts were replaced by the need to consolidate captured ground. Special Pioniere, or military engineers, were given the responsibility for constructing multiple and consecutive defence lines. Seemingly countless rows of barbed wire, machine gun posts and concrete bunkers followed the topographical contours and connected tactically important features on the landscape. Four defensive positions were developed between the front line and Passendale. The Albrecht Stellung and Wilhelm Stellung were massively expanded into a network of trenches and dugouts, the two Flandern-Stellungen being more bunker lines. Deceiving the enemy played an important role; for example fake trenches were used to deceive aerial observers. Riegel, or smaller connecting lines (switch lines), acted as fortified connections between the major defence lines. The newly adopted concept of elastic defence, combined with these lines, assured the Germans that during an allied offensive they would be able to fall back on yet another defence line; one from which a counter attack could be launched. These developments played a crucial role during the Third Battle of Ypres in 1917.

These defence lines included numerous buildings and shelters. Whilst the Allies believed more in dugouts of varying depth (to a great extent because they regarded their positions as temporary and operated on the understanding that they would always be seeking to recover capture territory lost to the invader), the Germans put their main effort into reinforced concrete bunkers. Wherever possible, ferro–concrete constructions were built inside existing and relatively undamaged housing. To deceive allied aircraft, the roofs of the houses were repaired; or free standing bunkers were disguised as houses by painting windows and doors and were topped off with imitation gabled roofs, complete with wattle-work. The Germans used concrete blocks to build bunkers from 1915 but from 1916 most bunkers were built as monoliths, with poured concrete and iron rebar cages. Close to the front line, however, pouring concrete was not an option and concrete blocks continued to be used.

Today many of these relics are still visible in our landscape and the ones in Zonnebeke can be visited and explained by using a visitor's guide produced by the Memorial Museum Passchendaele 1917.

Logistics - the supply of men and materiel - were an important factor in the construction of defence lines and fortifications. The most important building materials, such as timber, iron, cement and sandbags, had to be shipped in from many places to satisfy the needs of the Salient. For example, the fence around the chateau park in Zonnebeke was pulled down to be reused elsewhere. Oak beams and blocks of ashlar were valuable and were recycled for fortifications. Most of the building material was brought in via a complex network of railroads of different gauges. The pre-war tramline from Ypres to Menen, for example, played a crucial role. During the night the heavily loaded tram thundered along with its valuable cargo up to the Pionier Park at Veldhoek. Pionier Parks, of which many could be found in the Zonnebeke area, were dumps or storage areas where the building material was gathered; in this case mainly transported to them from Roeselare or Menen. From the Pionier Park it was taken to the trenches using small roads, narrow-gauge tracks, mules – and a lot of manpower.

Apart from supplies, labour was an essential factor in building the front line. The German army had special units at its disposal for such work: Armierungstruppen, unarmed conscripts, unfit for armed service in the front line. Basically they were military workers, lacking a military training and were used for all kinds of jobs and tasks. Belgian forced labourers, or Zivilarbeiter, were also deployed as part of the German workforce. Over 100,000 Belgians endured this fate and had to perform heavy labour in Germany's service. The Zivilarbeiter from the Operationsgebiet (the zone of the field army, which extended up to twenty-five kilometres behind the front line) were used exclusively within this zone to help to build the German defences. In this way the traffic of people from and to the Operationsgebiet would be limited, essential for military secrecy and to avoid espionage.

Billets were available for the German soldiers in Passendale (which remained relatively intact until the summer of 1917), Dadizele and Moorslede. There they could find entertainment and rest from the many tiresome tasks they were called to do. Along with popular cinemas, there was the possibility of a swim and there were plenty of pubs for the NCOs and an officers' mess. The many soldiers who worked around Zonnebeke and Passendale also needed a place to sleep. Several hutted camps arose, usually close by farms or hidden away in small areas of woods. The camps had electricity and shops, offices and sick bays.

Building the front line was a hard and prolonged assignment. The Germans eventually planned no less than six defence lines. When the (largely) British offensive was unleashed in mid 1917, the positions were not yet finished, especially the rear most ones. Yet the Allies got bogged down by the German defences. After the Third Battle of Ypres, the British appreciated the importance of defence in depth when contemplating the inevitability of a German offensive in the spring of 1918. They started to build a similar defence scheme themselves. Effective consolidation of captured ground became an important factor in warfare.

This study is the result of intensive research done by Jan Vancoillie and Kristof Blieck, exploring a largely underexposed subject in the literature of the First World War. We hope that this publication will lead to a better understanding of the how and the why of battle zone construction and how it related to the conduct of the war and how it was fought.

Steven Vandenbussche
Director
Memorial Museum Passchendaele 1917

Foreword by the Authors

The concrete bunkers along the former front line of the First World War might seem to many passers-by to bear a passing similarity to the Moai, the statues of Easter Island, the pyramids in Egypt or the Chinese Wall. They are somewhat mysterious, silent witnesses of a bygone and especially turbulent age. The grey concrete monoliths seem to have been built as monuments for eternity; monuments that remind us of a time when the whole area was blasted to pieces. But what is in fact the real story behind these constructions? Many publications have been written in the past about these buildings, albeit mainly with an eye to the tourist.

When the Memorial Museum Passchendaele 1917 decided to start an in-depth historical study of these bunkers some years ago, we had no idea at first about the number of such constructions that had been built. However, we soon came to realise that in the combined commune of Zonnebeke alone hundreds of concrete bunkers must have been built during the war years. A comprehensive inventory of all bunkers within its boundaries, even for Zonnebeke alone, would be just impossible to make.

The German strategy of elastic defence, fully embraced by the field army by early 1917, relied not only on these bunkers, but on a complex combination of barbed wire entanglements, trenches, supply lines, rest camps and more. This book tries for the first time to present an image of the immense building frenzy on the German side of the front line. It is not an encyclopaedic enumeration of constructions and units, but more a general overview of them, explained and illustrated regularly by specific examples.

We hope that this study may be a starting point for further detailed studies and act as a kind of manual for historians and others looking for specific bunker types or who are researching the evolution of construction in a defined geographical area. The possibilities for further research are almost endless, only limited by the sometimes difficult archival situation. As is known, a very substantial proportion of Germany's Great War military archives were lost because of allied aerial raids on Germany during the Second World War or because of drives for paper in the years of wartime scarcity. Yet we managed to find dozens of sources for this study, which are sometimes surprisingly interesting and detailed. The book is not exclusively based on German archival sources, but includes an extensive literature research and field research on the ground.

Our attention in this publication is limited geographically to the front zone of the German Fourth Army between the rivers Lys and Douve in the south and Diksmuide in the north, which can loosely be regarded as the Ypres Salient, though strictly speaking it ran in an easterly arc from St Eloi in the south through to Bixschoote in the north. The flooded area at the Yser front, the North Sea coast and the border area of Belgium and the Netherlands are each of them very specific 'front zones' with their own typical constructions.

We also want to launch a call, through this book, for a thorough evaluation of the remaining cultural property from the First World War and to prepare a programme for a comprehensive system of protection and preservation of such structures. Unfortunately, many unique constructions have been demolished in the recent past and with the rubble of the structures the story of these buildings disappears as well. These demolitions continue to this day. Even though the Great War heritage of the area is fairly well inventoried, it is time to protect and schedule certain exemplar construction types, particularly the last remaining complexes of bunkers and associated works.

Jan Vancoillie
Kristof Blieck

Foreword by Nigel Cave, Editor of the English Edition

It is now almost fifty years since my first trip to the Western Front – a long weekend with my father, travelling from BAOR in Germany, where he was posted. I was the same age (fourteen) as he was when my grandfather, who served for over three years on the Western Front during the Great War, took him to visit the battlefields in 1937. To help us find our way around we were equipped with an excellent, multi-lingual guide book, *Ieper en de frontstreek*, complete with a very handy map that thoughtfully included the location of several remaining bunkers. Apart from the delights of finding caltrops, good chunks of rum jars, bits of German equipment and shrapnel balls, there were also opportunities to explore several of these bunkers. Even then I vaguely wondered how it was possible to build these impressive constructions when the lines were so close together. This book provides some long awaited answers, to which I shall return in due course.

I first became aware *of Bouwen aan het front: loopgraven, schuilplaatsen en betonbunkers van het Duitse leger aan het Ieperfront 1914-1918* in the spring of 2016, soon after it was published by the Memorial Museum Passchendaele in Zonnebeke. A quick look through it suggested that it might well have the answer to my question of almost fifty years earlier, which had continued to niggle away at the back of my mind ever since. But there was obviously far more in the book than merely the matter of bunker construction in close proximity to the enemy.

The first impression was that the photographs and mapping in it are outstandingly good. I did not need more than the haziest knowledge of Dutch to appreciate straight away how valuable an addition it would be to the literature of the Great War related to the Ypres Salient: and that it would, indeed, provide the answer to my long standing question. However, it does far more than that. What is described is the evolution of the defensive system that the Germans put in place in Flanders, with the focus very much on the Ypres Salient. The authors provide an account of the development of simple trenches that were all that were available when the front solidified after the desperate fighting that characterised the First Battle of Ypres in the dying week of 1914, through to the complex bunker lines at the peak of sophisticated trench systems in 1917 and on to the 'open' battlefield that characterised the war, essentially of manoeuvre, in 1918.

The problem was that it was in Dutch; fortunately the authors both have an excellent command of English and thus it was that Jan Vancoillie (mainly) and Kristof Blieck took on the task of translating the book. The result is this English edition, with a number of additions in the main body of the text and, we hope, a useful tour section to enable the visitor to the Salient to see some of the variety of concrete defensive works that the Germans built there.

This study is, in itself, an interesting way of examining the war on the ground. The book traces the organic nature of defensive operations in the war through the prism of field defences and fortifications. In reality this can best be done by looking at the German army for, with some notable exceptions, it was broadly on the defensive on the Western Front for most of the war; whilst the allies were determined to break through. It follows, therefore, that the Germans had to develop their approach to holding their line to take into account the rapid evolution of weaponry, techniques and expertise that were available to those who took up offensive operations. By following how they dealt with the developing threat it becomes ever more clear that the conduct of war in the field in the West was transformed almost beyond recognition in the four years of the conflict.

The Flanders front in Belgium provided unusual problems for the combatants. In previous wars Flanders had been an area in which to manoeuvre and rarely one for lengthy operations, apart from sieges. In 1914 it was equipped with good infrastructure for the period, notably in the matter of railway lines – particularly so on the German side of the wire. However, because of the low lying nature of the ground and its proximity, therefore, to the water table and the fact that blue clay dominated much of the sub surface ground, there were considerable problems when it came to developing semi-permanent field fortifications. This blue clay is a marine geological formation that is known as Ypresian (which name is the first clue to its dominance in the area of the Salient), in Britain commonly known as London Clay. Amongst its other properties is that it is virtually impermeable – yet on the other hand it shrinks considerably during prolonged dry periods. Put these two factors together and there is a ready explanation for much of the misery endured by the troops in the trenches over and above enemy action.

Although, certainly, the area of the Salient is low lying, there are locally significant rises, a series of low ridges, each one somewhat higher than the other, forming a semi-circle to the north, east and south of Ypres. This explains, for example, the significance of the Gheluvelt Plateau to both sides; from here there were excellent views over the Allied positions to the west and south, in particular; whilst at its eastern end there were equally good vantage points overlooking the rear of the German position.

The country provided a mixture of large villages and hamlets, isolated farmhouses, numerous hedgerows and (perhaps surprisingly) a substantial number of chateaux, whose occupants made good use of the extensive woodland that would become a common part of the accounts of the fighting in the Salient. Between them they could easily be adapted and developed to suit the needs of the defenders, providing concealment, cellars for shelters, potential accommodation and so on.

All of these features combined to determine the nature of the defences that the Germans put in place. From an Anglocentric perspective, to many the Salient always appears to have been an active battle zone – from First Ypres in 1914, through to Second Ypres in April-May 1915, the German limited offensive of June 1916 at Mont Sorrel and then, in quick succession, Messines and Third Ypres in the summer and autumn of 1917. The reality, of course, was that, with the exception of the German offensive of spring 1915, until the summer of 1917 Ypres was a 'busy' sector but there were other parts of the Western Front where the French were operating, such as Artois, Champagne and the Argonne, which were often more active. However, the nature of the line and the conditions, where British troops could often be fired on from three sides, meant that it held a horror for them unsurpassed by other parts of the line, even in 'quiet' periods.

Although it had been established by the German High Command very early on that the Flanders sector would not involve major attacks (Second Ypres was something of an aberration and it is not completely clear what the strategic objective of the attack was meant to be), they had to contend with the fact that it would be a natural focus of British strategic planning. This meant a sophisticated defensive system and one that could adapt to the development and expansion of offensive weaponry, most notably the weight and accuracy of the enemy's artillery.

It soon became evident that trenches – even lines of trenches and the development of second and third lines behind the first line system, needed to be bolstered by shell-proof shelters. The Flanders front witnessed a building frenzy of concrete shelters, which went through repeated design changes to cope with the weight of shells that might fall on them and an evolution in their function. In the end, even these mighty constructions proved to be inadequate and, with the return to a war of manoeuvre, dominated by the deployment of mass artillery increasingly well directed, field fortifications very often regressed almost to where they had been at the beginning of the war, with quickly erected sheets of iron providing shelter for the defenders, who tended to operate from shell holes and any available natural cover rather than from carefully established trench systems.

The book has (excuse the pun) been carefully constructed. It seeks to look not only at the what and the where of defensive lines and field works but also the who, the logistics and the operational reasons behind these systems. It does this by looking at four key components, taking each through the war time period: how (and why) the defences were developed; the 'bunker' phase, which dominated later 1915 to the end of 1917; who was responsible for all of this building, how the construction was carried out and by whom; and where the huge volumes of building material came from and how the operation was organised, a monumental logistical task.

By a skilful use of a mixture of contemporary reports, regimental histories and personal anecdotes, the authors provide a fascinating account of how the Germans managed this extraordinary feat of defending the Salient, maximizing the use of all the means available to them and successfully fending off the British (and to some extent the French) attempts to breach the line, never greater than during the Battle of Third Ypres. In the end, the system crumbled unexpectedly quickly; the nature of the war by late 1917 meant that rigid – or even elastic – defence lines were no longer a match for the tilt of the scales that had put the advantage with a well coordinated offensive; the shift had been very slow, lasting over three years, from the establishment of the line in November 1914 until, by the end of Third Ypres and with the dramatic (albeit short lived) success of the artillery and massed tanks at Cambrai, it had become clear that a passive conduct of the war was no longer a viable option.

It seems to be a national trait of the British in sport to decry the efforts of their own teams in defeat, placing all the blame for the outcome on the inadequacies of their players and management; much less common is an acceptance as a key factor in that defeat of how very good the opposition might be. Anyone who reads this book will be better informed as to the scale of the problems facing the British when they attempted to break the German lines; and of renewed respect for the German soldiers who designed their defences and then had the military capability to hold them. In the end, however, no matter how sophisticated the defence, lacking manpower and faced by the full weight of a well planned and directed, all arms assault, spearheaded by numbers and weights of guns, fed by huge quantities of ammunition – quite unimaginable in 1914, it simply disintegrated.

This is the story of the fortifications that defended the German Ypres Salient.

Nigel Cave
Ratcliffe College, Christmas 2017

The Origins of the Front Line in Flanders

It is very important to appreciate the human, geographical, geological and topographical reasons for where the front line was formed, where trenches and hut camps were built or why concrete bunkers were constructed instead of deep (or, as they were often termed in the latter years of the war, mined) dugouts.

Topography and Geology

Even in antiquity the landscape played a large role in the construction of military buildings. Sites like Mounts Kemmel and Cassel are classic examples of military settlements. Height provided dominance over the surroundings. Whoever occupied the high ground had dry ground, could see greater distances and had a greater range for their artillery (as projectiles have a longer falling curve). Moreover, any attacker had to deliver physically more effort during an uphill attack. Height was one of the more important considerations in warfare.

This was even more pronounced in what soon came to be known as the Ypres Salient (for the British, the front had many salients, but there was only one Salient), where the Germans managed to occupy the ridges around the north, east and south of the city by the spring of 1915. They established themselves on the higher ground and prepared defensive works; it needs to be kept in mind that the Germans, with a few exceptions – one of which was the Second Battle of Ypres – adopted a defensive posture on the Western Front in 1915. The German positions were more or less in the form of a mirrored or reversed 'S', following the ridges. Even though the differences in altitude were quite small (not more than a few dozen metres), they were sufficient to be determinative. When building their defence lines, the German tried to make optimum use of these differences in altitude. In the beginning, defence lines were built as high as possible on the forward slope (the so-called 'forward military crest'). Later on, the main defences were built just over the crest, on the reverse slope (the so-called 'reverse military crest'), to give themselves protection against observation and enemy artillery fire.

In the northern part of the Ypres Salient, the Germans built their front line on Pilckem Ridge. This barely visible ridge offered protection to their hinterland (or rear areas) up to the so-called Midden-West-Vlaamse Heuvelrug (the 'Central West Flemish Ridge') against direct observation by the French and British. The German artillery had their observation posts on this higher ridge and thus had the situation at the front line perfectly under control.

In the central part of the Ypres Salient, the Germans controlled the Gheluvelt Plateau, a ridge to the west of Geluveld running up to Hooge, with Zandberg (Clapham Junction) as the highest point, along with the Tower Hamlets Spur. Together with Houthulst Forest, Gheluvelt Plateau was of the utmost importance to the German position during the Third Battle of Ypres, fought in the summer and autumn of 1917. If the Germans lost this ridge they would be deprived of good observation, whilst their complete rear area towards Menen would be open and exposed, in turn, to British observation. The Germans built their defence system here with considerable thought and extremely well, constructing three strongly fortified lines and the Gheluvelt Riegel (switch line) to protect the area from a direct attack from the west or from a flanking attack from the south.

Further to the south, in the Wytschaete Salient, the Germans also occupied high ground that gave them the ability to observe the British rear areas. However, the Wytschaete Salient was not as favourable as it would seem at first sight. The British also had some excellent observation possibilities at their disposal on Mount Kemmel and Hill 63 (Le Rossignol, to the north west of Ploegsteert Wood), from which they could look over the German front line and the rear area that slowly descended from Messines Ridge down to the River Lys. The potential for the Germans to construct strong defence lines in the Wytschaete Salient was limited and, in particular, locations for good observation posts for their artillery were rare.

The problems of underground working and groundwater cannot be underestimated in Flanders. Just below the soil (a layer only about one metre thick) is a layer of sandy loam, with underneath that a layer of clay. The sandy loam has a limited permeability, but the thick layer of blue clay (called locally Ypresian Clay) is a hard layer of compressed clay, usually over a hundred metres thick and through which hardly any water can penetrate. This combination of layers has made the area very fertile, but also very marshy. Draining this wet ground for agricultural purposes started in the High Middle Ages, accomplished by digging ditches and canals; but it was only from the middle of the nineteenth century that drainage was carried out efficiently by the use of earthwork tubes (ie field drainage). This network of tubes and ditches was destroyed during the First World War. Heavy shelling destroyed by far the greater part of this infrastructure and thus the efficient draining of water, both groundwater and rainwater, from the area. Therefore, as soon as the first shelters and trenches were dug in late 1914, water gathered in them. Consequently, trenches were often out of necessity built only partially below ground level and mainly above ground level – in effect they were breastworks. The fact that surface concrete bunkers were favoured in the area instead of deep (or mined) dugouts was mainly determined by the geology of underground Flanders. The British, when it came to the tunnelling war, were perhaps quicker to grasp the possibilities of mining practices that suited these conditions – Colonel Norton-Griffiths recruited the first members of British tunnelling companies from men engaged in underground workings (for sewers, mainly) in similar geological conditions under London and Manchester.

The many ditches and small streams cutting through the Flemish landscape that divert the water to the Yser or Lys drainage basin, formed barriers that were easily adapted to military purposes, providing ready constructed – if rather wet and muddy – trenches. When developing defence lines in the rear areas, the Germans used the shallow valleys to improve their defensive capabilities. Because of the destruction of the drainage system and the waterways during the Third Battle of Ypres, small streams were swollen into wide, seemingly impassable, swamps. Behind these streams the Germans build their barbed wire entanglements to protect the defence line on higher ground. The attacker had not only to battle uphill – even if it was only a slight rise – but also had to cross wide, marshy valleys and then find a way through a labyrinth of barbed wire before eventually reaching the German trenches. This was an almost impossible task. The most dramatic evidence of the efficiency of all this can be seen in the New Zealand Division's attack of 12 October 1917, launched across the Ravebeek Valley in the direction of Bellevue Spur near Passendale. In only a few hours some 850 New Zealanders were killed.

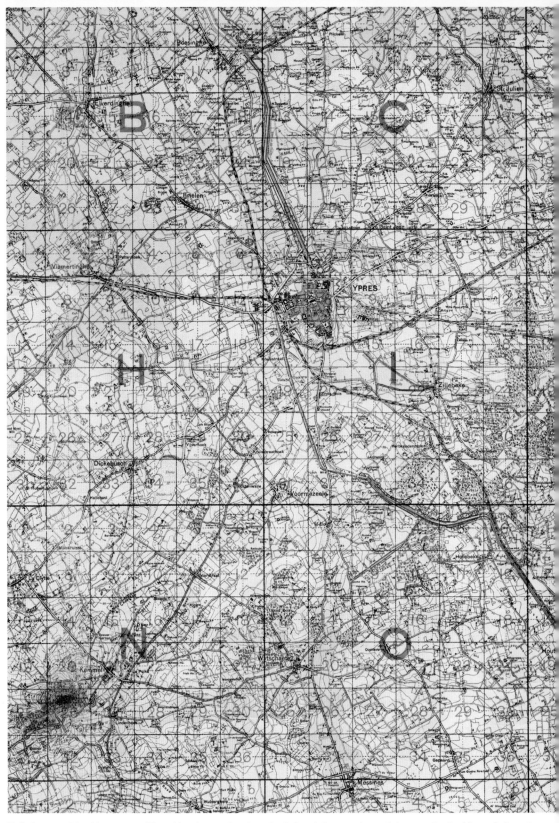

Relief map of the Ypres area. The ridged area that largely defined the conduct of the war in the Ypres Salient is clearly highlighted, running south from Passendale via Geluveld to Wijtschate and then splitting, west to Kemmel and south to Messines.

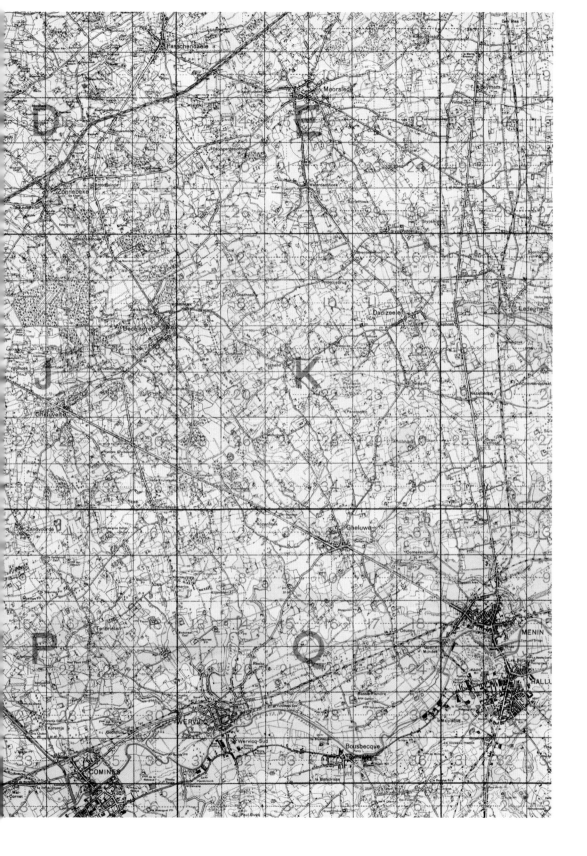

Groundwater and the sub-soil layers played an essential role in the construction phase of all types of buildings. Geologists first investigated every location where a concrete bunker was planned from late 1916 onwards to determine whether a construction would be hampered by groundwater (and if so, to what extent) and to make sure that the sub-soil could actually carry the heavy concrete construction.

Vegetation, human habitation and traffic infrastructure.

Landscape considerations were – and, indeed, are – very important when choosing the location of trenches and military constructions. The Flemish landscape in 1914 was divided into small areas by countless hedges, hedgerows and tree lines, forming a type of *bocage*. Modern agricultural methods, with its concentration on large fields, the reduction in the size of some woods (for example and most notably, Houthulst Forest) and the disappearance altogether of some of the small copses and woods are economic and topographical aspects which are all too often forgotten nowadays: the landscape is very different today from that facing the soldiers of 1914.

German soldiers working in a trench. Note the water pump in the centre. Maintaining trenches was a constant battle against water, requiring increasingly sophisticated methods to deal with the problems it caused. (*Vancoillie*)

The German mass attacks in October and November 1914 stalled in this closed landscape, ideally suited for a robust defence. Practically as soon as the war bogged down into trench warfare, trenches and military structures were often constructed close by or along these linear landscape structures. The hedges largely hid the immediate area from ground observation and even to some extent from accurate aerial observation. For the same reason, the edges of woods were considered suitable places along which to dig in, for instance along the edge of Polygon Wood and Bayernwald (Bois Quarante). The trees offered cover for both defensive and offensive purposes. Troops could be assembled more or less out of sight inside extensive woodland in the immediate lead up to an attack – in the autumn of 1914 there is the example of the Worcesters in Polygon Wood just prior to their counter-attack towards Geluveld; whilst Sanctuary Wood became a holding area for stragglers before they were redeployed.

While Houthulst Forest was left in October 1914 to the Germans without any opposition, the woods to the east and south of Ypres were scenes of heavy fighting. Woods offered excellent defensive possibilities. Attackers had a very difficult time trying to keep an effective degree of control when attacking into or through woodland – and, even worse, extensive woodland, something which was made apparent time and again in October and

An oblique aerial picture of Beselare (c.1915-1916) showing the village centre looking towards the northwest. Most of the darker areas were woodlands and forests, many of which were not replanted after the war. Clearly visible are numerous hedges (very few of which remain) and lines of trees bordering the meadows and plots of farmland. (*Vancoillie*)

November 1914. A German assault into Polygon Wood in October 1914 led to an almost certain death or imprisonment for those who got into it; whilst the German attacks around Wijtschate were seriously hampered by the many woods in the immediate area. Even the renowned Prussian Guard was halted and then routed by resolute opposition in Glencorse Wood and neighbouring Nonne Bosschen; units were very disoriented when attacking through woods – and some of these were (and still are) of a substantial extent. The front line stabilised in November 1914 in large part along the edges of these larger woods – examples such as Polygon Wood, Glencorse Wood, Inverness Copse, Herenthage Forest and Shrewsbury Forest all spring to mind.

The many smaller isolated woods and copses in the Salient were very soon used to shelter troops. In many of the forests and larger woods, rest camps were built to accommodate reserves.

The advantages (or disadvantages, depending on your perspective) of such a landscape was supplemented by the nature of human settlements in the area. The Salient had a number of small villages, hamlets in reality, often associated with a major chateau – such as those of Hooge or Polderhoek; there were also plenty of isolated farm complexes. They provided the basis for establishing numerous strong points. The many small farms and rural dwellings were fortified with ferro-concrete in 1916 and 1917 and offered excellent resistance points for the Germans during the Third Battle of Ypres. The number of scattered hamlets allowed both sides to billet their troops in the early days of the war without having to worry overmuch about providing temporary housing in the form of tents or huts. Only after the battle zone suffered more and more destruction by shelling did the need to build tent or hut encampments increase. In the Salient and nearby areas the German army in particular benefited from existing satisfactory infrastructure further from the front – but close enough to it – to house troops and store supplies. Only in 1917 did it become necessary to build larger camps further from the front.

The importance of Houthulst Forest to the Germans during the Third Battle of Ypres cannot be emphasised enough. The German Fourth Army underscored its importance in an Army Order issued after the first days of fighting in late July and early August 1917:

Der Besitz des Houthulster Forstes ist für den Feind bei der Fortführung seiner Angriffe von ausschlaggebender Bedeutung, für uns aber unbedingt nötig zur Aufstellung der sonst in dem offenen Gelände nur schwer Deckung findenden Artillerie. Es ist deshalb erforderlich, den Ausbau des Houthulster Forstes auf Grund einer jetzt schon aufzustellenden Organisation der Verteidigung und unter Ausnutzung der in dem Forste vorhandenen artilleristischen Anlagen für die spätere infanteristische Verteidigung einheitlich zu regeln.

[The possession of Houthulst Forest for the continuation of the enemy's attacks is of the utmost importance; for us its possession is imperative for the deployment of our artillery, which can otherwise find no shelter in the open landscape. It is therefore necessary to arrange homogeneously the fortification of Houthulst Forest on the basis of a defence organisation which should be laid out now and with preparations made for the use of the artillery positions already present in the woods for a later defence by the infantry.]

Consequently, several trench lines were built in front of the forest, whilst inside it everything was put in place for its defence.

Logistical, including transportation, infrastructure is a further factor which has a determining influence on the location of fortifications. Major roads, cross roads, railroads or waterways often play a crucial role in warfare. For the Germans, the Menin Road is an example of such an important vital supply line, along with the railroads running from Roeselare to Ypres or from Menen to Roeselare. In a part of the country where most roads were only dirt roads for farm vehicles (and those horse powered and not particularly heavy), the availability of adequate transport infrastructure was essential to be able to conduct war on an industrial scale. These roads had to transport huge numbers of men and quantities of materiel to the front line; rail links provided flexibility as well as transport of materiel. They were both necessary to conduct large offensives or to maintain one's defences properly. Many of the smaller roads were improved; but these large traffic arteries remained of the utmost importance. Beside these major roads and the spur lines from railways, large dumps were established from where building material (not to mention ammunition and rations, as well as manpower) could be spread over a large area.

Most of these major roads were put in a state of defence by the Germans to deny their use to the enemy. They were at first blockaded by big *chevaux de frise*. During the summer of 1917 most of the important roads were blown up at various points (invariably cross roads received this treatment) by the Germans in advance of the allied offensive, thus creating a large crater – sometimes called a 'tank trap' by the British, which in turn was often brought into a state of defence to act as a strongpoint.

A German Gulaschkanone (soldier's slang for a field kitchen) on the Menin Road near Geluveld in early 1916. The Menin Road was one of the few wide and paved roads in the Salient and was therefore logistically very important. (*Vancoillie*)

Massive chevaux de frise block the Menin Road near Inverness Copse, west of Geluveld. The road was later prepared for destruction, in particular to deprive tanks of its use, during the Third Battle of Ypres. The mine was blown in the autumn of 1917. (*Vancoillie*)

55. I. 1177.
20.R. ROULERS
21. 9. 17.

Aerial picture of Roulers (21 September 1917). Roulers was of great importance to the Germans. Not only were its buildings used to house German troops and various headquarters, it was also a major logistical hub, with important land roads, railway lines and waterways. (*McMaster University*)

Chapter 1

The Development of the Defences of the Ypres Front

The beginning of the fortification of the Ypres Salient.

To protect themselves against bullets, artillery and enemy observation, both sides began digging in early in the war; historians often consider the Battle of the Aisne in September as marking the beginning of the trench warfare that has become the dominant image of the war for following generations. These early trenches were the prelude of a trench war on the Western Front that would last for almost four years, only broken by the war of movement that commenced in the spring of 1918 with the German offensives. During this long period of static warfare, however, a clear evolution can be identified in the construction and use of trenches by both the Germans and the Allies.

Autumn 1914 – Spring 1915.

When the war started, many people on all sides believed in a swift war of manoeuvre that would overwhelm the enemy; it would all be over in a few months. In fact not everyone thought like this – for example, many of the senior British generals, including Kitchener and Haig, predicted that it would be a long and costly war, lasting for as long as three years.

In September 1914 the initial German offensive stalled in France and the Germans withdrew to positions that were easier to defend and which safeguarded important territory, such as strategic railway lines and places of economic value and of use to the war effort. What then followed was the so-called 'Race to the Sea', a series of flanking movements, in the desperate hope of gaining a decisive advantage before the bad weather set in. This was not achieved and the 'race' ended up with both sides exhausted and occupying positions from the Channel coast to the Swiss frontier.

On the Yser Front the Germans were halted with the help of a large scale inundation of territory, achieved by opening the sluices in Nieuwpoort. From the end of the First Battle of Ypres onwards, towards the end of November 1914, the troops in the Ypres Salient dug in deeper and deeper to defend themselves against the enemy's rifle fire and frequent shelling. Ditches, field boundaries, tree lines and hedges were used as points to excavate simple shelters in which two to five men could be accommodated. These holes were gradually connected and primitive, straight trenches, dug in a hurry, resulted. These trenches had neither wall reinforcements nor drainage. Because of the high groundwater level, a characteristic of the Salient, the trenches could not be dug to any great depth and walls – or breastworks – were (partially) built above ground by the use of sandbags. These were at first made from any material that could be found: bed sheets, curtains or any other handy pieces of fabric. Many of these trenches were quickly destroyed by shelling or by collapses caused by rain, the effects of frost, groundwater – or a combination of them.

With the major offensive action over by about 20 November 1914, the Armee Oberkommandos and Generalkommandos issued orders that every able man was to work on improving the trench system under the supervision of the engineers. Orders stated that not an inch of ground was to be given to the enemy; the line must be defended at all costs. A continuous combat trench was to be constructed, defended by barbed wire entanglements on the enemy side, which would have concealed paths in them to enable offensive action, such as patrolling and limited attacks. Shelters were to be constructed as part of the trench system to protect against enemy artillery fire and to provide some shelter against poor weather conditions.

In combat trenches, loop-holed steel or iron plates were positioned to protect sentries and riflemen; the aim was to maintain the dominance of the Germans over No Man's Land. Support trenches were to be connected to the front line trench by a number of communication trenches. To prevent an enemy breakthrough, a second parallel battle trench (a Support Trench) close to the front line was constructed; the aim was that this would allow flanking fire during enemy attacks and provide a base line for any counter attacks that might be necessary. The first German trenches were constructed along the lines of these orders; but often the support trench was lacking because of a lack of materials and the shortage of manpower.

The sides of some trenches were reinforced with beams and doors, salvaged from destroyed farms, houses and outbuildings close to the front, so that rain, rising groundwater and frosts would not result in them constantly collapsing. Straw was often thrown onto the bottom of the trench, but this was usually insufficient to keep the feet of the soldiers dry. Most of the trench walls, in fact, were not reinforced and were just excavated from the earth, so that after even moderately poor weather the garrisons of the trenches were left up to their knees in the mud, which in turn led to problems with trench feet. Shelters were usually nothing more than a hole

A combat trench of Reserve Infanterie Regiment 245 at 'In de Ster', near Beselare, during the winter of 1914-1915. Note the simplicity of the trench wall, particularly evident on the rear (left), the parados, which lacks supports other than sandbags. (*Schmieschek*)

scraped out of the wall of a trench (and which, in turn, weakened the trenches' structure). Soldiers more often than not had to make do with inadequate shelter, often provided simply by their ground sheets.

To give an example of this development, 1st and 2nd Reserve Kompagnie Pionier Bataillon 11, 25th Reserve Division, were at first deployed in the line near Wijtschate in early November 1914 with the task of supporting attacks, being used to cut the enemy's barbed wire defences, throwing hand grenades – originally a Pioneer responsibility, and deploying boards over obstacles such as ditches, etc. However, from the end of offensive operations in late November it soon became apparent that the knowledge of field defence construction among the infantry (which in the Salient at that time was made up largely by reservists and older men) was insufficient to develop decent trenches and therefore the Pioniere were called in to direct operations. They helped the infantry to build a solid front line near Wijtschate and were also active during the night in installing the first barbed wire entanglements in No Man's Land.

By the end of January 1915, given winter conditions, it became quite clear that construction methods were inadequate and the bottom of trenches were often reduced to becoming the bed of what were, in effect, small streams. Around Plugstreet Wood, for example, Kavallerie Pionier Abteilung 3, which had been detached to XIX Armeekorps since mid November 1914, was ordered to construct new trenches a short distance behind the existing flooded front line trenches. The new trenches were only dug half a metre deep, the main construction being above ground. In places the new and old trenches were linked so that the old trench acted as a drainage ditch in which to divert water from the new trenches; but it also provided a defensive use, rather like moats around medieval castles.

A trench of Reserve Infanterie Regiment 245 at Broodseinde in the spring of 1915. A couple of simple shelters are visible to the right, using unprotected corrugated iron as a roof. (*Schmieschek*)

A primitive trench of Reserve Infanterie Regiment 236. Note the basic shelter in the side of the trench, separated from the trench by a groundsheet. (*Vancoillie*)

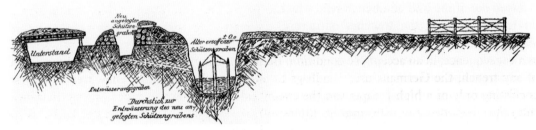

Cross section sketch of a front line trench near Ploegsteert Wood, as constructed by Kavallerie Pionier Abteilung 3 in late 1914. To the right is the barbed wire entanglement in No Man's Land, in the middle the first, flooded trench and to the left the new, partly breast work, combat trench with a typical shelter of this stage of the war. (*Pionier Bataillon 11*)

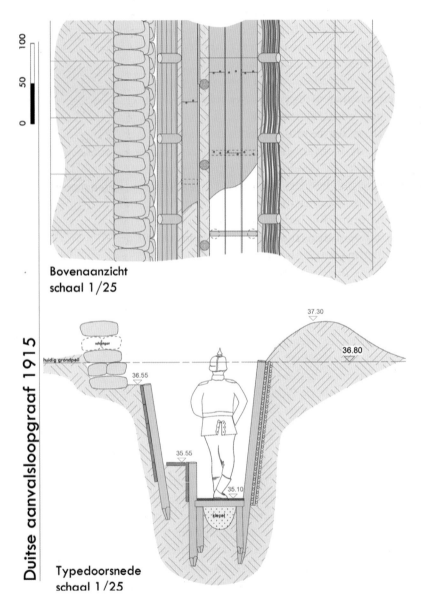

Cross section and bird's eye view of a German combat trench from the spring of 1915 as reconstructed at the Memorial Museum Passchendaele 1917. (*MMP.1917*)

Thus the front line combat trenches in the beginning were often nothing more than a straight ditch. During the winter of 1914-1915 breastworks were constructed and trenches were generally reinforced and improved. By the spring of 1915 most German trenches were, as a consequence, in an acceptable condition. Because the high water table restricted the depth of any trench, the Germans used sandbags to build a wall above the shallow trench, at first consisting only of a high parapet (on the enemy side) and a lower parados (facing their own side). As mentioned, in the beginning most sandbags were not made from the standard hessian but any kind of available fabric. Reserve Jäger Bataillon 18, active in the region of Het Sas (Boezinge) during the summer of 1915, noted in its battalion history:

'The look of these sandbag walls is remarkably colourful and unmilitary. Thousands and thousands of these bags were sewn in the Etappe [ie a base area to the rear] using fabrics and colours of all sorts. Some are made from blue and white linen, others made from mattress ticking, curtain fabric or even fabric for elegant costumes. One can study the wall forever and thus dispel boredom.'

These sandbag walls (ie breastworks) were not at all strong; the bags were filled on the spot and built up like brick walls, using stretcher bonds to hold the structure together. To offer a reasonable degree of protection, these sandbag walls were built more than a metre thick when above ground level, a necessary depth as otherwise bullets and shrapnel would penetrate the breastwork wall. Enemy action, such as grenade explosions, bullet impacts and occasional shell fire, damaged these defensive works and constant maintenance was required. Nature also played havoc with the breastworks; rain, snow and humidity rotted the fabric of the bags, including hessian when this became available. Sandbags were never envisioned as being the means of creating semi permanent defensive systems and certainly not for years on end. Rainfall and moisture in general also meant that the earth was constantly being washed out of the sandbags, weakening the structure.

German trench supported by a motley collection of sandbags. (*MMP.1917*)

Trenches had to be adapted for a particular purpose in the spring of 1915; the digging in of chlorine gas cylinders in the forward German trenches. In the early days of gas warfare, gas was released from steel cylinders and so in preparation for the gas attack and the opening of the Second Battle of Ypres thousands of cylinders, filled with chlorine, were dug in. The main brunt of the attack was focussed at the northern end and beyond of the Ypres Salient. Only a week before the attack, German Pioniere, supported by the infantry holding the sector, dug in more than 6,000 gas cylinders. It was evident that at least some of the German infantry were dubious about the cylinders: in fighting at Hill 60, the British noted that the Germans opposite had shown an uncharacteristic tendency to disappear during bombardments of their line – obviously concerned that one or more of the cylinders might be broken in their own trenches. Yet although some strange smells were noted by some of the British, these were put down to the explosive used in projectiles; and no cylinders were located, which would certainly have given the game away.

Spring 1915 – June 1917.

The Ypres front stabilised and became relatively quiet again after the 1915 gas attack and Second Ypres, although this did not preclude some quite significant local actions around Bellewaarde, for example, by the British in the autumn of 1915 and by the Germans before Mount Sorrel in the summer of 1916. Both sides continued to improve their trenches. Initially the German trench walls were strengthened by wooden planks; but this method was soon given up. When shells exploded they scattered the wood, the splinters from which could be dangerous to the trench occupants; whilst boards had to be replaced, which in turn put pressure on the limited supplies of timber that were available. The Germans started using wattle-work instead, indeed from quite early in the war (as did the French), to reinforce the trench walls. The semi breastwork part of the trenches continued to be built up with sandbags. This work was mostly carried out by the units occupying the trench system, sometimes supported by the divisional engineers.

The use of traverses, which gave trenches the characteristic crenelated appearance when viewed from the air, was not always as effective as expected. Artillery bombardment, ever increasing in strength and accuracy as the war progressed, and harsh weather conditions often led to their collapse. They made movement through trench systems more difficult and reduced the length of the firing line. From mid 1915 on trenches were built more and more in a zigzag pattern and the traditional type of traverse became rarer.

In the early days of trench warfare in the Salient, from late 1914 to early 1915, loophole plates (often, and inaccurately, called sniper plates) were very popular; but as time went on they largely fell into disuse. The plates stuck out above the trench, which acted as a marker for the enemy opposite and became ever more vulnerable when mortars (with their cheap but accurate bombs) became increasingly widespread. Well trained snipers could see whether a loophole was open or not, which put the soldier behind the plate in danger, though there were solutions to this problem. Loopholes and loophole plates gradually disappeared and were replaced by a fire step that allowed the defenders both to fire and to look over the parapet while standing or kneeling – and since the fire step stretched along the whole length of trench facing the enemy, this meant that any sentry could appear at any point along it: far less conspicuous than the use of plates. The arrangements meant that, in the event of an attack, all of the defenders could bring their weapons to bear; as yet the skills of the gunners opposite were not sufficient to

Stellung bei Ypern.

German combat trench in the Ypres Salient with a fire step and a parapet built with sandbags. The walls of the trench are reinforced with wattle-work. (*Deraeve*)

force the trench garrison to keep their heads down and in shelter whilst the opposing infantry advanced under its protection.

Duckboards, sturdy wooden constructions, loosely ladder like in shape, were increasingly positioned on the trench floor; underneath there was a drainage system, usually made of wooden planks. The boards on which the men walked could be placed across the width or along the length of the trench, depending on the type of construction and dictated by local needs. The duckboards were mostly made and stored behind the lines in pioneer parks and were transported from there to the trenches; for the final stage they would usually be carried into the line by support troops.

The same principles were applied in the construction of trenches in the Second Line and in further defence lines to the rear. Newcomers to the war, adapting to the front and trench warfare, and specific labour units, such as Armierungstruppen, were in charge of constructing the depth position lines. Gradually the defensive system expanded in depth, culminating in 1916 with three positions: the front line, the Albrecht Stellung and the Wilhelm Stellung.

Communication trenches were dug to connect these Lines (and the trenches that existed within each of them). These allowed reinforcements, reliefs, supplies and wounded to be brought up or moved to the rear in relatively safety circumstances, offering some protection against small arms fire and shelling. These communication trenches were wider than combat trenches, allowing an easy passage, sometimes in two directions. In many places the trenches were covered with branches, camouflage nets or camouflage hurdles (essentially wattle fences) to hinder enemy observation from the air. Because the location of these trenches was known to the enemy, they were shelled during any form of attack, local or more widespread along the line, so that they became a far less safe route to bring in reinforcements or supplies. One rather unusual supply line was the Hooge Tunnel, built under the middle of the Menin Road, which ran from Kantintje Cabaret to beyond Clapham Junction. The tunnel was built as an adjunct to the surface supply lines, which were well known to the British.

German soldiers assembling duckboards behind the front. (*Deraeve*)

German recruits of Reserve Infanterie Regiment 247 get used to being close to the front line by building second and third line trenches near Zonnebeke during the latter half of 1915. (*Vancoillie*)

Above left: A communication trench near the Ypres-Comines Canal. The wooden beams above it and connected to the vertical beam supports for the trench wall. This system prevented the trench walls from collapsing because of the pressure from the earth and groundwater. However, in time it was officially condemned because the struts were vulnerable to shelling and fragmented segments and splinters could cause casualties. Note the telephone lines attached to the trench walls. (*Vancoillie*)

Above right: A 'model' communication trench, near Geluveld. (*Vancoillie*)

Left: Interior view of Hooge Tunnel. This tunnel was approximately 1,500 metres long and ran under the centre of the length of the Menin Road from Kantintje Cabaret to Hooge. (*Grenadier Regiment 119*)

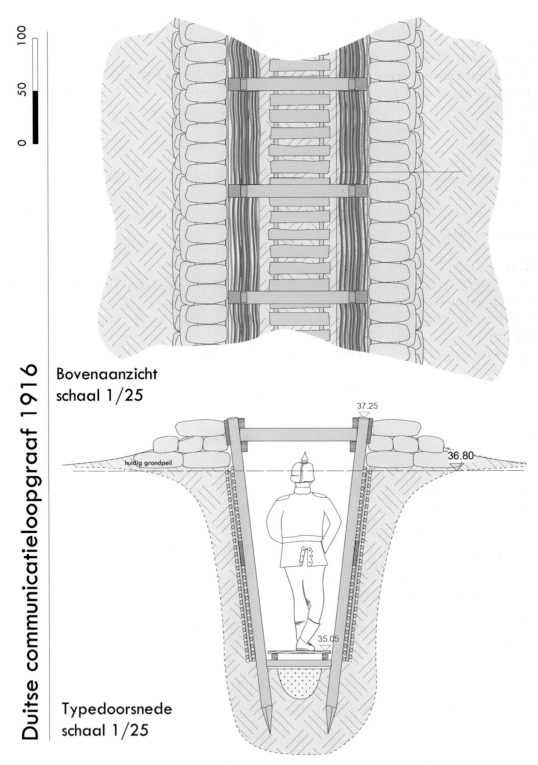

Cross section and bird's eye view of a 1916 German communication trench as reconstructed at the Memorial Museum Passchendaele 1917. (*MMP.1917*)

The Germans held the higher ground around Ypres (the Salient consisted of a series of low ridges, generally speaking each rising higher as one went to the east). They built their front line trenches on the forward slopes of the ridges, ie on the enemy side of them. This offered good observation and an excellent field of fire. However, this kind of position (Vorderhangstellung) had the disadvantage that the enemy could observe the German trenches directly and could shell them by direct observation (and, in due course, subject them to a machine gun barrage). However, this was not much of a problem in the generally calm period of mid 1915 to mid 1917, especially in the early part of this period, not least because the British lacked sufficient artillery and machine guns to do this effectively. In any case, during this period major British military offensive operations took place to the south, in battles such as Neuve Chapelle, Aubers Ridge, Loos and, in 1916, the Somme. Thus, until the summer of 1917 there were few changes to the method of constructing the trenches and the thinking behind their positioning and function.

The period 1915 – mid-1917 was marked by quite extensive underground warfare in the Ypres Salient. This kind of fighting required considerable resources, more so here than in other heavily mined parts of the Western Front to the south, such as around Arras, the Somme, Champagne and Argonne, amongst others. This was due to the geological nature of the ground: whereas chalk was close to the surface in areas such as Arras and the Somme, which made for rapid digging of stable tunnels, the Salient had clay – in particular blue clay. This was notoriously difficult to excavate through safely and any workings required substantial quantities of timber to support them.

Generally starting in the front line trench or from the support trenches in the rear close to the front line, shafts were dug vertically several metres deep. Tunnels were then excavated that ran towards the British line, occasionally underneath them. Listening posts were installed in order to track British mining operations. To construct these shafts and tunnels a lot of timber was needed, mainly prefabricated frames using timber 25 centimetres wide. The frames, which were made available through pioneer parks, existed in three sizes: 1.80 metres by 1.20 metres, 1.80 metres by one metre and 1.60 metres by 0.90 metres. As mentioned, the shafts were mostly excavated straight down [whereas the British tended to use an incline system] and sometimes steel rings or concrete blocks were used to support the shafts. The earth (mostly blue clay) was, preferably, transported as far away as possible from the excavation site because its particular colour would give away indications of the underground activity to the enemy. Mining warfare was originally undertaken by infantrymen who had experience in the mining industry (it needs to be kept in mind just how extensive mining was in pre war western Europe); but from early in 1915 special units were formed, so-called Pionier Mineur Kompagnien. They remained active underground in the Salient until June 1917.

For a variety of reasons, the Germans lost the underground war strategically; but they were often victorious in tactical mine warfare. In particular, the Germans were expert in reacting to the detonation of mines, both those fired by themselves or by the enemy, and more often than not succeeded in capturing mine craters, occupying them and transforming them into small fortresses. However, after the Battle of Messines (7-14 June 1917), which marked the last great mining attack, and the opening of the Battle of Third Ypres on 31 July, mine warfare effectively came to an end in the Salient (as, indeed, it did to a considerable extent along the entire Western Front).

A mine crater fortified by the Germans, photographed in September 1915. Timber for the typical mine frames can be seen to the right. The German soldiers on the left are building a roof using beams and rails. Note the variety of material still being used to make sandbags. (*Vancoillie*)

According to the caption on the rear of this photograph, this is Hooge Crater when held by the Germans. Note the numerous sections of wattle-work. A Förderbahn is visible on the right, used for the transportation of building material for the underground war; its return journey was not wasted, as it was used to remove excavated earth. (*Vancoillie*)

1917-1918.

During the preliminary artillery bombardment for the Battle of Messines, the British artillery destroyed the laboriously built and maintained trenches in the Wijtschate area. Because of that the German defenders would crawl some distance every day before dawn – maybe fifty metres or so, into No Man's Land and take cover there in shell holes. At dusk they returned to their trenches; but as the state of these trenches got ever worse, they increasingly stayed in the shell holes and prepared these for defence. During the preparatory shelling of the Third Battle of Ypres the same development took place in the Salient.

The development of this so-called Trichterstellung (shell hole position) went back to the big battles of 1916, the Battles of Verdun and the Somme, when trenches were completely destroyed after days or weeks of incessant shelling. Repairing trenches was almost impossible during the constant bombardments. The Germans took cover in shell holes near the trenches instead, which were less targeted and certainly did not appear on trench maps. At first they tried to connect shell holes by shallow trenches; but this quickly led to losses caused by sniper and artillery fire, attracted by the work. The Germans therefore limited themselves to putting up barbed wire obstacles around their occupied shell holes and digging out basic shelters inside the craters.

The use of shell holes had a number of advantages. It fitted perfectly the strategic and tactical vision that was developed by Ludendorff of the so-called 'empty battlefield'. Troops were spread out over the depth of a battlefield so that the enemy artillery no longer had large and/or clear targets to shoot at. The diffused spread of the soldiers was also hard to detect by observers

A German strongpoint during the Third Battle of Ypres. A group of concrete bunkers provided protection and shelters for the defenders. Clearly defined trenches were a thing of the past by this stage of the battle. (*Deseyne*)

on the ground or in the air. The possibility of creating strong points remained, usually as a location from which to harass the enemy in the immediate aftermath of an attack. In addition, the construction of fake trenches (ie trenches that were unmanned) remained important as a means of tricking the enemy into squandering its shells and mortar bombs on them.

The main problem with these scattered positions in shell holes was that of control and command of the troops. There was a considerable debate amongst the German staff when this approach to defence became almost a necessity in the last weeks of the Somme. In the end these battle tactics could only be used because the German army had a strong tradition amongst its officers of decentralised command and personal initiative before the war. Indeed, every soldier was encouraged to make his own decisions when needed, which allowed, at least initially, for a rather successful application of these tactics. However, from the earliest days there were concerns expressed about the quality of soldiers coming to the Front; 1916 marks the year when the German army began to face ever more serious manning issues and a perceived diminution in the quality of the new recruits.

However, the German army intended to construct trenches once more after the fighting and shelling lost intensity and the enemy's offensive action had ceased. This was the case in the Salient after the Third Battle of Ypres drew to a close in mid November 1917. After the Battle of the Lys, however, and more particularly during the summer of 1918, no significant new trench works were constructed. The German army lacked the manpower to carry out such work, both in combat troops (as a consequence of the great losses during the Spring offensives and of the rapidly spreading Spanish 'flu pandemic) and those allocated to act as labour troops. (Russians PoWs, often used in the construction of defensive lines, had to be returned to Russia after the Treaty of Brest-Litovsk was signed on 3 March 1918 with Soviet Russia.) Given the complete change in positions after the Battle of the Lys, when the German line advanced almost to the walls of Ypres, new lines would have needed to be constructed almost from scratch. The logistics challenge was huge, as everything had to be transported across a ravaged countryside and a destroyed infrastructure – and that was always assuming that the necessary construction materials were available. Not only was there now a chronic shortage of manpower for the German army, but also the *materiel* war had been lost. The allies, on the other hand, could call upon a seemingly endless supply of both, now that the United States was beginning to make its presence felt on the battlefield.

The German army before Ypres was to collapse during the Final Offensive in Flanders, which got under way towards the end of September 1918, largely fighting from inadequately strengthened shell holes. During the German retreat in October and on to November 1918, the troops could only fall back on hastily prepared defence lines, which were in reality usually nothing more than a pencil line on a staff map, and some hastily erected barbed wire entanglements.

The Development of the Positions and Lines at the Front.

The Front Line.

Very soon after the front stabilised after the war of manoeuvre of 1914, a number of positions or defence lines (Stellungen in German) were created in addition to the front line, each of which in turn was usually made up of several trench lines (Linien or Graben in German) when they had reached full development. The troops in the battle zone, especially in an area of major tactical and, indeed, strategic importance, such as Ypres, often had three such positions at their disposal, which were separated from each other by anything up to two and even three kilometres, but were more usually a thousand to 1,500 metres apart; they were also often connected to each other by trench systems commonly called switch lines. The degree of development of these positions varied, however. Even further away from the front line there were still operational and strategic defence lines, mainly developed as from late 1916. In part this reflected the decision by the German commander, Falkenhayn, to concentrate the major efforts of Germany in the east at least until the opening of the Verdun offensive in February 1916, along with one or two notable exceptions.

The number of positions and lines depended completely on German tactical and strategic guide lines that were in force at that particular time. In general, the Germans employed a rigid defence of the front line until late 1916, after which they applied defence in depth as their core strategy. The rigid defence system allowed for and even required multiple trench lines in the front line, to be able to cope with temporary successful enemy attacks, although

A British oblique aerial photograph showing the German trenches in the Verlorenhoek Sector (on the Ypres-Zonnebeke road) in May 1917. Note the huge crater in the road; a mine had been blown so that British tanks would not be able to use its solid surface. (*McMaster University*)

the actual construction and the development of a front line system might take a considerable amount of time. The third trench line of the front line in the sector of XXVI Reservekorps (from Verlorenhoek to Pilkem), for instance, was only finished in the spring of 1916; it was located on the reverse slope of a ridge. This line accommodated the command posts of the Kampftruppenkommandeure (KTK, commander of the front line troops), communication posts and the medical aid posts.

The front line needed to be defended, so the doctrine went, until the last man; it was never to fall into enemy hands. This was the prevailing rule until late 1916. From late 1914 until late 1916 a huge amount of construction material and labour was used to keep this front line system in the best possible condition. After every bombardment it was essential to repair all damage that had been done to the shelters and trenches; whilst continuous efforts were made to improve and develop the position.

The construction, maintenance and improvement of the trenches in the front line were the task of the infantry that was defending that particular part of the line. To get an idea of the excavation work that was needed for this, a simple calculation can be performed. A company that dug out a trench 200 metres long by two metres deep and 1.50 metres wide moved some 900 tonnes of earth!

As soon as the preliminary bombardment for the Battle of Messines started in late May 1917 (a bombardment of unprecedented ferocity in the Salient), the Germans changed their defensive system to one of defence in depth, based upon defending from shell holes and pill boxes, making as much use as possible of barbed wire obstructions and camouflage. Large, perfectly built trench lines, certainly at the front itself, were no longer constructed from the summer of 1917. Even the support position, the so-called Artillerie Schutz Stellung (artillery protective line), where the reserve battalion was assembled, had become nothing more than a collection of shell holes and shelters that were hidden from enemy observation.

The Albrecht Stellung.

This defence line gets its name from the commander (until February 1917) of the Fourth Army: Albrecht, Duke of Württemberg. Initially, in the summer of 1915, this line was conceived as a third line of defence, about one to one and a half kilometres behind the front line position. The location of this line was a Hinterhangstellung (a position on the reverse slope of a ridge), so it could not be targeted by direct artillery fire. Even in the case of a gas attack at the front line (at a period when gas could only be delivered by canisters and not by shells), this line was far enough away from the immediate front line to be safe. By this stage, enemy use of poison gas in any attack was a realistic scenario during the planning and construction of this defence line in 1915.

The Albrecht Stellung mostly comprised just the one trench line, a continuous combat trench protected for most of its length by an electrified barbed wire entanglement. A significant number of concrete, reinforced bunkers were incorporated in the Albrecht Stellung, mainly shelters (so called Kasernen, barracks) for the reserve troops that were deployed in this defence line, but were also provided as medical aid posts.

By mid-1917 this line was often known as the Zwischen Stellung (intermediate position), because it was located between the front line and the Artillerie Schutz Stellung (named in the

A German trench map from late 1916, showing the German defence lines (in blue) east of Ypres. The front line and its trench system is clearly visible. Some distance behind the front line is the Albrecht Stellung (right of centre); on the right is the Wilhelm Stellung, which comprised a continuous trench in the south and a series of strongpoints further north. (MMP.1917)

Salient the Wilhelm Stellung). By this stage it did not fit with the ideal of the defensive scheme for the Salient. However, the Germans used the Albrecht Stellung very skilfully during the Third Battle of Ypres. The barbed wire defences that protected it were by that time no longer electrified; but they had been substantially expanded in depth. Between the front line and the Albrecht Stellung concrete machine gun posts (designed for one or two machine guns) were built in carefully located positions, while the Albrecht Stellung itself was seen as forming part of the Großkampffeld, which stretched up to the Wilhelm Stellung. The Großkampffeld was the battlefield during the first weeks of the Third Battle of Ypres and its numerous bunkers offered excellent defensive possibilities to the Germans from the very start of the battle on 31 July 1917.

A section of trench of the Albrecht Stellung near Kantintje Cabaret and the Menin Road, west of Geluveld. The trench has been constructed according to the book; note the proximity of a battlefield cemetery. (*Vancoillie*)

The Wilhelm Stellung.

The Wilhelm Stellung, named after Kaiser Wilhelm II, was constructed and developed as a Third Line by the local divisions from the spring of 1916 on. Because every division or army corps had its own vision about the ideal defence system in depth, the outcome of the works varied from one sector to another, though the location and purpose of the line was clearly laid down by higher command. XIII Armeekorps, for instance, built its section of the Wilhelm Stellung as a powerful continuous combat trench from the Ypres – Comines Canal to Polygon Wood. A lot of the spade work was done by recruits from the Feldrekrutendepot, thereby getting used to living and working close to the front; but Armierungstruppen were also employed in the development of this line.

The division in the sector near Zonnebeke had another view of this defence line. Several strong points, Stützpunkte, were constructed, with ample barbed wire entanglements in front of them, rather than a continuous line. Further to the north, near Langemark, there was again a continuous combat trench, strengthened by concrete bunkers. In front of the line a wide belt of barbed wire defences was laid out (and by this stage in the war these belts of wire could be very deep indeed, often fifty metres and sometimes repeated again, forming two zones of barbed wire) and concrete bunkers were constructed in and just behind the position itself.

After the Battle of Messines in mid June the Germans briefly considered the option of withdrawing to the Flandern I Stellung or to the Wilhelm Stellung to frustrate the enemy's offensive planning and out of concern of further massive mines. Because the advantage of having the front line on the first ridge around Ypres did not outweigh the possible disadvantages of keeping the current front line, the plans were quickly shelved. During the summer of 1917 the Wilhelm Stellung was turned into the Artillerie Schutz Stellung and became the area where the reserve battalions (Bereitschaftsbataillon), which acted as counter attack troops, were gathered.

On 31 July 1917 the German Eingreif [ie counter attack or rapid response] Divisionen carried out counter-attacks only after the British troops were advancing towards the Wilhelm

Recruits and Armierungssoldaten, pictured in early 1916 working on the third line, later called the Wilhelm Stellung. (*Grenadier Regiment 119*)

Soldiers of Reserve Infanterie Regiment 235 in one of the strongpoints (Grotemolen, south of the Ypres-Zonnebeke road – see map overleaf) of the Wilhelm Stellung in the spring of 1916. Note the elaborately built trench walls, making full use of wattle-work. Note also the lack of steel helmets (though admittedly this was then some distance behind the line) – these were not widespread in the German army, apart from those serving in Verdun, until the later summer of 1916. (*Vancoillie*)

A German trench map, dated from the end of 1916, showing the German defence lines (in blue) northeast of Ypres and west of Zonnebeke. It shows the front line, here called Schloß Stellung, with its complex of trench lines; behind it lies the continuous Albrecht Stellung, with some strongpoints; whilst to the east of it is the Wilhelm Stellung, built in the south, particularly along the Ypres-Zonnebeke road, as a series of unconnected strongpoints and further north more as a continuous fighting trench. (*MMP.1917*)

A German messenger with his bicycle stand in front of a well concealed shelter of the Wilhelm Stellung (note the sign on the bunker) in late 1916. This may be either a machine gun post or an observation post, judging from the wide slit (at the bottom) in the construction. (*Vancoillie*)

Stellung. These German counter attacks pushed the British back beyond the Albrecht Stellung. In the end, capturing the Wilhelm Stellung became the hardest nut to crack for the British attackers during the summer and autumn of 1917. The strong points of the Wilhelm Stellung near Zonnebeke, for example, for weeks resisted the relentless British attacks. The British called these strong points the Bremen Redoubt (Brandenburg-Werk), Potsdam Redoubt (Schwabenhof) and Zonnebeke Redoubt (Grotemolen Süd); and suffered heavy losses by the time that they finally captured these positions in September 1917. West of Geluveld there was fighting until October 1917 before the British captured the last section of the Wilhelm Stellung, with Tower Hamlets its most notorious stronghold.

South of the Ypres – Comines Canal.

Between the Ypres-Comines Canal and the Lys (Leie), the Germans organised their defensive system differently because of the different topographical situation. While the Germans situated their front line to the north of the canal on a ridge, with even higher ground in the rear, the

A German trench map of December 1916 showing the German defence lines (in blue) between Wytschaete and the Ypres-Comines Canal. (*MMP.1917*)

front line south of the canal was located on high ground but with only lower ground in the rear. Losing the front line position south of the canal would have severe implications on retaining control of the area between the front line, the Ypres-Comines Canal and the Lys.

The first trench line (named Ia and Ib) of the front line was positioned on the forward slope of the ridge running from Sint-Elooi over Wijtschate to Messines. The second trench line, the Sonne Linie, was located close behind the first line. On top of and just behind the ridge was located the Höhen Stellung (Second Line). This position was much closer to the front line than its counterpart, the Albrecht Stellung, to the north of the canal. The Höhen Stellung comprised two trench lines. The majority of the reserve troops in the Höhen Stellung were located in its second trench line, just behind the ridge on the reverse slope, which offered better protection against enemy observation and artillery.

Behind the Höhen Stellung, itself situated on an arc-shaped ridge, was the Sehnen Stellung. It formed the string to the bow, running from Château Mahieu (White Chateau) to Basse Ville. The British called this line the Oosttaverne Line because it passed through the hamlet of Oosttaverne. Behind the Sehnen Stellung was the 3. Stellung, basically an extension of the Wilhelm Stellung and which ran from Kortewilde, through Garde-Dieu and on to Warneton.

Most of the German defence system fell into British hands within half a day on 7 June 1917 after a painstakingly prepared attack, firing deep mines that had been dug and prepared months beforehand, deploying a perfectly orchestrated artillery barrage that threatened to completely overwhelm the German artillery, with an infantry assault that was supported by tanks. It was a fine example of the execution of an offensive with limited objectives.

The front line and the Höhen Stellung comprised well established, maintained and developed trenches, defended mine craters and concrete bunkers. The Sehnen Stellung and 3. Stellung were less developed and defences mainly consisted of barbed wire obstacles, although there were some bunkers, especially in or around the scattered farm buildings, a feature of the landscape. With the loss of their main defence lines, the Germans continued the battle from occupied shell holes, supported by strong points based around bunkers. The Germans considered for a while a retreat to the other bank of the Lys and behind the Ypres-Comines Canal, where defensive lines were available. The plan was quickly shelved when the British started to dig in and consolidate their gains during the afternoon of 7 June 1917 and did not push the attack further with any great effort.

Defence in depth: 1917-1918.

The strategic-tactical move towards defence in depth, adopted in the summer of 1917, had major consequences for both the front line and the rear defence lines. The whole Kampfzone (Battle Zone) was now conceived as an 'empty battlefield'; there was no place for trenches, only for strong points based in shell holes and around bunkers, surrounded by barbed wire. Behind the front line, now more like a zone of defended shell holes, the Artillerie Schutz Stellung was located about one and a half kilometres further back. The area in between was, of course, also occupied and defended by strong points according to the same principles. The use of numerous machine guns was of the highest importance.

The Artillerie Schutz Stellung was conceived as a Hinterhangstellung, formed of three lines. Trenches could be built here if there were sufficient available resources, notably labour and suitable materiel. Of more importance were the simple reinforced shelters; there was a maximum of a sixth of these in the first line of the system, with more in the second and the third lines. A continuous and suitably deep barbed wire entanglement, with enough gaps and paths through it to allow for counter attacks in the direction of the front line, had to be built in front of this Artillerie Schutz Stellung.

This re-evaluation of the defensive system had huge consequences on the nature of defensive construction work. In the Salient from the summer of 1917 the Germans effectively ceased to construct complex trenches apart from some short stretches here and there. Shallow trenches, however, were still dug. From the air some of the lines deep in the German rear looked like magnificently built trenches, whilst in reality they were nothing more than shallow ditches, designed to attract the attention of the allied artillery and of air observation and thereby distract them from more effective and destructive work. Nearly all efforts in defensive works were therefore diverted from mid 1917 towards the construction of shelters, whether built with ferro-concrete or not. The Germans learnt that well-hidden shelters made from corrugated iron plates or sheets, accompanied by barbed wire obstacles, were more efficient, safer and more defensible than the strongest concrete bunker, which stuck out from the surrounding landscape and was a natural target for concentrated artillery fire.

The Kampfzone (battle zone) comprised three lines from the summer of 1918, all constructed on the principles of defence in depth: the Franken Stellung, Preußen Stellung

An oblique aerial photograph, dated October 1918, showing the Kezelberg area (Hill 41) between Dadizele and Moorsele. The Menen-Roeselare road is visible in the centre and, just to the west and parallel to the road, the railway line. The (new) Flandern I Stellung is clearly visible; a shallow trench defended by three lines of barbed wire entanglements. Note that there are camouflage nets over Oude Ieperstraat, which provided some cover from allied observation for traffic on the road. (*McMaster University*)

and Bayern Stellung, named after three of the constituent peoples of Germany. The Franken Stellung was comparable to the former outpost line. It had a forward area (in fact largely No Man's Land) and a main resistance line. It served mainly to delay the enemy advance. The few German defenders in it were to withdraw to the Preußen Stellung in case of a large scale attack. This Second Line comprised a forward area, a main resistance line, an intermediate area and the Artillerie Schutz Stellung, which was in effect the Third Line, the Bayern Stellung. The main resistance line of the Preußen Stellung was the most important line to defend; but in a worst case scenario the defenders could fall back on to the Artillerie Schutz Stellung (Bayern Stellung). Here, reserve troops were assembled and with their help a counter-attack would be launched to recapture the main resistance line of the Preußen Stellung. It is important to note that in the summer of 1918 none of these lines in the Kampfzone was recognisable or seriously developed, except for some scattered strong points and barbed wire entanglements. The concrete bunkers, pieces of trenches and shelters that were present mostly dated from earlier periods in the war and some of them were re-used and adapted British constructions.

The Flandern I Stellung and the Flandern II Stellung, constructed in the winter of 1917-1918, were located behind the operational defence lines. Both Flandern Stellungen formed the strategic defence lines; the Flandern I Stellung served as the German front line from late September 1918 to mid October 1918. Nothing had been done for the improvement of this line since spring 1918, which reduced its defensive capabilities.

Passive Defence.

Barbed Wire.

Barbed wire was first patented in 1874 by the American Joseph F. Glidden, developed as a cheap and effective way to demarcate properties and contain grazing cattle in the prairies of the United States of America. Until then small walls were built with rocks or thorn hedges were planted to separate the different meadows. Because both of these options were practically impossible in the open plains, where construction materials were scarce and difficult to import and where hedges did – and do - not grow well, Glidden found a solution in barbed wire, which was easily and quickly placed. He earned a fortune from his patent. Very soon it was realised that if barbed wire could stop animals then it could also stop humans. Thus during the Spanish-American War of 1898 the Americans used barbed wire in the defences of Santiago (Cuba). In 1899 it was used by the British to enclose and secure camps where Boers in South Africa were being detained.

As soon as the fighting in the First World War became bogged down in a stalemated trench war, barbed wire defences were erected to protect the trenches, though admittedly quite primitive and thin in these early days. The fences did not need to be very high; fifty to ninety centimetres would be more than enough to slow down and even halt the advancing enemy, if only temporarily. Because there was often a shortage of barbed wire, smooth wire was mixed with barbed wire in the obstacles. Between the different lines of barbed wire trip wires were placed. These were made with smooth wire and were difficult to detect when there was low vegetation. The main goal of these wire defences was to keep the enemy at a distance and impede him so he could be kept under fire for a longer time. In fact it is a military maxim that such obstacles have to be under effective fire as else they are largely ineffective. The barbed wire entanglements needed to be positioned far enough in front of a trench to make sure the enemy could not throw hand grenades into the trenches from behind the wire. Having the enemy caught up in wire at a distance also meant that more firepower could be brought to bear from a longer length of the trench – if it were too close and too shallow, then fewer defenders would be able to tackle such an attack. It was also necessary to keep enough open space between the wire obstacle and the trench to allow for effective observation of No Man's Land and of the enemy during any attack.

Building such obstacles in No Man's Land was not an easy job. The enemy had No Man's Land under observation and everything that moved in it was liable to be shot at. Building a wide and effective barbed wire defence system was a very tricky task, not least because the wooden stakes needed to be hammered in the ground, which could hardly be done silently. Cloth bags were placed over the pickets to try and silence the noise of the hammering with a mallet. To make the task of building a barbed wire fence easier, *chevaux de frise*, prefabricated behind the front line, were sometimes used. These were then dragged out into No Man's Land at night. These *chevaux de frise*, also known as Spanish riders or knife rests, are made of two wooden or steel crosses connected by a long wooden beam or a bar of angle iron of approximate 2.5 metre in length. Barbed wire is then strung all over. Because of their size (1.2 metres across and 2.5 metres long) it was far from simple to carry these *chevaux de frise* along the communication trenches into the front line. The soldiers occasionally pushed the obstacles into No Man's Land using very long rods to keep enough distance between the barbed wire and the front line trench. Later on the obstacles would have to be secured to the ground to make sure that the enemy could not simply drag them to his side or push them back into the German trench.

Hammering pickets into the ground was obviously unsatisfactory and it was realised that steel pickets (made from angle iron) were much stronger than wooden stakes because they could withstand an explosion, were harder to spot and could be more easily got into the ground. From

No Man's Land somewhere on the Ypres front in 1915; note the extensive use of chevaux de frise, as extensive fixed barbed wire entanglements were still a thing of the future. (*Deraeve*)

Barbed wire entanglements in front of the trenches of Infanterie Regiment 172 between Hooge and Klein Zillebeke in 1915. It comprises a mix of Drahtwalzen (a system to fix coiled barbed wire) and chevaux de frise. (*Vancoillie*)

late 1915 and early 1916 the typical steel corkscrew pickets were widely introduced (known as 'pig tails' by the local Flemish population). These could be screwed into the ground silently and quickly, even from a lying position. However, it was often the case that these screw pickets could not be secured firmly enough in the ground, so it was recommended to use wooden posts as well as corkscrew pickets. This was especially the case when erecting the barbed wire defences for a defensive line that was being prepared behind the front line. The system became increasingly sophisticated as the war went on – for example pickets of different sizes were used, which made the entanglements even more difficult to penetrate. A further advantage of the screw picket was that it could be relatively easily transported up to the front: a single man could carry as many as fifteen to twenty of them. Finally, they were durable – evidence of this can be occasionally seen in the boundary fencing of many of today's farmers' fields; here and there a screw picket is still supporting barbed wire.

Another form of barbed wire entanglement was made by using concertina wire (Drahtwalze, barbed wire cylinders): spiral shaped coils of barbed wire that can be expanded like a concertina. These coils, measuring about a metre across, were prefabricated in Pionier Parks behind the front and could be carried by one person. The wire was already attached to three screw pickets and it was a simple task for three men to expand the concertina and fix it. In a matter of minutes such a team could erect a fence some seventy five centimetres high and fifteen metres long.

Barbed wire defences provided the trench garrisons of both sides with a reasonable degree of security against sudden attack and raids. However, it was essential that there were systems in place that turned barbed wire from a passive defence into an active one – for example by constructing saps from the front line into the barbed wire system for sentries, by putting patrols out into No Man's Land at night, and for a comprehensive defensive fire plan that could

A wiring party near Oosttaverne (east of Wijtschate) in 1916. (*Vancoillie*)

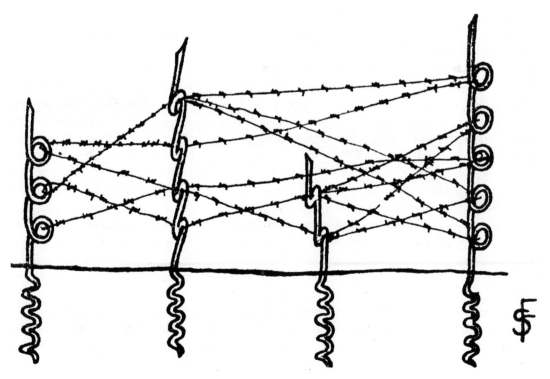

The pickets to which barbed wire was attached came in different sizes to make the obstruction more complex and therefore more effective as an obstacle. (*Seeßelberg*)

Narrow-gauge railway wagons propelled by manpower are being used to transport barbed wire to the front line. A shallow trench has been dug along a line of trees to conceal this track. The Drahtwalzen are clearly visible, as are rolls of smooth wire to the right of the right hand man sitting on the wagon. This type of wire was used together with barbed wire for entanglements or to make trip wires. (*Deraeve*)

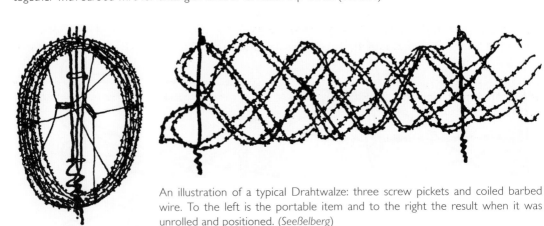

An illustration of a typical Drahtwalze: three screw pickets and coiled barbed wire. To the left is the portable item and to the right the result when it was unrolled and positioned. (*Seeßelberg*)

bring down artillery and machine gun fire on a threatened area very rapidly. Trench raiding became relatively common as the war progressed and the techniques to counter the raiders consequently became more complex.

Barbed wire obstacles became even more important during major fighting in a sector, most especially in the opening phase of an offensive, becoming an essential part of the defensive system at the front. Planning for a major attack (and, in reality, even a trench raid) was influenced by the problem of barbed wire; any attack had to work on the basis that the barbed wire entanglements had been presumed to be destroyed. For raids the requirements were different, but for an attack along a length of line the integrity of the barbed wire defences had to be destroyed if the impetus of the attack were not to stumble – almost literally – at the first hurdle. Special shell fuses were developed for shells (for instance the British N° 106 fuse), that were very sensitive and which detonated as soon as the barbed wire was hit. This aimed to destroy barbed wire entanglements; other, less sensitive, fuses only exploded after contact with the ground and would often only scatter the barbed wire around in piles. In this case the wire got more and more entangled, which actually worked to the advantage of the defender instead of the attacker. The British also deployed the recently invented (1912) Bangalore Torpedo to clear paths through the barbed wire. This could be very effective, but had limitations, such as the circumstances in which it could be used.

Another approach to the problem included sending wire cutting parties out immediately ahead of an attack; their objectives was to cut gaps (or paths) through the wire to make sure that their troops could assault the enemy positions without being delayed or hindered by wire. To counter this, one defensive tactic was deliberately to leave some gaps in the wire defence to lure the enemy towards these openings. These gaps would be well covered by machine guns – note the plural, usually with pre arranged firing lines that could even be used at night, and which could take the attacker under cross-fire. The arcs of fire of machine guns were usually arranged so that all parts of the line could be covered by at least two machine guns and thus the orders to the various gun crews would reflect this need. The gaps in the wire were also required for their own counter-attacks or for their various night patrols – patrols that included those dedicated to protecting those mending or developing the barbed wire defences.

A good example of a well organised barbed wire defensive system in action, as it were, took place during the Third Battle of Ypres. The New Zealand Division launched an attack on the German positions near 's Graventafel, not far from Passendale, on 12 October 1917. A barbed wire entanglement, that varied in depth from twenty-five to fifty metres and which had not been destroyed by the preparatory artillery bombardment, soon held up the division. The Germans

German soldiers constructing a barbed wire entanglement. Both iron and wooden pickets are being used in the same entanglement. Note that the wire is being loosely strung; it would be more easily destroyed by shell fire if it was made too taut. (*Deraeve*)

were able to fire freely from their positions on the higher ground at any movement made within the area of the barbed wire entanglement. The New Zealanders experienced their blackest day of the war in this engagement: 845 men were killed in only a few hours in the mud and barbed wire before Passchendaele Ridge. The reason for the extent of these losses was exclusively attributed to the German barbed wire defence:

'Neither the deep mud, however, nor the pillboxes, nor the machine guns, nor the weakness of supporting artillery would even conjointly, as Cockerell's attack in the marshes demonstrated, have held our attack. The direct cause of failure was the wide unbroken entanglements against which infantry resourcefulness and fortitude broke in vain.'

At the beginning of the war, when attacks were not preceded by large artillery bombardments (both sides had a relative shortage of shells and of guns of heavy calibre, at least as compared to what was available to the French and the Germans by mid to late 1915 and to the British by autumn 1916), some barbed wire entanglements were put under high voltage. The most famous example of this was the so-called 'Wire of Death' (Dodendraad) on the Belgian-Dutch border. There was also such a wire fence along the Swiss-German border. However, the Germans even experimented with electrified fences at the front. Along the Ypres-Comines Canal they built an electrically charged barbed wire fence in the spring of 1916. A similar fence was also constructed that spring in front of the second line of defence (Albrecht Stellung) in the sector of XXVI Reservekorps. The fence was still functioning in late 1916 when the 17th Reserve Division was deployed in the area of Zonnebeke – Sint-Juliaan. The electricity could be switched on and off via switch boards located in the reserve trenches. The increasing strength and volume of artillery bombardments before attacks make these systems obsolete in the Salient during 1917.

It appears that one of the few victims of these electrically charged fences was a German soldier who was working on it. Armierungsoldat Theodor Lindler, of the 4 Kompagnie Bayerisches Armierungs Bataillon 1, was mortally wounded (by fire) after touching the wire accidentally on 27 September 1915 in the area of Sint-Juliaan. He was buried the next day in the German military cemetery at Poelkapelle, but has since been moved to the German military cemetery of Menen Wald, Grave O/1681.

When the different defence lines behind the front line were constructed, the accompanying barbed wire obstacles would, naturally, be built at the same time. The entanglements were best placed in an area forty to sixty metres in front of the combat trenches, in multiple lines of some five to ten metres wide and with a similar interval between them to reduce the effect of shell blasts. These different lines of barbed wire would be connected periodically by a belt of barbed wire to limit the freedom of movement of the attacker within the barbed wire field. It was very important that the wire was not stretched too tautly. Barbed wire under tension was easier to break, even by the concussion from bursting shells, than loosely suspended wire. And loosely suspended wire was more of an obstacle to troops.

Because these defences were easy to spot and measure by air reconnaissance, some of the wiring was strung into existing hedges and bushes. The working parties had to take care to suspend the wires from the branches of the hedges and not build the barbed wire entanglement just behind the hedge, where it would be easier to spot.

In 1918 the Germans switched their policy as regards wire to 'less is more'. Wide barbed wire entanglements were too easy to spot from the sky and the enemy's artillery had become more proficient and had a wider range of ordnance at its disposal to deal with such obstructions. By October 1918 fighting was taking place over an area that had been barely damaged by the fighting (well, certainly when compared to the ground around villages like Langemark and Geluveld). Here only limited barbed wire defences were erected, usually hidden in hedges and along rows of trees. Of course this was also a reflection of the shortages that the German army faced of manpower and of materiel. But the reality was that the weapon systems of 1918 could overcome wire belts no matter how thick (in fact some of the greatest early success of the tank was in crushing barbed wire defences) and this method of deploying barbed wire brought in an element of surprise.

Barbed wire entanglements in the Salient, from the earliest days of static warfare in the winter of 1914 and right through to the allied Final Offensive of autumn 1918, provided the basis of the security of the German defence system.

Hiding and concealment.

An important aspect of passive defence was the hiding of all sorts of constructions and the active disguising of them. The First World War was the first war in which there were such extensive possibilities for observing the enemy; most importantly these were not restricted simply to the ground but from the air (although observation by balloon, of course, had been around for a while). Very soon the necessity arose to hide both construction and men.

Active camouflage.
The first thing soldiers do to escape enemy fire and observation is building or searching for a shelter. This is often best done by hiding in or under the ground. This way the first trenches, scrapes (what would late be described as fox holes) and dugouts were created. Because of the increasing fire power and its growing precision, just digging in was no longer sufficient as the rising quantity of artillery, shells and improved accuracy made shallow shelters more and more vulnerable. The constructions needed camouflaging. Initially this was done very primitively. Twigs and branches were arranged to break up the outline of a construction that would otherwise stick out from the background. As long as the terrain still had a regular covering of growth, then the problem was minimised.

Because the enemy could not shell everything constantly, the Germans considered it sufficient to screen constructions just enough so that the enemy could not see whether somebody was inside the building. Screens were very soon used in large numbers. For example, along the main supply roads that could be observed directly by the enemy, large poles were placed along their length to hold netting (an often photographed example of this was the netting used by the British to conceal movement along the Menin Road). Important communication trenches were often excavated deeper than normal so that mats or nets could be laid over the trench and therefore disguise/hide movement in them.

In the case of bunkers a layer of earth of varying depth was built up on its top and the sides in order to disguise it and in an attempt to make it blend in with the nearby landscape. Camouflage nets and wattle-work sections were also used to hide dugouts. With bunkers or other defences that made extensive use of concrete, there was the problem that its colour and, especially when first built, brightness, made them stand out against the brown earth. A variety of ingenious methods were developed – for example, bunkers were built within existing buildings, observation posts were established in metal tubes disguised to look like trees, bunkers were given the appearance of a normal building by giving them a roof and painting on fake doors and windows and sometimes even 'dazzle' camouflage (of a similar type to that used on ships) was painted on, as well as using camouflage 'splotches' of paint that served to break up the shape of a bunker.

Varying types of camouflage were used during the construction of the site, but it was often the case that some form of permanent camouflage was needed. The need became especially apparent further to the rear of the German line after 31 July 1917; considerable parts of this German hinterland, which had remained hidden from direct observation until then, now became visible to allied observers on the ground because of the slow, gradual move of the front eastwards during the Third Battle of Ypres. Thus during the second half of 1917 the Germans had to divert considerable labour and resources in camouflaging as best as possible their new roads and camps. Camouflage nets and wickerwork mats were not only used alongside roads but also above railroad tracks and even to cover piles of building material.

German soldiers (note that the one on the left is wearing puttees) enjoying the fine weather in their chairs in front of a hut. It is camouflaged by a mixture of branches and paint applied in what became to be known as a dispersal pattern. (*Deraeve*)

German gunners posing near their gun position sometime after the autumn of 1916. The position is built in a wood to avoid observation from the air. When the gun was not in action the mat in the foreground was put over the gun and associated bunker to make it more difficult to spot. (*Vancoillie*)

Passive hiding.

Besides the active measures to hide construction work, completed buildings and fortifications, movements of supplies and troops, both sides took maximum advantage of the possibilities provided by the Flemish landscape. The advantage of this particular protection was that it involved minimal – if any – extra resources, a very important consideration for the Germans.

In the early stages of the war, in late 1914, woods, which were still plentifully present in the area of the Salient (pre-war this part of Belgium was notable for the number of large residences and many woods were used for hunting), were used to hide troop concentrations. Many of the semi permanent camps were erected in the existing woods. Houthulst Forest, from its sheer size, was not only effectively a gigantic camp for troops who were resting or not deployed in the battle zone, but was also home to numerous heavy artillery pieces, as was the case for other woods in the area. Houthulst had the advantage of scale, its location outside the range of all but the heaviest artillery and the possibilities of adding infrastructure – notably varying types of rail.

Hedgerows – of which there were many more than there are today – were used to hide barbed wire entanglements or acted as cover from observation for trenches, which were often dug immediately next to them.

The landscape was taken into consideration when planning the location of concrete bunkers, with the aim of blending them into the scenery. Many bunkers were constructed in or close to existing buildings. Wooded areas served to conceal bunkers from observation. It is one of the myths that Flanders is uniformly flat; in particular, the Salient is relatively hilly – or at least has low level ridges – and the Germans made full use of the topography to hide their bunkers.

Sections of wattle-work have been placed on the roof and against the walls of this bunker. It has been built close to the existing farm building (and in a similar style) to conceal it. (*Vancoillie*)

Loop-holed plates and armoured cupolas.

The use of loop holed plates, popularly, if mistakenly, known as sniper plates, was not something new in warfare. At the outbreak of the First World War the French already had two sorts of shields: an offensive shield, small and portable; and a defensive shield, larger and heavier. The Germans had the Schutzschild 08, designed for machine guns. Early in the war they designed and brought into production a so-called Schutzschild mit Schießscharte (armoured shield with loophole). It was small but very thick (15 mm) and was made of soft steel, making it very heavy. It had no supports and was designed to be wedged into position between sandbags.

After a year of war, all the belligerent countries had developed trench shields to protect their troops. The shields were mainly designed to offer extra protection to the rifleman in the trenches – particularly those who were sentries – and those manning the advanced listening posts, used for observation and as advanced sentry posts. This led to the rather misleading (to put it kindly) nickname 'sniper plate' for these protective chunks of metal.

From 1915 on there were experiments with portable shields, equipped with a handle, that could serve as protection when fixed into the ground, the so-called Schreitschild (advancing shield). Behind this shield an infantryman could take cover and fire through a small aperture that could be opened and closed, even when advancing into No Man's Land. The French experimented with an extraordinary looking contraption, a sort of inverted cut away bathtub mounted on wheels, in an attempt to provide protection for infantry in the attack.

All of these shields were heavy and had only limited efficiency. Bullets and shell fragments penetrated these protective means. The shields soon became obsolete. To observe No Man's Land and the enemy trenches it was recommended to use trench mirrors or trench periscopes during day light hours, safer to use for sentries as they did not put themselves at risk when using them.

A German front trench, whose walls have not yet been reinforced, during the winter of 1914-1915 in the woods near Herenthage Chateau, south of the Menin Road. Several 'sniper plates' can be seen fixed to the parapet with rifles ready to fire on the opposing British and French positions. At least two of the soldiers pictured have been awarded the Iron Cross. (*Vancoillie*)

From late 1914 until mid 1917 high trees were used to build observation posts for artillery units. In the upper reaches of large trees a wooden, open platform was built by using wooden planks attached to the trunk. If there were no high trees present where an observation post was needed, engineers build a wooden, open observation tower, where observers could stand on a platform. Closer to the line wide metal tubes, disguised as shattered trees, were occasionally used.

In due course there were trials to armour the German soldier himself with the so-called Stirnpanzer (a thick steel plate attached to the front of the helmet) and the Brustpanzer or Sappenpanzer, body armour for the front of the body made of several elements. These steel plates seriously limited the mobility of the wearer and were too heavy to wear. They did not protect against direct bullet hits. The experiment was not practical and the plates were soon discarded or only used by sentries in quiet regions and occasionally by machine gun operators in fixed positions.

An observation tower, to some extent disguised by the use of a tree, near Nordhof (Passendale). (*27th Infanterie Division*)

British soldiers investigate a 'Fahrpanzer' close to Stirling Castle after its capture in August-September 1917. These armoured cupolas were used by the Germans for anti tank guns. Note the concrete blocks scattered around it. (*Vancoillie*)

The only more or less successful armour came in the form of steel observation cupolas, integrated in concrete bunkers. From mid 1917 on this kind of armour was increasingly standardised. The steel plates were four centimetre thick, with openings only five centimetre high and of a limited width, sufficient to allow the use of a Scherenfernrohr (stereo-telescope).

The Germans used in some locations the Fahrpanzer, an armoured cupola armed with a 5.3 centimetre gun. This piece of artillery had been in development from 1878 by the German Grusonwerk, which became a part of the Krupp industrial conglomerate in 1893. This type of armoured gun was used in the Salient as an anti-tank gun. The cupola could be integrated within a trench; an example of this type was installed in Beukenhorstkasteel (Stirling Castle).

Constructions and shelters at the front.

Shelters in and above the ground

The men who occupied the trenches at the front were, of course, in need of some sort of shelter. These shelters were placed into categories according to the degree and type of shelter that they offered: protection against the weather (regensicher); protection against shell splinters (splittersicher); protection against a direct hit of small shells up to fifteen centimetres in calibre (schußsicher); or protection against direct impact by a heavy calibre gun (bombensicher).

In the beginning troops dug out holes in the side of the trenches. They put straw on the floor and covered the aperture with a groundsheet. These primitive shelters offered minimal protection – they were not even very good at keeping men dry. The holes were improved and strengthened by a roof made of trunks or wooden beams, preferably with a layer of roofing felt on top and a layer of several feet of earth, usually a minimum of half a metre. If rails were available, a layer of these were added to the roof. This was how most of the early shelters were made at the front and were believed to be bulletproof (schußsicher); but this was not always the case and they were certainly not shell proof. In addition, in most cases there was no drainage for groundwater or rain, which gathered on top of the roofing felt and finally found its way down into the shelter.

The walls of the constructions shelters provided a problem as well. The pressure of the soil and the groundwater forced the soldiers to build walls made of trunks or logs to support the heavy roof, weighed as it was by a mixture of tree trunks, earth and rails. Even a close miss by a

A shelter used by Landwehr Infanterie Regiment 77 close behind the front line near Wallemolen (between Passendale and Poelkapelle) during the winter of 1914-1915. This kind of shelter was supposed to offer protection against shells; something of a pious hope. (*Landwehr Infanterie Regiment 77*)

heavy shell created sufficient extra pressure on these walls that they often gave way to it. These relatively primitive shelters often collapsed and they then turned into a tomb for those inside unless their comrades were quick enough in digging them out.

On the other hand, the enemy did not have mass quantities of heavy artillery (ten centimetres or 4.5" or more) in the first years of the war, which allowed these early shelters to be in use for some time. However, it became clear early on that such shelters in the front line should be kept small and should be spread out along the length of the trench as much as possible, to avoid too many victims at once from a direct hit by a heavier shell. It soon became the practice that such shelters were moved to a second, parallel, fighting trench, dug behind the forward combat trench. This had all sorts of benefits, not least in allowing a sheltering garrison time to emerge from the protection of these shelters and to take their place in the firing line.

Shelter could also be provided by making use of damaged civilian buildings close to the front; these were adapted for a more war like use. Windows and damaged walls were sealed up and the interior of the building and its roof reinforced, with sandbags at first but in due course complete concrete structures were built within a house. Cellars were especially prized and these were later often covered with an extra layer of concrete to transform them into a dugout. Piles of debris on top served the dual purpose of an extra layer of protection and camouflage. During the early years, the houses close to the line mostly served to provide housing for the local unit headquarters (after

After the line stabilised and time and resources allowed, shelters in trench walls were fortified by the use of ferro-concrete. (*Vancoillie*)

A 'shellproof' shelter from the winter of 1914-1915, built against a ruined farm and making extensive use of tree trunks, earth and wattle-work. These shelters were, in fact, nothing more than a waste of the valuable timber used to build them; they offered no protection against a direct hit by a shell of even relatively small calibre. (*Vancoillie*)

A shelter of an artillery unit near Calvaire Ferme, between Zandvoorde and Klein Zillebeke, in the spring of 1915. The damaged farm building has been repaired on the side facing the enemy by the use of tree trunks, sandbags and wattle-work in the hope of offering some protection against artillery fire. (*Vancoillie*)

all, officers have a right to more comfortable and safer shelters!). The artillery, positioned further away from the front, became particularly adept at restoring these damaged buildings; there were, naturally, more to choose from, given the level of destruction closer to the line.

The main building materials for these early shelters were wood, iron (rails and later corrugated iron sheets) and in due course concrete. Timber was cut from woods in the immediate area, but soon it was brought up from the rear to the front to spare the woodlands at the front, as these provided good camouflage. Timber shortages soon became an issue for both sides.

From mid 1915 on the Germans used armoured concrete blocks to build shelters that were, consequently, much stronger. Gradually the types of shelters became more diverse, built to serve a specific function. To guarantee that they were schußsicher (what the British would call blast proof), ferro-concrete was used in the construction of most of the shelters built from 1915 on, even though in many places shelters made of wood or corrugated iron, built in or on the ground, were still being used. The use of concrete during the war was so vast that it justifies a chapter devoted to this subject later on in this book.

From 1915 on more and more corrugated iron was used to build shelters. Despite the fact that corrugated iron existed before the war (for example the Feldbefestigungs-Vorschrift [the Field Fortifications Manual] of 1893 describes shelters constructed with corrugated iron), it took time before German industry could produce enough of it to keep up with the demands of the military. Corrugated iron was eventually produced on a massive scale and became widely available, especially after Hindenburg and Ludendorff took control of the German military effort in late August 1916 and immediately set about reorganising the German war economy.

A partially sunk German shelter, constructed from sheets of corrugated iron and strengthened by a colourful collection of sandbags on top. (*Deraeve*)

Underground Shelters.

Underground shelters were nothing more than a logical evolution of the inadequacies of shallow shelters. To obtain greater protection, shelters were dug ever deeper. However, because of the high groundwater level in the Salient it was no easy task to build deep dugout shelters, miniterte Unterstände (or mined dugout). German sources indicate that there were few deep dugouts excavated in the Salient until 1917. The Germans did dig dugouts in banks there, ie horizontally, for instance along the Ypres-Comines Canal or in railway embankments. The standard minimum requirement for a mined dugout was at least five to seven metres of earth above the top of the shelter. A dugout that deep underground in the geological conditions of Flanders was very difficult to keep dry. However, the construction of such deep shelters was relatively easy and could be done quickly by the infantry, given technical supervision.

Wooden frames 25 centimetres thick were designed for these underground constructions; they were prefabricated behind the front in three sizes: 1.80 by 1.20 metres, 1.80 by 1 metres and 1.60 by 0.90 metres. A deep (or mined) dugout always had at least two entrances a distance apart so that a direct hit on an entrance would not block it completely. The main compartment of the dugout was located in the gallery between the two entrances.

A 'horizontal' dugout was excavated in 1996 near Potsdam Redoubt (Schwabenhof, in the Albrecht Stellung). On both sides of the railway embankment of the Roeselare-Ypres line, the Germans built concrete bunkers; in between a dugout approximately eighteen metres long ran between them, under the central part of the railway embankment. The entrances were located on both sides of the embankment; two in the direction of Ypres and one in the direction of Zonnebeke. On one side of the tunnel there were seven double bunk beds (though often in these shelters the beds were arranged in three tiers). The limited depth of the shelter proved to be its undoing. A direct hit partly destroyed it and killed six Germans soldiers who had been resting or sleeping on the bunk beds at the time. Their remains were still present when the dugout was unearthed in 1996.

After the Battle of Messines in June 1917 the Germans halted underground warfare completely in the Salient and, indeed, in much of the rest of the front, although not entirely. [As did the British; the last major mine fired by the British was at Givenchy in August 1917.] The units that until then were in charge of tunnelling operations, the Pionier Mineur Kompagnien (Pioneer Mining Companies – the British equivalent were the Tunnelling Companies), were immediately reassigned to other tasks. They were attached to the Stabsoffiziere der Pioniere (Stopi) (ie the Pioneer Staff officer) and most of them were tasked with assisting in building the rear defence lines. A number of these companies got the assignment of

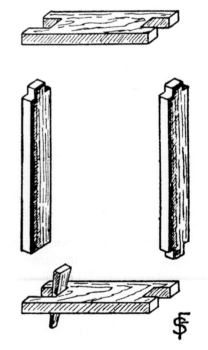

Minierrahmen, a frame used in underground constructions (including tunnelling). This frame could be easily assembled by the use of a bridle joint; the outer corner was fixed by using a wooden wedge. (*Seeßelberg*)

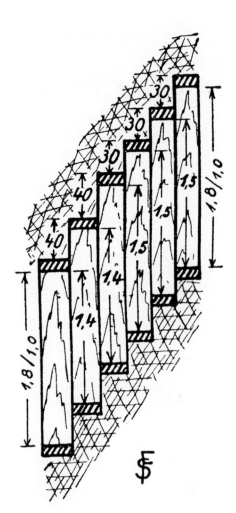

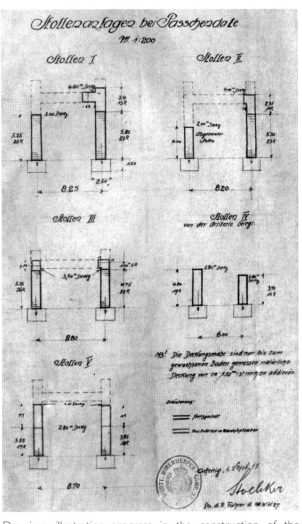

A diagram illustrating how an incline staircase could easily be built by using these frames. (Seeßelberg)

Drawings illustrating progress in the construction of the dugouts, built by Minenwerfer Kompagnie 27, near Passendale in August 1917. (HStAS)

constructing minierte Unterstände (mined dugouts) during the summer of 1917. In the Gruppe Ypres sector, Pionier Mineur Kompagnie 322 (stationed in Passendale) built deep dugouts in the sector of the 233rd Infanterie Division in the area near Mosselmarkt (Passendale). Pionier Mineur Kompagnie 294 (stationed in Moorslede) worked on deep dugouts in the Verlorenhoek sector of the 17th Infanterie Division. In the area of Nordhof (Passendale, near Veal Cottages), there are indications that deep dugouts were excavated there.

From August 1917 on more and more minierte Unterstände were built in the Salient; from October 1917 onwards the emphasis on the construction of this type of shelter was further emphasised, mainly because of the fact that suitable locations for them were now closer to the front line. Minierte Unterstände were easier and faster to build than concrete bunkers and when made well were also safer. Pionier Kompagnien, as mentioned, were ordered to build these deep dugouts, but a lot of Minenwerfer Kompagnien (Trench Mortar Companies) were also set on this task.

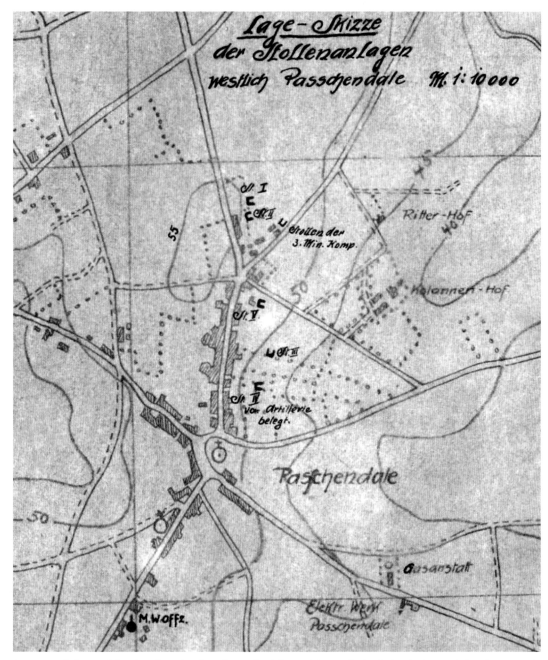

A map of Passendale showing the location of minierte Unterstände (mined dugouts) in the area in August-September 1917. (*HStAS*)

Mined dugouts could be constructed in places where the underground clay layer touches the surface, something that is the case in the area of Westrozebeke and Passendale. In most cases in the Salient underground water-bearing layers (aquifers) lie on top of the clay layer, so that suitable locations for such workings are rare. When the aquifer is shallow it was possible to sink a straight shaft through this layer to reach the clay layer below. The higher ground between

Stadendreef and Moorslede was suitable for the excavation of mined dugouts. In some locations in that area there are dry sand layers of six to ten metres depth, in which deep dugouts could easily be built. The disadvantage lay in the fact that surface water oozed through the sand layer into the minierte Unterstände, which needed to be pumped out constantly during rainy weather (which it was, more often than not).

Although most mined dugouts were relatively small, some larger systems were constructed, for instance in the railway embankment to the northwest of Stadenberg, where an underground tunnel system with six entrances was built with a total length of over a hundred metres.

Shelters from late 1917 onwards.

The increasing weight of artillery fire from mid 1917 on destroyed a large proportion of the existing shelters and complicated the construction of new shelters. It became very hard to get the necessary building materials to the front and every evident change in the landscape came immediately under fire. The Germans rethought their system and developed new types of shelters, relatively easy to construct, requiring few materials and which could be hidden in the moonscape to which the battlefield had been reduced. It became typical from mid 1917 on that protection did not depend on ever more reinforced constructions but on actively or passively concealing them.

Thus a new type of shelter was adopted, one within a shell hole. With very limited means (a sheet of corrugated iron, some steel plates, some timber, a duckboard and some branches) a shelter could be made in which three men could lie down. These 'hiding holes' – what might later be described as fox holes – were mainly made using the so-called Heinrich Wellblecheinheit, a curved corrugated iron sheet 2.3 metres in length, one metre wide and with a 0.55 metres curve. More complex shelters, constructed with what the British sometimes described as elephant iron, were called Siegfried Unterschlupfe.

The most used shelter from late 1917 was one made of Siegfried corrugated iron sheets (Schurzblechrahmen). These corrugated iron sheets were 0.28 metres wide and could be bent in a U-shape of approximately 1.4 metres high and 1.10 metres across. These sheets could be easily connected to each other by means of small iron bars. They were attached at the bottom to wooden planks (to silence the noise and to avoid condensation on the iron). Putting seven of these plates together, a standard-size shelter of some two metres long could be swiftly and easily constructed (the estimated construction time for such a shelter was four to six hours). Up to three soldiers could be

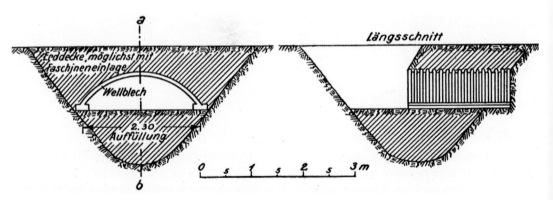

A diagram showing a shelter that could be easily and quickly built inside a shell hole. (*Seeßelberg*)

housed in the shelter; this type was first used in the Wotan Stellung and the Siegfried Stellung in the spring of 1917 and soon appeared along the whole German front. There was another option for a similar shelter for three men, using three sheets, that could be built even faster; but this type allowed sufficient space for seating only for the three men. The depth of this shelter was about 1.20 metre. Such a shelter could be constructed in less than two hours. These Siegfried Schurzrahmen were available in huge numbers from the spring of 1917.

By early 1918 the artillery needed to take up new positions in the destroyed landscape. The gunners were forced to build simpler basic shelters, using timber and corrugated iron sheets. These huts and shelters were no longer built according to standard types or plans and were put together by making use of whatever materials were handy.

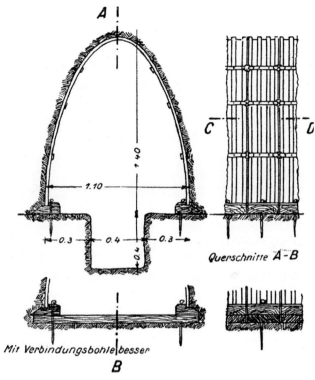

Technical drawing for building a shelter using Siegfried sheets of corrugated iron. (Seeßelberg)

German soldiers in front of their Siegfried shelters in the Ypres Salient during the winter of 1917-1918. (Vancoillie)

An 'unofficial' shelter, which provided cover for several soldiers. Most of the protection it offers is because of its location near a hedgerow. (*Vancoillie*)

From Tented Encampments to Hutted Camps: Accommodation Behind the Front Line.

Development of different types of Accommodation.

As soon as the opening moves of the armies ground to a halt in the winter of 1914 and were transformed into trench warfare, there was a growing and immediate need for satisfactory billets in what turned out to be a harsh winter. A relief system of rotating troops in the front line zone was introduced, with troops in the front line, troops in reserve and troops at rest. The latter were called Ruhebataillone and they needed a roof over their heads. At first existing buildings in the villages and farms close behind the lines were used to billet these troops. However, some of these villages had been severely damaged in the fighting or were regularly under enemy artillery fire (eg Zandvoorde), whilst others rapidly became overpopulated (eg Ten Brielen) Such a situation did not contribute to providing the well earned rest that the soldiers needed. Therefore it became inevitable that appropriate housing would have to be built, preferably in wooded areas. And so, for example, at Doornkapel (Chapelle d'Epines, between Zandvoorde and Kruiseke) a military camp grew up in late 1914; elsewhere similar camps arose, such as at Kalve, to the east of Passendale, or within Houthulst Forest, whose huge area enabled several camps to be erected and hidden under its trees.

Individual buildings in these camps were usually constructed by soldiers from the units in the camp who had experience in the construction of wooden houses. The style of these buildings was very similar to a typical forest hut or log cabin. The construction demanded considerable knowledge and skills; whilst the style of the buildings differed greatly from sector to sector, depending on the origins of the builders. A notable feature in this time of relative plenty was that building material was not used very economically and the process itself was not particularly efficient, however architecturally pleasing the outcome might have been.

Front line units in the Ypres Sector soon applied to Armee Oberkommando 4 (Fourth Army headquarters) for huts that could be constructed easily by less experienced men. The army staff passed the requirement on to Baudirektion 4 (Construction Directorate 4) to develop this special type of hut. This department drew up plans for a standard construction, known as 'Genter Baracke' or 'Genter Unterkunftshütte' (Ghent hut or Ghent refuge, named after Ghent, the city where Baudirektion 4 was based). The hut was basically made of wooden boards, planks and roofing. Standardised windows, doors and furniture (tables, seats and beds) were delivered together with the huts. The huts could be heated by stoves (safely installed, of course) and were electrically lit. The hut was a very successful development, was easy to maintain and to keep (relatively) clean.

A residential hut was sixteen metres long by five metres wide and could house forty to sixty men. Inside were beds for forty to sixty men, four tables and eight benches. There were also two types of huts for stabling horses. These stables were eight metres wide and 17.5 or 32.6 metres long. Inside was room for twenty-six or fifty horses. Window/ventilation openings were integrated on the long side. In addition to these types, a more permanent hut was developed, measuring 16.26 by 6.26 metres. This building was split in two by a wall, so that there was room for twelve bunks in each room. There was room for tables and benches in the middle. In order for these huts to be used rather comfortably in more wintery conditions, an extra wall could be constructed against the outer walls, using cement blocks or bricks.

Soldiers of Infanterie Regiment 143 in front of their log cabin in 1915, located somewhere between Zandvoorde and Zillebeke. Note how the roof has been constructed by the use of lengthy logs, roofing felt and layers of sandbags. It is probable that rails have been inserted between the layers. (*Vancoillie*)

The regimental staff of Infanterie Regiment 125 in the first half of 1916 was based in this imposing building, looking like a log cabin, somewhere in the area of Herenthage Wood. (*Vancoillie*)

A typical Genter Baracke in the Ypres Salient. The various sections of these huts were fabricated in the Gent area by Baudirektion 4 and then sent to the front. (*Vancoillie*)

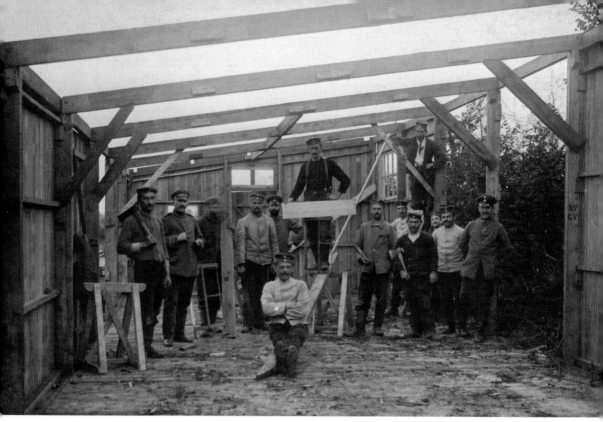

Interior view of a Genter Baracke in the course of construction. (*Deraeve*)

All the components were prefabricated in the area of Gent (Ghent) in east Flanders. In the spring of 1916 it was decided to deliver these huts not only to the German Fourth Army but to make them available to the other German Armies on the Western Front. By mid April 1917 some 25,000 Genter Baracken had been delivered, 20,000 to shelter men, 5,000 for horses. This made it theoretically possible for up to a million men and 200,000 horses to be housed in Genter Baracken. Seventy eight (Belgian) companies in the area of Gent were employed, under German supervision, in fabricating the parts for these huts. These companies employed 8,675 Belgian civilians, while 170 German soldiers supervised the proceedings. During 1916 some thirty to forty huts were produced every day, a number that was to increase! By the end of July 1918 some 50,000 Genter Baracken had been produced.

The system of constructing huts using prefabricated parts was far from new. In the 1880s a Danish cavalry captain, Johan Gerhard Clemens Doecker (1828-1904), designed a medical hut that could be easily assembled. He immediately filed the relevant patents. In 1883 he received the gold medal at the Hygieneausstellung (Hygiene Fair) in Berlin for his invention. The hut consisted of a modular system of panels, of which the parts were very easy to transport. Even non-professionals could assemble the hut with these panels within four to five hours, after which the building was ready for immediate use. The Danish company Christoph & Unmack bought the exclusive rights to the huts. To meet the large demand for them by the German army, the firm opened a factory in Niesky (Saxony). Elsewhere in Europe subsidiaries were established. The huts were widely used by different armies from all over the world and were also used for fast-expanding residential areas and in the colonies. During the First World War these Doecker Baracken (sometimes called Doeckersche Baracken) were used as extensions to many German military hospitals in Flanders and not as normal military billets.

A group of German soldiers engaged in building a hutted camp. Some of the finished buildings are visible in the background. (*Vancoillie*)

A completed Genter Baracke in use. (*Vancoillie*)

Huts used by a Feldlazarett (field hospital) in West Flanders. Doeckersche Baracken can be seen on the right hand of the photograph. (*Vancoillie*)

Other semi-permanent constructions were also developed: huts to serve as magazines, kitchen huts, aircraft hangars, etc. These were usually built further back from the front line.

During the Third Battle of Ypres new types of shelters and housing were built. Building above the ground was getting more and more difficult due to the increased shelling and the development of aerial bombing capability, which quickly destroyed such types of buildings. The construction of concrete bunkers took too much time, required a lot of building material that was, in any case, in short supply, whilst it was very difficult to build in the battle zone because of enemy observation and artillery fire. The construction of deep dugouts was limited because of the high groundwater level. This left the Germans in the battle zone with no other option than to seek shelter immediately below ground level close behind the front. They constructed shallow shelters in shell holes and so-called Erdhütten (earth lodges). The construction pit for an Erdhütte was only about one metre deep, leaving only the gable roof sticking out above ground level. The gable roof was covered with brushwood and earth on top of that. Erdhütten were very hard to spot by aerial observation, as there was only a mound of earth visible (though strict rules had to be put in place so that tracks to the entrances would not make their presence obvious from the air). This type of construction was used extensively on the Eastern Front during the First World War and even for prisoner of war camps; it was to be found in France before 1917 and in Flanders from late 1917 on.

The number of hutted camps in Flanders close to the line increased significantly from the summer of 1917; they were built over a large area behind the front. There was a severe need for more housing at this point because the number of units deployed on the Flanders front increased dramatically. These camps also housed the Eingreif Divisionen (counter-attack divisions) and many thousands of other soldiers, PoWs and labourers employed behind the front line.

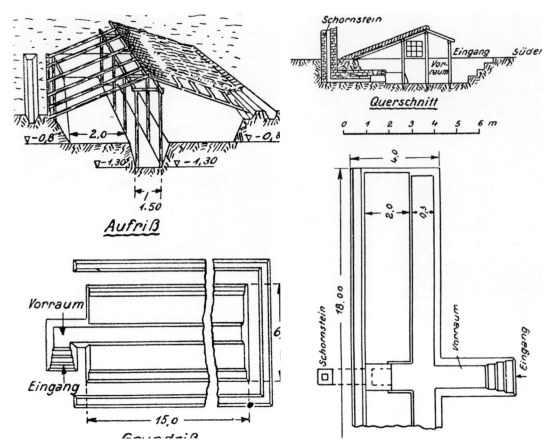

Technical drawings for building Erdhütten. (*Seeßelberg*)

As circumstances and the opportunity allowed, a brick wall was built in front of the wooden wall of huts. This was usually done to make the huts more weather and wind proof and therefore more comfortable in winter conditions. (*Deraeve*)

A hutted camp in the Diksmuide area; note the addition of the 'extra' brick wall, which naturally made for much better accommodation in the winter months. It did not stop there; attempts have been made at landscaping, complete with a pair of ornamental garden lions, probably salvaged from the grounds of a local mansion. (*Vancoillie*)

Because these camps were often targeted by air raids and long range artillery, there was a growing need to reinforce the huts. The worsening weather conditions and the coming winter encouraged the Germans to improve the existing huts by adding an extra outside wall of bricks or a thin layer of poured concrete between the existing external walls and a wooden formwork.

Some examples of Hutted Camps.

Kalve (Landwehr Infanterie Regiment 77).

Because Passendale was often shelled from late 1914, the battalion of Landwehr Infanterie Regiment 77 that was out of the line moved in December to Kalve, a hamlet about two kilometres to the northeast of Passendale. Some ruined houses and farm buildings were put back in order and made habitable. Apart from these, building material for eleven barracks was delivered, which were erected alongside the road from Oostnieuwkerke to Mosselmarkt. Both the barracks and the old farmhouses offered only poor protection against wind and rain, something that the Germans were not used to before the war, as their houses at home were better insulated. The walls were thin; the doors and windows did not close properly; during stormy weather the wind blew the rain and snow straight inside because of the unsatisfactory roofs etc. On the other hand, the sight of shells falling on Passendale and the growing destruction of that village provided some consolation to the German soldiers quartered at Kalve: at least they had a relatively safe, if far from weather-proof, shelter.

A few houses and huts were used for specific functions. There was a hut that served as a medical post, where lightly wounded and sick men could be treated. Officers had separate messes and relaxation rooms from the other ranks. A cemetery was developed near the camp. The dead of Landwehr Infanterie Regiment 77, who were brought back by the men who came to rest in the camp, were buried here. Regimental comrades took care of the layout of the graves and the development of the cemetery; carpenters made grave markers, built fences and made coffins; stonemasons provided headstones; gardeners maintained the plants. Next to the cemetery an open air altar was erected for church services. A training ground for the men out of the line was laid out, with trenches, ranges and an area for hand grenade practice. They even built all the facilities for training the men in the different elements of horsemanship, including a riding school. After all, all officers (and many senior NCOs) were supposed to know how to ride a horse – still the quickest means by which to get from A to B in most circumstances in the battle zone, a skill not that evident amongst many of the freshly promoted soldiers. When Landwehr Infanterie Regiment 77 left the area in May 1915, they bequeathed a very well equipped and organised military camp, complete with all the necessary infrastructure, to their successors.

Waldlager Melaene: Reserve Jäger Bataillon 18 and Landwehr Infanterie Regiment 35.
After the gas attacks of 1915, several camps, so-called Waldlager (forest camps), were erected in Houthulst Forest. Near Melaene Cabaret (a house near Ptarmigen Junction), a camp was built that was first occupied by Reserve Jäger Bataillon 18 on 5 May 1915 and which they called Barackenlager Melaene (Hut Camp Melaene). The huts had just been erected when they arrived and there were initially not enough beds for all of the men. Gradually the number of beds was increased. Embellishments were not forgotten. Among the first newly erected buildings were, of course, a Kantine (canteen, for NCOs and other ranks) and a Kasino (officers' mess).

The huts were spread out in between the trees, which could not be cut down for reasons of concealment. The trees did provide some issues – how could one organise a respectable troop inspection or parade in the camp? A short stretch of trench was excavated in close proximity to the huts so that soldiers could take cover in case of a bombardment. The most remarkable thing, perhaps, about the camp was the bathing installation. Initially there were only a few showers available; three men had to share one showerhead. Later some bathtubs were installed, which allowed for an individual bath. Before the company in the camp could bathe they had to collect wood in the forest and then needed to pump water to the boilers. The bathing installation was not particularly luxurious, but was obviously of hygienic value and a great luxury for men who would have endured the filth and muck of the trenches before they came to this demi paradise.

When Reserve Jäger Bataillon 18 left the camp it was named 'Jägerlager' in their honour. Landwehr Infanterie Regiment 35 then occupied both this camp and another camp close by. The huts each provided on average space for forty five men. In the summer the thin wooden walls were sufficient; but when winter came it was far from comfortable living in the wooden buildings. Each hut had two substantial tables and long benches, pallets (bags filled with straw to sleep on), positioned when not in use along the walls, and an iron stove in the middle of the hut. The washing facilities available in the camp, water wells and washing basins, were more than welcome for the soldiers returning from the front line. To improve the camp, craftsmen from the regiment stayed behind when the rest of the men moved up to the front line: carpenters, furniture makers, bricklayers, potters, basket weavers, broom makers etc. As winter

German soldiers photographed in front of their log cabin inside Houthulst Forest. (*Vancoillie*)

Hygiene was a major consideration when planning a hutted camp; they were usually quite overcrowded and therefore the risk from contagion was high. In Houthulst Forest (Barackenlager Melaene) this common Donnerbalken (latrine) was designed for the NCOs and men, officers usually had private toilets. (*Vancoillie*)

approached, in November 1915, the Germans decided to move the billets for the resting units to the village of Staden, accommodating them in repaired and requisitioned houses and partly in huts that still had to be constructed.

Stampkot, near Staden: Landwehr Infanterie Regiment 35.
An advance party of twelve men were sent to Staden on 26 November 1915 to construct a new hutted camp for the first battalion of Landwehr Infanterie Regiment 35. These men started by making tables, benches and beds to furnish the billets. They repaired the windows and doors of the damaged houses that had been assigned for use as quarters. In the evening the soldiers would go to the railway station of Staden, where four train wagons were located, fully laden with building material for huts. By 15 December two large barracks (Genter Baracken) were ready to be occupied. Each barrack could house sixty men and was equipped with all necessary beds, tables and benches. A large stable hut was built for horses next to the men's quarters, with a floor made of tree trunks. Three partly destroyed houses had been repaired and equipped with wooden dividing walls, stairs, doors, windows, beds, tables and chairs. At the disposal of the dozen craftsmen were: a hammer, two stonemason's hammers, two saws, pliers, a chisel, a joiner's plane, a block plane, a plane and a handsaw. By Christmas two more huts had been finished: a hut for the administration of the battalion and a first aid post. The first aid post had a double wall filled with earth, thus providing better insulation for the building.

Chapter 2

Defence by Concrete

The Scale of the Work

The number of concrete bunkers built by the Germans on the Ypres front was huge. A document dating from November 1916, pre-dating the start of the building of the many bunkers in the different Flandern Stellungen, provides the staggering total of 4,465 concrete bunkers for the whole of the German Fourth Army. This number can be sub-divided into: 768 bunkers built in the Marinekorps area (near the coast); 403 bunkers in the sector of the 20th Landwehr Division (Yser front); 518 bunkers in the sector of the 19th Landwehr Division (Diksmuide area to Bikschote); 1,773 bunkers in the sector of IX Reservekorps (northern part of the Ypres Salient); 500 bunkers in the sector of the 207th Infanterie Division (central Ypres Salient); 118 in the sector of the 204th Infanterie Division (southern Ypres Salient); and 385 in the sector of XIX Armeekorps (Wytschaete Salient).

The huge number of fortifications within IX Reservekorps' area, which held the sector between the Ypres-Roulers railway to Bikschote, is especially striking. There were 757 concrete bunkers in the first two lines of the front position alone and another 245 in the Third Line. 633 bunkers were in the second position (Albrecht Stellung) and 123 in the third (Wilhelm Stellung). At that stage, only fifteen machine gun bunkers had been built between the different positions.

Later counts have not been found as yet in the archives but, considering the German building frenzy in the area from late 1916 until the summer of 1917, undoubtedly several hundred bunkers were built in the first Flandern I Stellung and Flandern II Stellung and between the two positions. From late 1917 until early 1918 – confusingly – a new Flandern I Stellung and Flandern II Stellung were built, again containing several hundred concrete emplacements. It would seem justifiable to state that from late 1916 at least as many bunkers were built as were already finished at that point, which suggests a minimum total of 9,000 bunkers.

Constructing with poured concrete and building with prefabricated concrete bricks.

Prefabricated concrete bricks/blocks.

Two ways of building with concrete can be distinguished: building a concrete emplacement with prefabricated concrete bricks or pouring concrete in a mould (creating a 'monolith'). Bunkers built with concrete bricks were mostly to be found at places where it was too dangerous or too difficult to pour concrete in a form. This kind of emplacement was mainly built in or close to the front line, although sometimes bunkers made from poured concrete could be found there as well. In addition, on occasion concrete brick bunkers were built far from the front line (for instance, in the Holland Stellung on the Belgian-Dutch border) because some units preferred building with concrete bricks or blocks. The peak of this method of building bunkers was in 1916.

The idea of using prefabricated concrete parts emerged in 1915. At that point, the Germans filled sandbags and barrels with concrete and built simple walls with these; these were stronger and more lasting than walls built with normal sandbags or wood. However, these buildings made from unreinforced concrete could not withstand artillery fire. Furthermore, proper masonry construction methods required for these concrete sandbags and barrels was not easy.

The Germans started making prefabricated concrete blocks in early 1915. These blocks were cube shaped and made from ferro-concrete. The cubes were then stacked loosely without cement or any form of joining them with iron rods. The roofs of these constructions were still made of wood with earth and debris piled on top. Archaeological digs near Pilkem (Fortin 17) have found remains of this type of building very close to the former German front line.

To increase the strength of the constructions, bigger blocks had to be developed, ideally eighty by forty by twenty centimetres. However, transporting these very heavy and large blocks through the narrow trenches was a very difficult job. The cubes were replaced by cuboids made from ferro-concrete during 1915. The Allies (especially the Belgian army) also developed similar concrete bricks. These ferro-concrete cuboids were installed in stretcher bonds, with cement in between the bricks. The wooden roof in due course made way for a roof made out of rails or I-beams, with ferro-concrete blocks on top. The limited bearing capacity of the rails or beams was a serious defect as they had to bear both the weight of the concrete blocks and the

A German shelter in the Ypres Sector, constructed with loosely stacked concrete blocks. (*Vancoillie*)

force of an explosion. Only small chambers could be made in this way and the thickness of the roof was limited. The fact that the concrete bricks were joined only by cement further limited the strength of this emplacement when hit by a shell. The Germans tried to solve this problem by developing a ferro-concrete block with holes. These blocks could be used in stretcher bonds using cement and placing iron rods through the holes, holding the bricks together. This type of construction was a lot stronger. The roof was still resting on rails or I-beams lined up above the chambers, but some experiments were performed using long concrete lintels. The limitations in the size of the chambers continued to be a problem, as a result of which no larger or more functional bunkers could be built using these ferro-concrete blocks.

The blocks themselves were fabricated on an industrial scale in concrete factories behind the front. For the Flanders area, such factories existed in Wervik, Roeselare, Koekelare and Einsdijk, where German military workers and Belgian civilians made thousands of them. These blocks were transported to the front line using narrow-gauge tracks. To build a small personnel bunker, measuring 4.12 by 5.12 metres near the Bluff in May 1916, 2nd Kompagnie Pionier Bataillon 13 calculated it would need 580 full, 210 half, 110 oblique full, sixty oblique half and twenty corner blocks. In addition to these, twenty I-beams (total length fifty six metres) and numerous iron rods, with a total length of over 1,000 metres, were needed.

A German bunker, probably built in 1915 using massive concrete blocks. The rails supporting the roof are clearly visible. This kind of bunker was not particularly strong and was vulnerable to a direct hit by a medium calibre shell. (*Deraeve*)

German soldiers unloading building material (including ferro-concrete blocks) near Wijtschate in early 1916. (*Vancoillie*)

A German soldier-bricklayer working on a bunker using massive concrete blocks. (*IWM*)

Left: A German soldier carefully checking with an iron rod whether the concrete blocks have been placed correctly. The iron rods holding the construction together were probably inserted at the end and run through the wall laterally to avoid the need to slide heavy blocks over the rods every time one was added. (*IWM*)

Below: Experimental bunkers and shelters were made using different types of concrete bricks and beams. German construction soldiers, near Langemark, are here using concrete beams to build bunkers. Note the proximity of ruined buildings and woodland, which would both help to camouflage the completed work. (*Deraeve*)

It was possible to build small bunkers by using concrete beams relatively quickly. An iron rod was placed through each of the corners to hold everything together securely. The roof was also made of concrete beams. (*Deraeve*)

Belgian workers, under German supervision, fabricating concrete blocks in Wervik. (*IWM*)

The concrete blocks, pre-fabricated in Wervik, were then transported to the front line using a narrow gauge rail network. (*IWM*)

Bunkers built with concrete blocks are not as strong as monoliths; this weakness was also partly due to technical errors during the building process. This observation bunker was built inside Geluveld's church tower. (*Vancoillie*)

This big bunker (though not as large as some) near the railway station at Zonnebeke was built during the spring of 1916 using concrete blocks; however, this was a missed opportunity, as it was an ideal location for the use of poured concrete. (*Schmieschek*)

Although bunkers built with concrete blocks were clearly not as strong as monoliths, a large number were still being built in 1916 and 1917. The best known examples are the bunkers of the Holland Stellung. In autumn 1917 the use of ferro-concrete blocks to build bunkers was definitively forbidden, as they were for shelters close to the front line. By that time it was clear from research and first hand experience that these concrete block bunkers were far less strong than at first expected. This was also quite apparent to the British as a result of their investigation of captured German bunkers on the Ypres front. Most of the damaged or destroyed German bunkers, they found, were those built with concrete blocks.

Poured concrete.

At the outbreak of war, concrete as a building material for defensive works was well established and its use was widespread (for instance in the pre-war border fortresses). It was therefore obvious that concrete would be used to build all types of shelters and fortifications, although concrete had a poor reputation after the rapid destruction of forts in 1914. The earliest examples of poured concrete as building material on the Ypres front dates from as early as 1915. The front line units lacked a sufficient knowledge of reinforced concrete and as a consequence a lot of the building was done using simple concrete or by using ferro–concrete with too little iron or where the iron was applied incorrectly. For instance, iron surfaces that were too large (for example, by the use of sheets of iron in the concrete) resulted in too little adhesion and therefore insufficient strength. The use of a wrong combinations of material or bad ingredients (corroded iron, dirty water, coarse gravel, etc.) resulted in weak construction.

This monolithic bunker, i.e. one made with poured concrete, was constructed inside a mine crater in late 1915. Note that the walls and roof are not of the thickness that was the norm by 1917. (*Vancoillie*)

'Normal' concrete consisted of one part cement, two parts sand and four parts gravel or pebbles. A mixture of five bags of cement was enough to make a cubic metre of concrete suitable for bunkers. To make reinforced concrete, usually a mixture of one part cement, two parts sand and two parts gravel was used. The sand and gravel was normally mixed in the rear areas and the mixture was transported to the building places in or near the front line. In some cases ground up bricks were used; but this made concrete that was not as strong and the construction needed, as a consequence, a thicker layer of concrete.

Poured concrete was, preferably, made using a concrete mixer because the result was of a better quality than hand mixed concrete. A layer of up to thirty centimetres could then be poured into the formwork. After drying, a new layer could be poured. Ideally the concrete needed several weeks to completely harden.

For places where it was dangerous or difficult to work with a concrete mixer, the dry mixture was delivered to Mischplätze (mixing spots), where it was mixed with water. These places were close to the actual building sites. The mixture and the concrete were transported, preferably by Förderbahn (wagons on narrow-gauge tracks, pushed by man-power), but transport with wheelbarrows or in bags or barrels was also possible. The most important necessity was pure water on the building site. Normal rainwater, found in puddles and shell holes, could not be used as it was always polluted with soil. A particular problem, especially in Flanders, lay with the weather. When the weather was very wet, the concrete consequently had to be made a little bit drier. When the temperature dropped below 6 degrees celsius, no concrete was poured under normal circumstances. Should it be necessary in any case, gravel, sand and water were warmed in huge kettles before everything was mixed. Adding salt was another possibility. The mixture had to be kept out of the wind at all costs.

The concrete mixture had to be altered when it was used for ferro–concrete. The mixture had to be made softer by adding more water and less gravel, using a water to sand to gravel ratio of 1:2:2 instead of 1:2:4. Approximately eighty iron rods had to be used per cubic metre.

Building a solid construction with poured ferro–concrete demanded thorough technical knowledge and a lot of time and rest. Therefore these bunkers were usually built where the works were not likely to be disturbed, mostly from the second position rearwards. In the Zonnebeke area, this was the especially the case between the Albrecht Stellung and Wilhelm Stellung and further back from the front line, although many exceptions existed. Until late 1917 no standard model bunkers were developed and so, against all logic and regulations, concrete block bunkers continued to be built until well into 1917.

The building process of a bunker was phased and often several teams, each with their own specialisation, worked on a bunker. First, one team dug out soil to create an excavated site. Often civilian labourers and prisoners of war were used for this work, under German supervision. As soon as the ground was suitably excavated, a team twined iron rods into a mesh. Another team started pouring cement to create the floor plate, which served as a foundation. This mixture had less cement (one part cement, three parts sand and six parts gravel). While the floor-plate was being poured, iron workers started connecting the rods to the mesh where the walls were to be built. All the rods were connected to ensure the greatest possible strength. Wood workers then arrived to build the formwork. If necessary, the teams could work around

German soldiers building a bunker with poured concrete. Note the concrete-mixer at the top of the photograph, centre right. The concrete was poured into a narrow gauge rail wagon and then moved on rails to the appropriate point to be poured into the construction pit. (*Vancoillie*)

German soldiers standing in front of a bunker under construction near Langemark. The dry concrete mixture is taken to the building site by wheelbarrow, mixed with water and then used. Note that the chamber inside the bunker is being made with semi-circular corrugated iron sheets (type Heinrich) and that they are being as sparing as possible with the iron rods. This bunker, even though a monolith, would be easily destroyed by a direct hit by a medium to large calibre shell. (*Deraeve*)

This photograph illustrates the efforts made to camouflage a bunker construction site, which has been done here by the use of nets before any building work began, including the excavation of the foundations. (*Vancoillie*)

After the concrete for the ground plate was poured, the internal form work, in this case Heinrich sheets of corrugated iron, was put in place. The iron bars and rods to reinforce the walls were placed before the ground plate was poured so that the bunker would be one block of concrete. (*Deraeve*)

A view of the rebar beam cage of a bunker wall. Specialist soldiers made these cages by using iron rods that were bent to specific measurement in a Pionier Park nearby. Note the roof over the construction site so that the bunker was hidden from observation; and, just as importantly, so that the drying concrete would not get wet when it rained. (*Deraeve*)

The concrete was then poured into the form work layer by layer; the walls gradually built. The form work had to be braced to prevent it from collapsing under the pressure and weight of the concrete.

German officers monitored the construction closely so that all the work was done according to the methods laid down by higher command. The slide used to pour the concrete is on the lower right of the photograph. The soldier with the watering can had the job of making sure that the concrete did not dry too quickly. (Deraeve)

The rebar beam cage of this bunker has been completed; the next stage was for the concrete to arrive to complete the construction. (*Deraeve*)

Rails remained indispensable in building this type of bunker to ensure that the roof was sufficiently robust. (*Vancoillie*)

the clock. The concrete mixture was poured into the formwork whilst it was being finished and while the iron mesh was being twined. Before the roof was poured, I-beams and boards were put into position. The first layer of the roof had to dry first before other layers could be added to avoid collapse. Once this layer was dry, more concrete was poured into the formwork with the twined rods until the roof had the desired thickness. Afterwards, the pit was filled up with earth as necessary and earth was usually put on top of the roof as well. The wooden formwork was usually not removed for several reasons, which are described elsewhere.

Early in the war reinforced concrete buildings measured eighty centimetres in depth on the side facing the enemy lines and sixty centimetres on the sides. The roof was often eighty centimetres deep on the forward side and sixty at the back; whilst the reverse walls were only fifty centimetres thick. The use of iron rods inside the ferro–concrete was limited. The bunker was further reinforced by extra protective layers: on the side facing the enemy lines a layer of sandbags was stacked against the construction and on the roof layers of sandbags, fascines and sheets of (corrugated) iron were added. To protect the construction from enemy observation, a final layer of earth of variable depth was put on top of all of this.

A standard bunker, measuring approximately five by ten metres, required the following building material: ninety two cubic metres of concrete (approximately 830 bags of cement,

An Einheitsunterstand, near Ledegem, in the spring of 1918. The camouflage netting was left in place to prevent the bunker from being clearly identified on aerial photographs because of its brightly coloured, fresh concrete. (*Vancoillie*)

each weighing twenty five kilograms), 110 cubic metres of sand with gravel and 1,200 litres of water. Sixteen tonnes of iron rods were required. A real challenge lay in the fact that all the material had to be transported by narrow gauge tracks and by manpower to the building site. The minimum thickness of the roof and the walls was set at 1.5 metres by mid 1917. Only a minimum of 1.5 metres of ferro-concrete could withstand several hits by medium calibre shells or by the direct hit of one heavy calibre shell. Walls that could not be hit directly could be only one metre thick.

The German Fourth Amy had developed an Einheitsunterstand (a standardised bunker) by October 1917. This type of shelter used a concrete mixture of one part cement, two parts sand and three parts gravel. It measured 8.80 metres by 8.80 metre and had 28 m² usable surface. This type required 292 cubic metres of ferro–concrete made with 115 tonnes of cement, 245 tonnes of sand, 368 tonnes of broken stones and fifteen tonnes of iron.

Mixed and repaired constructions.

Some bunkers were built in different phases and by using different building techniques. Such a way of construction was not officially supported because there could never be an optimal connection between the layers and therefore this kind of bunker had several obvious weaknesses.

A group of German bunkers near the Hanebeek in late September 1917. The photograph clearly illustrates the use of different building methods (concrete blocks and poured concrete) in the construction of the bunkers within this group. (AWM)

Australian soldiers captured this bunker in the Hanebeek area in late September 1917. Some remains of the pre-war building in which the bunker was built can be seen to the left. An extra layer of concrete blocks built against the poured concrete construction is clearly visible on the right of the bunker. *(AWM)*

Some concrete brick or block bunkers had their roof (or at least parts of their roof) built with poured concrete. As explained earlier, building strong roofs using concrete bricks resting on rails or I-beams proved very difficult. The obvious solution was to use poured concrete for the roof.

Another frequently used technique earlier in the war was repairing damaged bunkers. In 1915 and 1916 bunkers were not that robust and were damaged more easily. To avoid having to build a completely new bunker, the soldiers regularly tried to repair the damage. Although reports afterwards claimed that the bunker was once more schußsicher (shell-proof), experience often proved that they were wrong and that they were engaging in hopeful thinking.

Earlier constructions made from poured concrete were often later reinforced with an extra layer of concrete blocks to make them stronger. It is clear that these mixed types did not accord with the rules.

In 1917 British and Allied troops captured numerous German bunkers and wanted to reuse these for themselves. As the entrance was now on the side of the Germans and the walls on that side were not as thick, the German bunkers were often adapted: a new entrance was created on the former British side (the former front) and the former rear was reinforced by an extra wall of ferro-concrete. This is an aspect that a visitor today has to keep in mind when looking at some of these bunkers; Among well known examples of a 'reversed' bunker are the Ziegler and Cryer Farm bunkers.

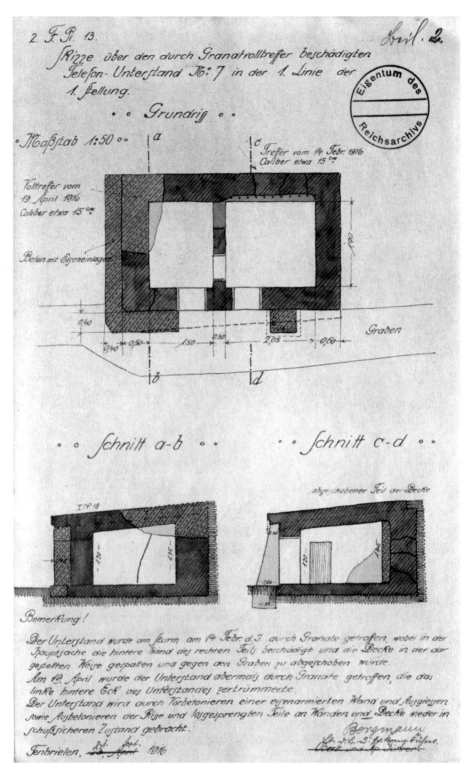

A technical drawing of the renovation of a German telephone bunker near Klein Zillebeke. The blue areas show the original construction, the red ones show the repairs. (*HStAS*)

Structural features.

Camouflage.

The principal aim of camouflage was to conceal bunkers from aerial observation; but the importance of being hidden from ground observation could not be neglected either. In this way, the element of surprise could be kept.

Many bunkers were built either close to or among buildings and disguised as similar buildings. In many cases, the builders went to the trouble of placing a wooden roof-like construction on top of the bunker and even added painted fake windows and doors on the walls of the emplacement. The effect was often improved by erecting barbed wire barricades shaped as small gardens. Some bunkers were constructed inside houses and farms, which made them even harder to spot – so long as the original building was still standing. In some cases the existing buildings were enlarged so that the bunker fitted completely inside it.

Formwork made of planks or wattle hurdles for bunkers that were more in the open served as camouflage. External formwork using wattle sections had an extra advantage: the uneven concrete surface facilitated plant growth after the hurdles were removed. The Germans sometimes added iron hooks or other means for fixing materials to the concrete so that camouflage netting, for example, could be attached. Many bunkers were given an extra layer of earth on top of the roof and/or against the walls. It served as an extra layer of protection and was often effective in concealing them.

This medical post was built inside an existing, partially destroyed, school building in an attempt to hide it from observation. (*Vancoillie*)

A well hidden medical post in the Houthulst area. It was built close to existing buildings and amongst trees and bushes, whilst camouflage netting has been spread on top of the bunker. (*Vancoillie*)

Regimentsgefechtsstand (a regimental battle headquarters) at Molenhoek, near Beselare, in August 1917. 'Windows' have been painted on the bunker wall to give the impression that it was an integral part of the farm alongside which the bunker was constructed. (*Vancoillie*)

A BTK (support battalion command post) near Beselare in the winter of 1917-1918. To camouflage the bunker, not only have 'windows' been painted on the wall, but a roof construction has been put on top of the bunker so that it would match that of a house. (*Vancoillie*)

A bunker built within a wattle-work formwork in the sector of Infanterie Regiment 188, near Woumen in the winter of 1917-1918. (*Vancoillie*)

These German bunkers near the Hanebeek were built with external form work made from wattle-work sections. This picture was taken after the Australians captured the area in late September 1917. (AWM)

The location of a bunker within the landscape was very important. Bunkers were almost never built on the crest of a hill, but rather on the slope. This made it more difficult to spot a bunker from ground level, as the bunker did not stick out so much against the background. The principle was the same as making the parados higher in a trench, so that soldiers looking over the parapet were not easy to spot. The height above ground level of most bunkers was comparable to the height of a parapet. Most of the fortifications only stood out about a metre above ground level, similar to the height of the breastworks of trenches.

From mid 1917 onwards the Ypres battle zone area increasingly resembled a lunar landscape. Bunkers that were either not disguised or from which the camouflage had disappeared (for example, the buildings around the shelter or the formwork) could be easily identified from a great distance. The fresh, pale grey concrete caught the eye against the brown sea of mud all around them. This turned the fortifications into magnets that attracted enemy observation and shell fire instead of them being safe shelters.

Development can also be seen in the level of concealment that was employed. From mid 1917 the Germans started hiding the construction site as soon as the bunker was planned. The site was shielded by a wooden construction over which camouflage netting was hung. These nets usually stayed there even when the shelter was finished. Concealment was extended to the building material dumps; whilst even the pathways used by the builders had to be hidden as much as possible.

Drainage.

Because of the sub-soil in Flanders (the impermeable layer of Ypres clay) it was not possible to dig a construction pit without ground water coming in. As soon as workers dug a hole a metre deep, inevitably ground water seeped up, a problem not only in low lying areas but on the ridges as well. However, a dry construction pit was essential for building a strong concrete bunker. The Germans started employing geologists from late 1916 onwards, during the construction of the Flandern Stellungen, to help in finding ideal spots for bunkers. These geologists investigated every building pit and gave advice. Through soil surveys, they checked whether the building pit could be deepened without hitting aquiferous soil layers. They sometimes recommended building a bunker nearby to avoid difficulties. Occasionally they advised digging ditches to drain the water. The water level of several waterways in the area was closely monitored and, if necessary, waterworks were ordered to increase drainage capacities.

Once the bunker was initially finished it had to be kept dry, an equally difficult task. Water slowly but steadily infiltrated, not only through the ground plate, but through the walls as well. In addition rain water entered the bunker during wet periods. All of this water had to be drained from the shelter whenever possible. Most bunker floors were not more than 1.20 metres under the surface. This was approximately the same depth as (or a bit less) than most trench floors. This was designed so that the trench drainage system could be used to remove the excess water from bunkers.

The rear of the German command post in Zandvoorde. The windows that allowed natural light into the bunker are clearly visible. The concrete wall on the right prevented shrapnel fragments from flying through the window openings; and, as importantly, prevented the pressure waves from exploding shells at the back from entering the bunker. The roof extends over the main construction so that rain water would not trickle down the walls. (*MMP.1917*)

It was of the utmost importance to get water as far away as possible from the bunker to prevent water collecting close to the constructions, which would eventually erode the soil from underneath it. This could lead to the bunker becoming unstable and thus become more vulnerable to tipping over.

In most cases, a gutter, which collected all the water from it, was added to the bunker. This gutter was then connected to the drainage of the trenches near the bunker or was connected to a waterway in the area. When no trenches existed in the immediate area, drainage towards a lower lying waterway was essential.

A command bunker, which still remains more or less intact in Zandvoorde, has a roof that is protruding from the back. This prevented rain water from running down the back wall and thus making the walls humid. Because of this particular method of construction, the water comes down at some distance from the wall. The water is then gathered in a gutter in a concrete gulley running behind the bunker and diverted away.

Another option for keeping bunkers dry was digging one or two sumps at the lowest points of the shelter. Such a sump measured 0.50 by 0.50 metres and was 0.70 metres deep. A pump, powered by electricity or by manpower, was then placed in the sump. The water was drained away through a hose towards a ditch or drainage system in the area. During the relatively quiet period of 1915-summer 1917 many bunkers, even in the front line, were connected to an electricity grid, installed to power these water pumps. From mid 1917 maintaining the electricity lines became increasingly difficult because of the incessant artillery fire. Manpower remained as the only possibility of keeping the pumps pumping.

Entrances, observation holes and loopholes.

Any openings, whether they be doorways, windows, loopholes or observation holes, reduced the strength of any concrete bunker. Therefore, as few apertures as possible were made and when they were, they were made as small as possible.

On the side facing the enemy, observation apertures and loopholes in observation bunkers and machine gun and artillery bunkers were included from 1915 to 1917. These relatively small observation apertures were used in bunkers in and near the front line. They were usually just big enough so that you could use a Scherenfernrohr (a binocular periscope) or simply binoculars. Loopholes for machine guns were somewhat bigger, but built conically, bigger on the outside than on the inside. The loopholes in artillery bunkers were usually significantly larger.

Building bunkers with any holes towards the enemy's side was strongly discouraged from mid 1917 onwards as these bunkers were too vulnerable, not just to a direct artillery hit but, more especially, to the pressure wave of an explosion in front of the bunker. Shooting from inside a bunker was also discouraged because of the very limited observation possibilities from inside it. It was, in fact, very difficult to observe the result of the fire.

Observation from inside the shelter was made possible from late 1917 onwards by using a small hole in the roof through which a trench periscope could be put. Every room in a bunker had one such observation hole in the roof (in case one of the rooms became unusable). Another option was a large hole in the roof into which a steel plate or observation turret was placed. From late 1917 shooting was from a platform at the back of the bunker or close by a bunker and no longer from inside the shelter.

Ideally, there would be two entrances to a bunker, sixty to seventy centimetres wide and 1.80 metres high. This prevented the bunker crew being trapped when an entrance was blocked.

An observation post at het Sas, near Boezinge. In fact, if the circumstances allowed it, observation from a position outside the bunker was much easier. The Scherenfernrohr (stereo-telescope), on the right, was used to observe the enemy positions and movements and to calculate the range. A telephone attached to the wall, left of centre, ensured that observations could be immediately reported to the relevant battery. (*Schmieschek*)

When there was, for whatever reason, only one entrance to a bunker, an emergency exit was normally available. This was a manhole measuring fifty by fifty centimetres. From mid 1917 on, the principal entrance door was a two-part stable door made from thick wood (five centimetres at least) and with strong hinges. A single–part steel door could be deformed by an explosion and thus block the entrance. The chances were better that at least one part of a two part stable door could be opened, even after damage by an explosion. Even if the wooden door would not open, the door could be smashed with an axe, something that would not be possible in the case of a steel door. To minimise the effect of the pressure wave of an explosion, the entrance was designed that it should not immediately give out to a room and there had to be a hallway. A bunker door also had to have a rim, so that that the door could not slam open inwards because of an explosion outside the bunker. The door was designed to open outwards to avoid any pressure wave of an explosion travelling into the bunker. The most deadly danger for a bunker crew was the high pressure wave of an explosion entering the confined space of the bunker.

Window openings to allow light to enter the otherwise dark bunker were usually to be avoided. Such window openings were, however, usually included at the rear of medical bunkers and command bunkers. To prevent shrapnel from flying into the bunker through these openings, a protective wall was built 1.50 to two metres from the rear of the bunker. This wall was usually poured at the same time as the rest of the construction and was built on the ground platform. A small hole was normally drilled into the back wall of a bunker to allow electricity or telephone cables to pass through.

A German observation post built inside an existing building. Remains of the original outside wall are still visible on the lower part of the building. The observation slit is visible on the upper right of the bunker. Note the wooden bunker door; the emergency exit can also be seen, also provided with a wooden door. This door opened outwards to prevent the concussion of an explosion from forcing inside the door inwards and, possibly, harming the bunker's residents. (*Vancoillie*)

German soldiers in front of a bunker at a Pionier Park near Westrozebeke. Note that the door stands open against the outside wall. It was probably made of wood and covered with a thin sheet of iron. An axe can be seen attached above the door. This allowed a trapped crew inside the bunker to hack their way out if the door was blocked. (*Deraeve*)

A German command post near Hollebeke, built into a road embankment. Several windows are visible at the back to allow natural light to enter the bunker. (*Vancoillie*)

Interior work.

In bunkers made with poured concrete, the wooden formwork was normally left inside once the building was finished. This wooden formwork was an important element, serving as insulation against cold and moisture. Usually a layer of roofing felt was attached to the formwork to keep the moisture out of the room. Attaching roofing felt to bare concrete was not possible.

The wooden formwork had extra advantages. A nail could be driven into the wood or a screw could be screwed in, which allowed telephone cables or electricity lines to pass inside bunkers. Shelves or small cabinets could be hung up so that personal belongings or military materials could be easily stored. If the formwork was not kept, niches were designed during the construction stage and inserted into the concrete walls, usually by placing ammunition cases in the poured concrete. These niches could be used to store a wide variety of things.

The most important advantage in leaving the formwork was safety. When a shell hit a bunker and exploded, it was not unusual for pieces of concrete to come off the interior walls and roof. Without the wooden formwork, these pieces of concrete would fly around the chambers, possibly causing injury to men in the room. If the woodwork was left in place the pieces of concrete were much less likely to move much. In some cases the formwork was intentionally removed and the walls cemented on the inside, to prevent water infiltration. Usually a similar thin layer of cement was applied on the outside wall as well (Zementglattstrich).

Because making a wooden formwork took both a lot of time and scarce material (particularly wood), the Germans used elephant shelters to make rooms (or chambers) inside a poured concrete bunker.

At least from 1917 on, the comfort of the bunker crew was improved by always ensuring that each room had heating. Therefore, each chamber had a place to put a small stove and a small opening in the side or the back of the bunker to allow the smoke to escape via a stove pipe. These stoves had three functions: for heating, ventilation and preparing warm food and drinks.

Obviously the stoves created some heat inside the bunker. Apart from the heat itself, the escaping warm air from the bunker created a natural air flow, as warm air rises. This flow of air helped the bunker to stay dry and drew fresh (cold) air into the shelter. The stoves (usually so-called Hindenburgofen) not only served to warm up the food, but were equipped with special hooks on which to hang mess tins. Thus, the contents stayed warm; and warm food is known to give morale a boost – a significant one in poor conditions.

The strength of the shelters.

Shelters were divided into four strength classes: regensicher (protects against weather conditions); splittersicher (protects against shrapnel); schußsicher (shell-proof, protects against direct hits by small calibre guns); and bombensicher (shell-proof, protects against a direct hit by heavy calibre guns). Concrete bunkers should always be schußsicher and bombensicher, although in fact this was far from always being the case, mainly because of faulty building techniques or the use of sub-standard building materials.

As building techniques improved over time, concrete bunkers become ever stronger. These improvements were trialled behind the front line in special test facilities. The best known of these test facilities was at Camp Marguerre, in Gouraincourt Wood near Loison, not far from Verdun. Technical officers performed all kinds of tests and shared the results with front line officers through courses and articles. The German High Command regularly updated their manuals and Merkblätter so that everyone was aware of the newest technical improvements as soon as possible.

This is what remains of a regensichere (weatherproof) or splittersichere (shrapnelproof) shelter after it had suffered a direct hit. This picture was taken near Anzac Ridge is late September 1917. (AWM)

Bunkers built with concrete bricks were not as strong as monoliths. This construction has been destroyed by a direct hit. The rails that supported the roof are clearly visible. (*Vancoillie*)

This monolothic bunker was destroyed by a shell. It is quite evident that the roof was not thick enough. (*Vancoillie*)

It was imperative that there was adequate connection work between the different layers and building phases. This was obviously not the case in this example. Weak spots could lead to the complete destruction of a bunker by a direct hit. (*Vancoillie*)

Originally concrete shelters had thin walls or walls made of concrete bricks, but by summer 1917 walls had to be made of at least 1.20 metres thick reinforced concrete (front and sides; the back wall could be 0.80 metres). The Einheitsunterstand, developed and built from October–November 1917 onwards, had front and side walls of 1.50 metres and a back wall of a metre. These concrete fortifications were constructed on a one metre thick reinforced concrete base plate or floor, which extended a metre beyond the building at the front and sides. This base plate prevented shells that ricocheted off the walls downwards from exploding under the bunker and toppling it over.

From late 1917 bunkers became the focus of particular attention by the British artillery (and thus of its observers, both on the ground and in the air) in preparation for an attack. Using observation planes and other means, the heaviest guns (those with a calibre over 28 centimetres) took concrete fortifications under fire one by one until one or more direct hits were observed to have destroyed the targeted construction, after which the next bunker came under attack. On 22 October 1917, three bunkers in the sector of 1st Kompagnie Bavarian Infantry Regiment 22, stationed near Passendale, were destroyed using this method. Twenty six German soldiers were killed and forty wounded, among them the company commander. However, precision artillery fire using heavy calibre guns was extremely difficult to achieve because of the huge distances involved.

One of the reasons why the British experienced difficulties in destroying German concrete bunkers had to do with the types of shells and fuzes employed. British HE (high explosive) shells usually had a fuze and detonator at the tip of the shell. As this detonator was usually made of brass, a rather soft metal, the shell did not penetrate into the reinforced concrete and thus the subsequent explosion happened on the outside of the concrete layer and did not penetrate it to any significant degree. At best, this kind of explosion caused some pieces of concrete to come loose on the inside of the bunker but it did not damage the integrity of the shelter. These loose pieces of concrete on the inside were mostly held in place by the formwork of wood or elephant shelters that had been left in place. To destroy a reinforced concrete bunker effectively, the projectile had to penetrate into the concrete and then explode; the same way that armour piercing shells work. During the First World War, Germans had shells with solid steel tips with a base fuze that had been developed to destroy fortresses; the British did not have this ammunition at their disposal for targeting German bunkers.

The main reason that the Germans built bunkers in the Ypres Salient above ground level instead of employing deep dugouts (from early 1917 on increasingly known as mined dugouts) was because of the high underground water level, itself a consequence of the underlying impermeable clay layer (generally known to the British as blue clay). This geological situation had consequences for the concrete bunkers. During the Third Battle of Ypres, aquifers became so saturated with ground water (because of the rain, but also because of the destroyed drainage system of the area), that bunkers became unstable. Many eyewitnesses described their experiences inside bunkers as like being on a ship on the ocean, a comparison that fitted the geological situation well. Many bunkers in fact sank in the mud.

German bunkers in the cratered landscape of the Ypres Salient in late 1917. The bright concrete of the bunkers stands out against the brown sea of mud all around them. During bombardments, these bunkers were likened to ships drifting on the ocean. *(Vancoillie)*

A further problem that arose because of these geological conditions was the fact that bunkers could tip over during bombardments. Because of the muddy ground, shells penetrated deep into the unresisting earth before they exploded. If this were to happen under a bunker wall, the resulting explosion fairly deep in the ground could tip it over. The use of standard ordnance by the British meant that their shells could be effectively used to create this outcome. In addition, a shell that ricocheted off the side of a bunker and exploded at the bottom of the wall could also tip over the shelter if the explosion were powerful enough (and hence the recommended extension of the base of the bunker beyond its walls).

A significant number of soldiers within bunkers thus got buried in a concrete grave; the Germans therefore came up with solutions to prevent their soldiers from being trapped in such a situation. The first solution was to include several entrances on multiple sides of the shelter. Traditionally, the main entrance was found at the back of a bunker, but a second entrance was now made in one or both of the side walls. Thus, there was the option of an exit should the shelter be pushed over on its back and the rear exit blocked. The second solution to the problem was to extend the reinforced concrete base plate on all sides of the construction. This base plate was approximately a metre thick and now extended up to 1.50 metres from the bunker. Thus, ricocheting shells could not explode under the bunker or at the bottom of the wall but, at worst – or best, depending on which side you were on – between the base plate and the wall. The constructions were designed to be able to withstand explosions of this type.

Destruction of bunkers by the defenders.

The Germans lost numerous bunkers during the Allied attacks in Flanders in 1917. The Germans were naturally unhappy that the enemy should get the benefit of strong shelters that they had built themselves. As a consequence, the Germans tried to ensure that bunkers were destroyed as late as possible before capture. Small local actions were also organised to recapture lost bunkers, even if only temporarily, and to place explosives and blow them up on withdrawing. The Germans detached some Pioniere (engineers) for such actions solely for this purpose.

The Pionier Versuchs Kompagnie was attached to the 3rd Marine Division (3rd Naval Division), then stationed near Poelkapelle, on 16 October 1917, when it received orders to prepare five bunkers for destruction. These bunkers were still in the German lines, but they imminently expected a major British attack and wanted to prevent the bunkers from falling into British hands relatively unscathed if they could not hold on to their positions. In total, some 750 kilograms of explosives were carried into the bunkers, which were only a few metres from the British outposts. It took an hour and a half to prepare the bunkers for destruction; as they were only to be blown up when overrun, a Pionier had to be left behind in every construction to detonate the charges if and when necessary. Three of the bunkers were, in due course, blown up during the British attack at the request of the infantry. The two other bunkers remained in German hands at first but were captured during later actions. Whether they were blown up remains unknown, as both the delegated engineers went missing during the fighting.

During this period, orders were issued that explosives with a time detonator should be put in position shortly before abandoning a bunker. As soon as the bunker was evacuated, the detonator was to be set. Future bunker/shelter design now had to take into account the possibility of demolition in the building process. In the master blueprint for the Einheitsunterstand (developed from October 1917 onwards), a niche, 50 x 50 x 50 centimetres, was included in the design of each room. Explosives could be placed in it to destroy the bunker in the case of withdrawal.

The types of bunker (shelter) according to their function.

In the following section we seek to categorise the bunkers built in the Ypres Salient according to their primary intended function. We are fully aware that many bunkers do not completely fit these various categories, not least because there was a considerable evolution in all aspects of bunkers and shelters in the period 1915 to 1918. In addition, many bunkers were built to combine several functions; whilst numerous bunkers got new functions because of the changing situation on the ground. This evolution became increasingly obvious to the Germans; their solution was to develop a standardised bunker by later 1917, whose particular function or functions would be decided by the locally engaged units.

Troop shelters.

These bunkers were built to provide relatively secure shelter for troops during bombardments. The first examples came into being when wooden shelters, built into the sides of trenches, were reinforced with concrete (i.e. at this time concrete bricks). Later, a lot of these troop shelters were built entirely made from concrete bricks. The Feldbefestigungs–Vorschrift (dating from 1893) described the option of building troop shelters using sheets of corrugated iron of the Heinrich type. Two of these sheets could be joined together to create a shelter in the form of a half circle. On top of this, a layer of concrete could be poured., At first during the war bunkers with one or two rooms were constructed. The side away from the enemy was often left open. A bunker of this type survives on Nonnebossenstraat in Zonnebeke. The construction consists of

A double troop shelter built using Heinrich corrugated iron sheets as the interior form work. The Germans built great numbers of this type of bunker between 1915 and 1917, not only in the Ypres Salient but on all fronts. (*Michael Sheil*)

a layer of reinforced concrete, a metre thick, poured on top of a semi-circular room formed by two Heinrich corrugated iron sheets. This type of shelter was very common in 1916, not only in the Ypres Salient but all along the German fronts, both western and eastern. Tests showed that this type of construction was capable of withstanding impacts from up to 21 cm calibre shells. However, the open rear created problems; an explosion at the back of this type caused a shock wave that could kill or wound the troops in the rooms.

When building the Albrecht Stellung, multiple similar rooms were built next to each other and were then linked up into 'Kasernen'. Some of these Kasernen remain, at least in part, in the Sint-Juliaan area, where Kaserne 2 Herzog Albrecht and Pond Farm are both of this type of design and construction.

English language literature (and consequently also Dutch language literature based on such works) often refers to the abbreviation MEBU, i.e. Mannschafts Eisenbeton Unterstand (reinforced concrete dugout). The various writers claim that the Germans themselves used this word as a synonym for reinforced concrete troop shelters. Although the abbreviation turns up in British sources during the war, we could not find one reference to this term in the many hundreds of pages of German source material that we came across relating to the building of bunkers in the German Fourth Army sector. Even the reference work relating to German trench building by Friedrich Seeßelberg does not use MEBU or Mannschafts Eisenbeton Unterstand. The word pops up in German slang, often in a rather sarcastic way, to refer to a very weak shelter. The word MEBU may have been used, however, for some of the constructions of the Siegfried Stellung (Hindenburg Line) in France.

Reinforced machine gun emplacement.

The importance of sufficient fire power cannot be overestimated and reinforced machine gun emplacements were built very early in the war to provide cover for machine guns against not only shrapnel and bombardments but also against mud. The first reinforced machine gun emplacements date from mid 1915. They usually consisted of two chambers: one for the machine gun and another room for the crew. The firing slit was to be found relatively high up the wall, as the bunker was built partly under the ground level and any firing, obviously, had to be above ground level. The machine gun itself was placed on a specially built strong 'table', usually made of wooden beams. To provide a decent field of fire for the machine gun, the slit was large (twenty to thirty centimetres high and often over a metre wide on the outside).

This type of bunker, in which a machine gun (MG 08) could be positioned to be able to fire through an aperture, was later called a Schartenstand (literally, a loop-holed bunker). These bunkers were built in large numbers from 1915 to 1917 in the Salient from the front line to the Wilhelm Stellung. The German tactics of defence in depth were very dependent on the widespread distribution of machine guns within the defence zone, i.e. not only in the different trench lines and positions but also in between them. The increasing number of machine guns in infantry regiments and the growing number of semi-independent Maschinengewehr Scharfschützen Abteilungen (heavy machine gun detachments) was the key factor that permitted the adoption of this new German defensive tactic.

A large number of heavy machine guns were spread out from behind the front line to the third position in so-called abgespaltene Maschinengewehrstände (literally, split away machine gun emplacements). In late 1916, orders were still issued emphasising the importance of these

A German machine gun bunker near Drie Grachten. Concrete blocks used to build the bunker are visible in the foreground. A MG 08 machine gun can be seen just inside right hand bunker entrance. Note the outward-opening wooden door. (*Schmieschek*)

emplacements being built as Schartenstände in order to protect the crews during fighting. These bunkers were to be built as strongly as possible (the walls and roof should be at least 1.50 metres thick) and that they were to be concealed using natural features and/or buildings. Enough earth was to be thrown against and on top of the emplacement to retain the cover, even after heavy bombardments. Next to the reinforced machine gun emplacement a machine gun position could also be dug outside, but the concealment of the hidden emplacement should not be endangered by this open position.

These concrete machine gun emplacements were built in significant numbers in the Flandern I Stellung. However, from the summer of 1917 the use of Schartenstände was no longer recommended for several reasons. The increasing use and distribution of the MG 08/15 (a light machine gun) by that time allowed a more mobile use of machine guns. The heavy machine guns (MG 08) could therefore be deployed in depth and not in the front line, where they were an easy prey because of their restricted mobility. In addition, a Schartenstand usually had room for only one MG 08, which hampered command and control. In machine gun units, a Zugführer (platoon commander) had two machine guns under his command. As there was only space and firing possibilities for one machine gun in a Schartenstand, the two machine guns under command of the Zugführer had to be deployed in two different bunkers, so that he could only directly command one of the two guns under his control at a time.

There were also some practical issues that had arisen with the Schartenstände. First, they were higher than normal bunkers, which made them stand out more. Secondly, the loopholes offered only limited observation and a restricted firing arc, making them easier to encircle. Thirdly, the limited field of fire, the cramped space, the noise inside and the generation of water vapour and gunpowder fumes in action made it very difficult for the machine gunners effectively to target anything satisfactorily.

Thames House, a German machine gun post in the Flandern I Stellung, built on the Ypres-Roeselare railway line. A concrete, open, machine gun position was integrated into the construction. (*AWM*)

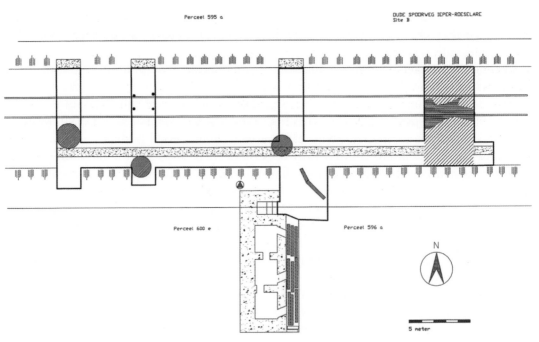

The excavation plan of the German machine gun post Thames House. The bunker had three chambers and an open machine gun position. (*MMP.1917*)

A photograph from the archaeological excavation of Thames House. The open machine gun position is visible to the right. (*MMP.1917*)

If the loophole was severely damaged the machine gun had to be taken off its sledge and fixed onto a Hilfslafette (auxiliary mounting) so that it could be fired outside the emplacement. Some machine gunners with a less soldierly spirit, it was found, preferred to stay inside the relative security of the concrete machine gun emplacements during attacks and bombardments instead of tackling the attackers with more effective fire from outside the bunker; whilst observation positions had to be in place outside the bunker.

From September 1917, new instructions stated that machine gun emplacements should be spread out more in depth, especially behind the front line and between the different lines and positions, preferably in a draughts/checker board pattern, so that they could fire independently and make best use of flanking fire, the ideal option for a machine gunner. Depending on the nature of the landscape (i.e. relatively open or closed country) bunkers were to be built further apart or closer together. Every machine gun emplacement had to provide shelter for a platoon commander and ten men and contain two machine guns with sledge and spare sledge, fifty boxes of ammunition, eight water containers, 6,000 unbelted rounds in boxes and a hundred hand grenades. There was to be room for tools and cleaning material and enough rations for the occupants for three to five days. In important tactical positions, extra platoons of infantry had to be provided with shelter. These bunkers were rapidly becoming strong points, effectively thickening the traditional lines of defence into a broad defensive zone, autonomous in ammunition, manpower and rations.

Because all infantry companies had several MG 08/15 at their disposal from the summer of 1917 and the MG 08 of the machine gun companies were to be placed in depth, extra machine gun emplacements had to be included in the planning when preparing the Flandern II Stellung

German machine gunners with their gun at the back of a bunker. The machine gun was attached to a Hilfslafette and could be fired from the roof of the bunker or from a nearby shell hole. (*Vancoillie*)

in September 1917. Therefore twelve machine gun posts were incorporated in each regimental sector between the second line of the front line and the Artillerie Schutz Stellung. As time was not available to build these concrete bunkers (Third Ypres was in full swing at the time), orders were issued to construct, as a temporary measure, well concealed and splinter-proof machine gun posts containing two machine guns. If Schartenstände were built, they were to have loop holes in the sides and rear – i.e. making them capable of all round defence. In any case, planning for such bunkers had to allow for deploying fire from outside the bunker, whilst the emplacement had to be easily defensible against encircling attacks.

Medical bunkers/dugouts

Concrete medical dugouts were to be found all along the evacuation routes for the wounded within any sector. These bunkers had several rooms. They were relatively spacious so that a number of wounded could be sheltered as well as treated. The medical dugouts had separate chambers for post treatment care and for the medical personnel. A most important aspect of these constructions was the wide entrances, broad enough so that a stretcher could be brought in without hindrance. Naturally, it was vital that there should be enough light inside; this was achieved by large windows at the back of the bunkers, whilst electric lighting was made available as a priority.

As many medical posts as possible were placed inside concrete bunkers in order to guarantee the safety of both patients and medical staff. The planners were naturally aware that during heavy fighting and bombardments the chances of being wounded increased. If the medics had to treat the wounded without adequate cover, the number of victims could only increase.

With the increase in artillery available to both sides, as well as mortars and a huge increase in machine guns, the period 1916-1917 saw a considerable number of medical bunkers built in the Ypres Salient. These usually had three to four chambers: one for the medical officer and his orderly; one for treating the wounded; and one or two where the wounded could be laid out on beds or mattresses. The wounded would not stay for any longer than necessary in these bunkers and would be evacuated down the line as soon as practicable. At least once a day, ambulances, either motorised or horse-drawn, were scheduled to remove all the wounded and sick who could not make their way back on their own. A telephone was always present in a medical dugout so that extra ambulances or medical help could be summoned if necessary.

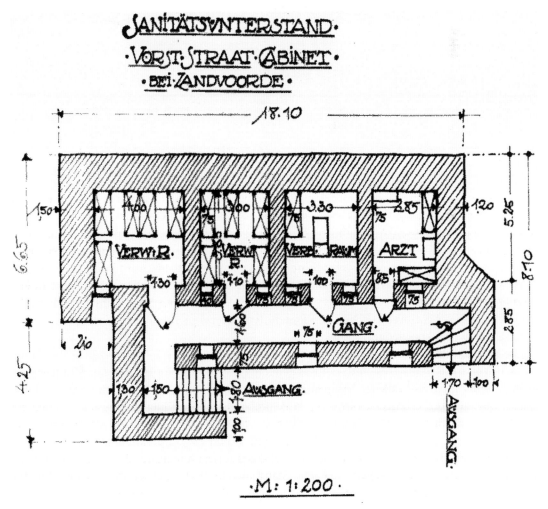

The construction plan of a medical post near De Voorstraat, on the road from Zandvoorde to Comines (some hundred metres south of the command post in Zandvoorde). This bunker was built between March and June 1917 by Sanitäts Kompagnie 563. (HStAS)

The medical post near De Voorstraat in June 1917. The exterior form work was not removed so that the fresh concrete of the walls would not reveal the bunker. In addition, a frame made with nets and branches was placed on top of the bunker to provide further camouflage. Note the Red Cross flag on the left of the photograph. (*Deraeve*)

Many bunkers were built by the Sanitäts Kompagnien (bearer companies) of the fighting divisions in the sector. If necessary they received help from labour units (Armierungstruppen etc.). The works were overseen by the Pioniere (engineers) of the division, who offered the necessary practical knowledge.

The time and the means for building any new bunkers were often lacking whilst the Third Battle of Ypres was in progress and so it was generally not possible for the Sanitäts Kompagnien to build extra medical bunkers. Medical posts had to be placed in temporary constructions, usually not shell-proof. This was seen as a huge problem and the issue was raised at the highest command levels in the autumn of 1917. When the new Flandern I Stellung and Flandern II Stellung were on the drawing board in the winter of 1917-1918, in the immediate aftermath of Third Ypres, an extra Einheitsunterstand was planned for each regimental sector to be used as a medical bunker and an extra Einheitsunterstand in each divisional sector to act as a shelter near the Wagenhalteplatz (halting place for ambulances).

Amongst the best known medical dugouts that can be seen today is the bunker at Cryer Farm, which was probably built as a Truppenverbandplatz (regimental aid post) by Reserve Infanterie Regiment 209 in spring 1917.

Storage bunker/ammunition dugout.

A bunker designed to be used as a place to safely store ammunition or other materiel was usually small. This type of bunker usually had only one entrance, no windows, nor any type of ventilation holes or other apertures. Ammunition bunkers were normally found close to artillery positions or in Pionierparke (pioneer dumps) along the main supply routes.

An ammunition bunker that formed a part of an artillery position was not, in most cases, a separate bunker but part of a troop shelter. The largest part of this type of bunker was meant for the gunners, with a smaller chamber to store ordnance. Both parts were completely separated and thus with their own entrances so that an explosion in the ordnance chamber would not have devastating consequences for the men sheltering in the other chamber.

In ammunition and pioneer dumps, several small bunkers were usually built, with space between them. These small bunkers were used to store ordnance of various types. The space intervals between these bunkers was designed to avoid serious consequences in the event of an explosion or accident in one of them.

A German ammunition bunker near Luigem (west of Houthulst). Note that both the wooden door and window shutter open outwards. The damage to the bunker over the door indicates that the Germans probably tried to destroy it when it became clear that they would lose it to the enemy. (*Vancoillie*)

German ammunition bunkers or huts forming part of the complex of an ammunition dump near Geluwe. These buildings are some distance apart to prevent a chain reaction should one of the buildings be hit and its contents explode. (*Deraeve*)

Gun emplacements.

A gun emplacement was a bunker in which a piece of artillery, including anti-tank weapons or Minenwerfer, could be placed. Typical of this kind of bunker were big loop holes and (usually) a large entrance.

Artillery bunker.

With the onset of static warfare in the autumn and winter of 1914, gunners tried to conceal their guns. At first they placed them in shelters built from wood and branches. These shelters were reinforced in early 1915: first they used thin concrete walls (either built with poured concrete or with concrete bricks), on top of which a roof made from wooden beams and rails and later from concrete beams was placed. Against the walls and on top of the roof earth was thrown to hide the construction from aerial observation (which took the form of air reconnaissance or by artillery observers in observation balloons). These shelters were often constructed inside existing buildings.

The disadvantage of this type of shelter lay in the fact that they had to have, both at the front and at the back, a large opening, which made them very vulnerable to bombardments and to counter battery fire, which became increasingly sophisticated as the war progressed. At the back a large entrance was needed to allow the gun to be manoeuvred into and out of the bunker. A concrete wall, as discussed, was often placed quite close to the rear of a normal bunker to shield the fortification from shrapnel and the shock wave from nearby explosions. This was, of course, not possible for artillery bunkers, as a gun needed several metres of free space in which to manoeuvre. At the front of the shelter a large opening was needed to provide the gun with a wide enough field of fire.

A German artillery bunker in Gapaardstraat, Wijtschate. A gun could be placed inside the bunker, which consequently has a large opening at the front and therefore made it very vulnerable. The Germans tried to improve the security of the bunker by making the walls thicker by building an extra wall from concrete blocks. (*Blieck*)

Because of the technological means that developed – such as flash spotting and sound raging – to determine the exact location of enemy guns from mid 1917 onwards, the Germans in the Salient opted to position their guns mainly in the open. Of course they tried to conceal their guns as much as possible against aerial observation and to move them around frequently; and would abandon a location once it had become evident that its position had been identified. Although this might sound a relatively easy process, the reality was that preparing an artillery position and ranging the guns was far from straight forward.

To fortify certain fixed artillery positions, the Germans continued to build bunkers into which artillery pieces could be placed. These guns were usually of heavier calibre and with a longer range. As soon as the enemy located them, however, they offered an ideal target. These bunkers were usually built on higher ground (which increased the range of the gun). As mobility and field of fire was limited, these pieces could only target certain areas, usually tactically important roads and positions. A good example of such a battery position that is more or less intact, complete with gun shelters, ammunition bunkers and observation post, can be found in Farbus Wood, on the eastern edge of Vimy Ridge; it was probably constructed in late 1916.

Usually a large number of these bunkers were specifically made to shelter a particular type of gun. It was only in 1917 that standardised designs for artillery positions appear, although these were usually open gun positions, near which bunkers were built for the gun crews and ammunition. The gun itself stayed in the open.

Another type of artillery bunker, if it can be called that, acted as a platform for a heavy artillery piece, mostly a heavy calibre naval gun. These were concrete, circular platforms onto which the naval gun would be placed. They were open, as the gun was usually protected by

A concrete gun emplacement from which the gun has been removed. These emplacements were mainly used for large calibre naval guns. (*Vancoillie*)

some kind of steel gun turret. Thus this type of 'bunker' provided negligible protection but served as an essential stable support for the gun.

Ammunition bunkers, troop shelters and other bunkers with supporting functions were normally to be found in the immediate neighbourhood of artillery shelters.

Anti-tank bunkers.

Anti-tank bunkers were constructed near significant stretches of important roads or railroads and were designed to accommodate an adapted field gun. These anti-tank bunkers had a horizontal aperture or a square loophole. The elevation of the gun inside the bunker was limited as it was only designed to fire at tanks or armoured vehicles moving along the road or railway line and therefore fired its shells at a flat trajectory. One of the guns frequently used for this task was the Russian Putilov 76.2 mm m/02 gun, which had a range of up to four kilometres. A lot of these guns were captured, together with plentiful ammunition, on the Eastern Front.

Sometimes the Fahrpanzer was also used as, in effect, an anti-tank bunker with gun. It was often built into the trenches.

The best known example of an anti-tank bunker in the Salient that is still visible today is Cheddar Villa. Its firing slit is aimed at Buffs Road, the only road in the area which had not been utterly destroyed and as such was still usable by tanks in the summer of 1917.

Minenwerfer bunkers.

Minenwerfer bunkers differ from artillery bunkers in that they were constructed as much below ground level as practicable. Because of the limited range of the Minenwerfer, they had to be built in or close behind the front line. By constructing the bunker underground, everything stayed more or less concealed from the enemy. A Minenwerfer bunker provided shelter for the Minenwerfer, its crew and ammunition. This type of bunker was usually built by the Minenwerfer Kompagnien themselves.

A Minenwerfer bunker for a mittlere Minenwerfer (17 cm calibre), near Diksmuide. (*Schmieschek*)

Minenwerfer bunker for a leichte Minenwerfer (7.7 cm calibre) near Diksmuide. (*Schmieschek*)

Observation bunkers.

An observation bunker was built to be able to observe the enemy safely from the security of the construction. The disadvantage of having openings on the side facing the enemy was that it created structural weak points. Originally, when bunkers were built an appreciable distance from the front line, large observation slits were possible as a direct hit by a shell of sufficient calibre was very unlikely due to a lack of precision in artillery fire and the limited availability of heavy guns that could reach deep into the enemy hinterland. Later in the war, precision bombardment of bunkers far behind the front and using heavy artillery became far more practicable.

However, at the front and close behind it, wide observation slits were impossible from the beginning. Observation bunkers in such locations were provided with openings measuring on the outside only five by five centimetres, an opening that then widened inside the bunker. There were usually multiple observation slits providing coverage in different directions at the front of the rounded bunker to allow for a panoramic view of the enemy lines.

As the Germans in the Ypres Salient usually occupied the higher ground, they could construct their observation bunkers close to ground level and yet still retain excellent observation. Observation bunkers for artillery and the staff were built further from the front and had to be higher to offer good observation possibilities. Most of such observation bunkers

German observation post built with concrete blocks after its capture by Australian troops in October 1917. This bunker was called Kit and Kat by the British. (*AWM*)

A German observation post built with poured concrete, photographed after its capture by Australian troops in October 1917. This one was named Anzac Strong Post by the British. (*AWM*)

were built on top of a ridge; but this was not always the case as some high points were often under fire (especially at times when accurate observation was most needed) and the Allies were well aware of the value of higher ground. There had to be a regular spread of observation posts, necessary for reasons of safety and to be able to measure accurately targets in the enemy rear areas by use of triangulation.

As most of the observation bunkers had to be built in an elevated area, using poured concrete in their construction was not always very easy; but this system of construction was necessary if there was to be sufficient protection. Existing high buildings were used extensively as a cover inside which the bunkers could be built. Houses were useful for this, but particularly valuable were windmills, church towers or factory chimneys. High observation bunkers had the huge disadvantage that they stuck out clearly above the landscape once the exterior building and any other nearby buildings had been destroyed by artillery fire. In addition, their extra height often made them very unstable as sufficient foundations could not be dug for them.

An option to avoid these vulnerabilities was to build small steel observation cupolas on top of normal bunkers, accessed by stairs on the inside wall. An observer could thus climb the stairs and watch the surrounding area through the slits in the cupola in safety. As the means of observation evolved, especially after the development of the trench periscope (including a specialist one for gunners), the need for observation slits or high observation towers diminished. A small hole in the roof was sufficient to stick the trench periscope through and provide an overview of the surrounding landscape. From late 1917 most Einheitsunterstände could be used as observation bunkers because of the choice of their location. Both chambers of this type of construction had an opening in the roof designed for a trench periscope, whilst stairs at the back of the bunker enabled anyone to observe the area from behind the shelter of the bunker. If these options were insufficient, it was always possible to add a small observation cupola during the construction of the bunker.

The Germans built this impressive concrete observation tower in Warneton. (*Schmieschek*)

Command posts.

A command post did not look much different from a troop shelter. The first command posts were nothing more than a normal troop shelter with one chamber in which an officer, usually the company commander, lived. These command posts were built in the front line. At that point in the war there was no need yet to build large bunkers for the higher staffs. They were still based in existing buildings close enough to the front for them to perform their command functions. Because of the increase in the means of communication, especially telephone lines, there was a growing need for a double bunker: one room for the commander (and sometimes his aide); and next door a communications room where the telephone (or a light-signal) detachment resided with its equipment.

Because of the increasing strength and reach of the artillery, the need grew for bunkers in which the staffs of battalions could be sheltered or to act as battle headquarters for regiments, brigades and divisions. Diverse means of communications (telephone, telegraph, pigeons, light signals, runners etc.), new specialist officers and the need to house one or more officers with supporting troops and, on occasion, even fighting units, increased the size of these command posts. Therefore, along the most important lines of communications, at some distance from the front line, large bunkers were erected, consisting of multiple chambers. In the case of significant fighting in a sector or during a state of tension, some staff officers took up position in these command posts. The communications lines (telephone lines, messenger dog lines or chains of runners) within the sector were concentrated to this point. The command posts enabled fast decision making by the different staffs in secure circumstances; whilst they were able to keep closer track with the fighting in a particular sector.

The German command post in Zandvoorde in 1917. (*MMP.1917*)

A German command post in Houthulst Forest, late 1917. (*Vancoillie*)

To house the officers in ideal circumstances, the rooms were usually larger than the ones in fighting bunkers. Telephone and electricity lines were incorporated in the structure when it was built. Large 'window' openings were let in to the rear wall so that there was sufficient natural light coming into the meeting and planning rooms.

The publicly accessible command post in Zandvoorde is a typical example of this type. This particular post was definitely used in 1917 for some time as a Divisionsgefechtsstand (battle headquarters) for the Division Zandvoorde. It was built in 1916 by Armierungstruppen. This bunker has six rooms and was built near the main road within the division's zone. Its position on the reverse slope of a hill made it a difficult target for enemy artillery, although direct observation was possible from the top of the bunker. Until the 1950s a similar type of bunker existed in Geluveld, along the Menin Road. This example was even bigger; it was dismantled during the Korean War to salvage the metal used in its construction.

Technical bunkers.

Numerous bunkers were built to house some specific technical installation. These bunkers did not have a standardised plan, but were built so that the installation would fit perfectly, along with adequate space for its operation.

Communication bunkers.

There were many different means of communication during the First World War – none of it very satisfactory by later standards and communications undoubtedly was one of the weakest,

A German telephone bunker near Oosttaverne, pictured in late 1916. Apart from the insulators and the telephone wires on the wall, there is no other indication to show the purpose of the bunker. (*Schmieschek*)

A German telephone bunker, clearly identifiable as such from the very large number of incoming and outgoing telephone lines. (*Vancoillie*)

if not the weakest, command and control element of the war. Communications included telephone, telegraph, earth current telegraph, light signalling, runners, pigeons, messenger dogs etc. As it was of vital importance to be informed quickly and to pass on information up the line of command as correctly and swiftly as possible, it was logical that these communication posts were placed close to command posts. Indeed, in many cases the communications function was integrated into or combined with the command post.

Several communication bunkers are preserved to this day. The one in the Kasteelhof (Cayennestraat 88, Langemark) is probably a communications bunker. There are several external openings, there is a communication hole between the two chambers and there is a shaft to the roof. The enemy was probably observed through a trench periscope and the information was despatched by using light signals, pigeons or messengers. The exact meaning of the openings is not known although the presence of two neighbouring openings in one chamber seems to indicate that light signals could be sent from this room.

A light signal post (or a Blinkstelle) can be identified by large openings in the walls in the direction of the German rear areas. These openings were hidden from the enemy, who therefore could not observe the signals sent from there. There does not seem to have been a standardised opening for a light signal device. The best known example of a light signal post is the Ziegler Bunker near Boezinge, which has a large trapezoid opening towards the German rear.

The 'Ziegler' Bunker near Boezinge. The large opening probably served to house a big signalling lamp, so that light signals could be sent to the rear. (*Blieck*)

Bunkers over an underground system.
Some concrete shelters served only to provide reinforced protection for an entrance or the shaft of an underground mine system or dugout. The German concrete counter mining shaft ('Dietrich') visible today near Wijtschate was built inside a concrete bunker, that had the dual task of protecting the shaft from enemy shell fire and from aerial observation.

Cookhouse bunkers.
As the adage says, an army marches (and fights) on its stomach, thus the importance of warm meals and drinks in the front line cannot be overestimated. As getting warm food up to the front line was often very difficult because of enemy shelling of the main routes forward both by day and night, the problem was partially solved by building fortified kitchens.

One of these bunkers is well known as it is documented through photographs and descriptions in several regimental histories. This kitchen bunker, near Ostermorgengut (Low Farm), was built in the winter of 1916-1917 between the Albrecht Stellung and Wilhelm Stellung (the Second and Third German positions). Warm food and drinks could be taken to the front line troops using insulated containers via communication trenches.

A German cook house bunker in Sint-Juliaan. This construction has relatively large chimneys, essential because of the smoke from the ovens. Note the upper layers of concrete, which are obviously of poor quality – amongst other things the gravel used is unsuitable. A narrow gauge railway goes past the entrance. (*Deraeve*)

German kitchen bunker near Ostermorgengut (Low Farm), Frezenberg, near Zonnebeke. This kitchen bunker operated four kitchens for the four companies deployed within the regimental sector. (*Deraeve*)

An electricity generator at Kruiseke. From here there was an electricity grid leading forward to the front, where several bunkers with transformers were located. These provided a low-tension electricity network to provide light inside bunkers, electricity for floodlights and to power water pumps. (*Deraeve*)

Bunkers for electrical installations.
This type of bunker was built to protect an electrical installation: examples include pumps to keep the water level under control; pumps to provide drinking water to reserve camps and the front line; generators and transformers for electricity, etc. These bunkers were always specifically built according to the installation inside. Many examples are known to have existed in the Salient through indications on trench maps: a Pumpkraftwerk (pumping station) north of Smiske; a bunker with electricity generator in Herenthagebos (Inverness Copse); or a bunker with a transformer in Wijtschatebos (Bois de Wytschaete), to name just a few.

Einheitsunterstand.

The troops that were engaged on the Ypres front in the autumn of 1917 urgently needed more bunkers as fast as possible. It was a matter of small concern to them for what purpose they were designed; all that mattered was that there should be plenty of them and that they were multi functional. The German Fourth Army decided in October 1917 to develop a standardised bunker that could be adapted for any function that was likely to be needed: command post, observation post, machine gun emplacement, troop shelter, communication bunker or ammunition bunker. This type of bunker was called the Einheitsunterstand. It had many advantages: it was simple to build and there was extensive standardisation of building materials, iron rods and formwork. This made it possible for the workforce to work faster (and that workforce could be less skilled), the supervision was easier, bringing up the necessary building materials could be organised better and, if necessary, other workers could easily take over a construction site in the middle of the work.

This bunker type was built from late October 1917 onwards, especially in the Flandern III Stellung and Flandern IV Stellung (alas, confusingly renamed Flandern I Stellung and Flandern II Stellung in November 1917), which were in the course of being built at that time. In principle, no other bunker types should have been built from then on, except for the bunkers for which construction had already started.

An Einheitsunterstand had two chambers, each measuring two metres wide, three metres long and 1.80 metres high. The roof was made of sheets of corrugated iron or 5 cm thick beams. At the rear of the bunker there were two entrances; between them, on the outside, were stairs, which allowed the bunker to be used as a parapet. The front wall, side walls, base plate (floor) and roof had a concrete depth of 1.50 metres; the back wall one of only one metre. The roof of the bunker sloped downwards on the front side and its corners were chamfered. Each chamber contained a heater, from which the smoke escaped through a pipe leading out of the side wall. The roof of each chamber had a ventilation hole, which also served as an observation hole for a trench periscope. At the back there were apertures to allow the easy entry of electricity and communication cables or for sending light signals. There were also two sumps, so that water could be pumped out of the bunker. Each bunker provided shelter for a minimum of twenty men, with room for extra personnel if necessary.

Rear view of an Einheitsunterstand in Dadizele. The raised platform between the two entrances allowed observation from here or it could be used as a fire step. (*Vancoillie*)

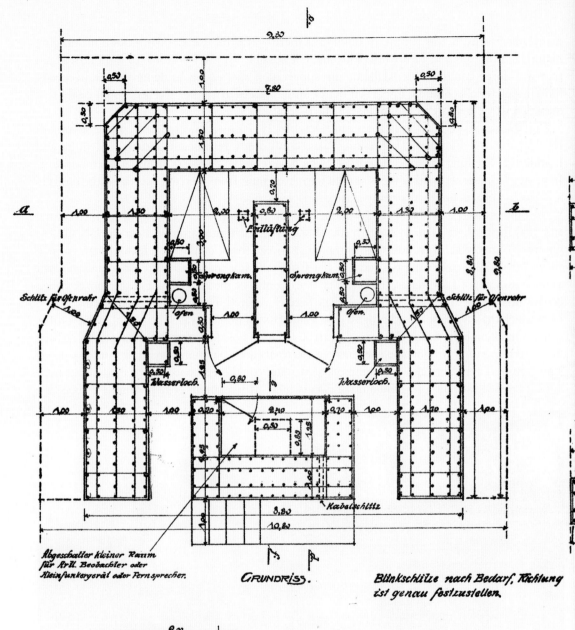

GRUNDRISS.

Abgeschalter kleiner Raum
für Artl. Beobachter oder
Kleinfunkergerät oder Fernsprecher.

Blinkschlitze nach Bedarf, Richtung
ist genau festzustellen.

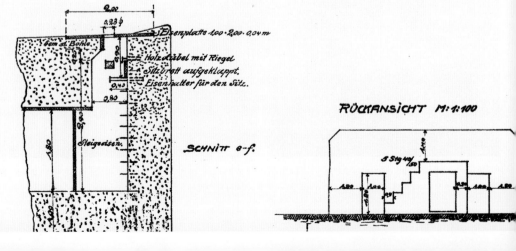

SCHNITT e-f.

RÜCKANSICHT M: 1:100

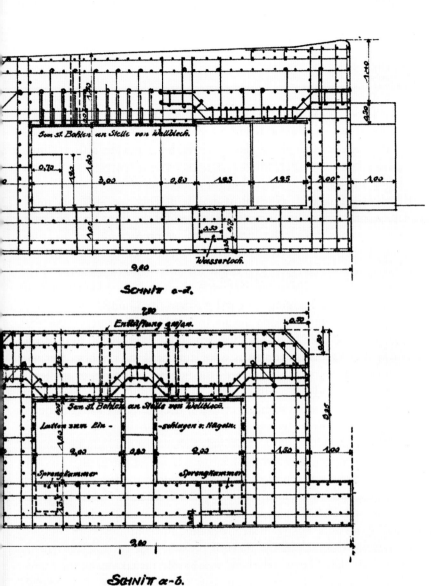

Som st. Bohlen an Stelle von Wellblech.

0,79   3,00   0,80   1,25   1,25   2,00   1,00

Wasserloch.

9,00

SCHNITT c-d.

1,40   2,00

Entlüftung $30/30.$ 0,50

Som st. Bohlen an Stelle von Wellblech.

Latten 2mm Ein-   -schlagen v. Nägeln.

2,00   0,80   2,00   1,50   1,00

Sprengkammer   Sprengkammer

3,00

SCHNITT a-b.

Baustoffbedarf:
292 cbm Beton.
28 qm nutzbare Fläche.
Mischung 1:2:3.
Cement   116 t.
Sand   245 t.
Schotter 368 t.
Eisen   15 t.

F.
Hopf

MASSTAB 1:50

0,5   1   2   3   4   5   7,5

Technical drawing for the Einheitsunterstand. This type of bunker was the only type that was built from November 1917 and were particularly notable in the new Flandern I Stellung and Flandern II Stellung. (*BayHStA/ Abt. IV*)

German Bunker Lines

Evolution of the doctrine.

Early in the war, around the winter of 1914-1915, the Germans understood the need to develop a defensive system based on several lines, each separated by a gap of significant distance. This was then expanded to allow for the concept of an elastic defence, which itself evolved from simple beginnings to a complex system. From late 1915, the first concrete bunkers were built that had to serve as strong points within this type of defence; but they also had to offer protection for the occupants against artillery fire. This early concept of mobile defence was still very much at an evolutionary stage. The second trench line, situated close behind the front line (or firing) trench, mainly served to shelter troops during the enemy's artillery preparation and to house reserves. Holding the front line trench securely remained essential. However, the possibility of a large and concentrated enemy attack, which could lead to the loss of a significant section of the front line trench, had to be taken into consideration. For these cases, considered at the time to be very exceptional, the Germans started building a second position from mid 1915.

The fighting on the Somme in the summer and autumn of 1916 made it very clear that occupying the front line with large bodies of troops and trying to hold on at all cost to the front line trench (thus, if lost, numerous costly counter attacks were launched) was inefficient against an increasingly well equipped opponent (notably as regards the number and types of artillery). In any case, the losses of manpower in 1916 as a consequence of the fighting at Verdun and the Somme meant that different systems had to be found. The use of deep dugouts was considered no longer effective; too much time was lost in getting out of the dugout to man the trench (and, though perhaps not publicly said, it was felt – rightly or wrongly – that a not insignificant number of men seem to have been inclined to stay down in the relative security of the earth). Towards the end of August 1916 von Falkenhayn was replaced as Chief of Staff of the German Army by the duumvirate of von Hindenburg and Ludendorff, at which point German defensive strategies were thoroughly revised. A true elastic defence posture was adopted and more depth was created in the battle zone. A thinly held front line, relying on strong points, and combined with counter-attacking formations and Eingreifdivisionen should make it possible that an attacking enemy would bleed to death in an empty battlefield in which there were hardly any targets for the enemy artillery. Although this was fine in theory, it is far from clear that this was ever fully implemented.

Somewhat in contradiction to this doctrine, the construction of an extremely strong, in depth fortified defensive position was prepared some distance from the front line in the autumn of 1916 (this was particularly true of the Somme, where the evacuation involved a withdrawal of up to thirty kilometres). The Hindenburg Line, as the British called most of its length, allowed the Germans to use defence in depth to the full; the end result formed a line of fortifications from the North Sea to Pont-à-Mousson (south of Metz). In Flanders (German Fourth Army) this position was officially called the Flandern Stellung and later the Flandern I Stellung when more fortified defensive positions were planned and constructed. In France the same strategic defensive position was called the Wotan Stellung [Drocourt – Quèant Line to the British] (German Sixth Army) and so on through the Siegfried Stellung, Hunding Stellung and Michel Stellung. Many new engineer and labour units were raised to build this strategic bunker position, as well as the redeploying of existing ones from different parts of the front – for example, the German mining effort along Vimy Ridge was notably reduced by redeploying skilled manpower to the construction of the new system.

Flandern I Stellung.

Building the Flandern Stellung from late 1916 to spring 1917.
In order to have enough manpower for the construction of the Flandern Stellung, which fully got under way in October 1916, a lot of units, some of them newly raised, were transferred to the Fourth Army. Not only were Armierungskompagnien (labour companies) sent to the Salient, but so were Pionier Kompagnien (engineer companies).

Amongst these Pionier Kompagnien was Pionier Kompagnie 334, also named Pionier Kompagnie 334 g.v.; the 'g.v.' stands for garnisonsverwendungsfähig (fit for garrison duty), which meant that the men were not fit enough for active duty in the front line, usually for medical reasons. The men were assembled in Roeselare and the company was formed on 7 September 1916. From 22 September 1916 it was ready to be deployed and the company was billeted in Hoogkwartier (Houthulst), where it was based whilst working on the Lützow Stellung near Smiske (northwest of Bikschote). Soon afterwards it was working on the Draaibank Linie (a defensive line along the Sint-Jansbeek and Broenbeek). From November 1916 all its attention was diverted to building the Flandern Stellung between Vla (a hamlet northeast of Houthulst) to the railway line connecting Staden to Vijfwegen. Three companies of Landwehr Infanterie and 430 Belgian Zivilarbeiter (civilian labourers) assisted them. During the first months of 1917, Pionier Kompagnie 334 was temporarily used to build several lines between the Albrecht Stellung and the Flandern Stellung but, from 20 May 1917, the company was working again on the Flandern Stellung, this time in the divisional sectors of Langemark and Passendale. Pionier Kompagnie 334 moved back to Roeselare in June 1917, from where it continued to construct the Flandern I Stellung and the Houthulst Riegel, between the railway line that ran between Staden-Vijfwegen and Westrozebeke. The company remained in the Salient, building bunkers in different defensive lines, until spring 1918.

The infantrymen of the 11th Landwehr Brigade (21st Landwehr Division) were withdrawn from the front line and deployed behind the lines to help build the Flandern Stellung. The companies of Landwehr Infanterie Regiment 35 were spread out over four divisional sectors. From early in the morning to late at night the men put up barbed wire entanglements and constructed concrete bunkers. Quite remarkably, the hard work was not rewarded with extra rations. The brigade was back performing infantry duties in the front line from February 1917.

Oskar Dennhardt, of 1st Kompagnie Landwehr Infanterie Regiment 35, was billeted in Klerken in early November 1916 and described his impressions of the building of the Flandern Stellung in the regimental magazine dated 1925.

Then started for us a strict work routine. The new position was laid out by engineer units, which were detached to our unit. We spat in our hands and started working. A special workplace produced custom made wooden boards for the formwork. The earth was dug out one metre deep at the chosen places and the wooden walls were put together in the excavation. At this point the real work started, constructing the shelter with concrete. The walls were made from 1.50 metres of strong concrete and, to increase its strength, iron rods were used in the concrete. A large Pionierpark [supply dump] was located in Klerken, where day in and day out lorries drove in and out, loaded with cement, gravel, wood and iron. These lorries were quickly unloaded. Do you, poor lambs, who were used only to holding a pen or governing a school or administering a solicitor's office, still remember those times and how much a 1.25 Zentner [a Zentner is approximately fifty kilograms] bag of cement made your back bend? And just when this treacherous bag was on your shoulder, every now and then a bag ripped open and the whole blessing poured out over the unlucky bearer. I pitied you regularly, but there was a war going on and all healthy hands could be used. Other teams worked on the double barbed wire fences, built twenty five metres wide and fifty metres apart. Some labourers dragged wooden poles, while other hands drove the same pointed poles into the ground using large wooden hammers, using a lot of swing. This was followed by the hard work of the wire pullers, who wove the wire criss-cross from one pole to another and whose hands looked like spider webs. The defensive line was built according to all the rules of the modern art of war and whoever saw those sophistically engineered heavy machine gun emplacements could not believe that such a strong position could ever be taken. The labour was heavy, very heavy, but whether it rained or whether the sun shone or whether it was cold, the daily task had to be accomplished. On top of this, the food was not very filling. There were a lot of turnips and marmalade, which with even the best will in the world no athletes could be fed. But the Landwehr 35 was a recognised labour regiment and we can still be proud today of the work that we performed then in such difficult circumstances.

When the 11th Landwehr Brigade went back into the line the workforce was not replaced. Other units that were already constructing the Flandern Stellung, amongst which were Pionier Kompagnien and Armierungs Kompagnien, stayed behind and continued the works, although they seemed to lack much enthusiasm from spring 1917 onwards. Gruppe Ypres (the army corps in the centre of the Ypres Salient) in early June 1917 had only three Pionier Kompagnien working on the Flandern Stellung. At the same time, three Pionier Kompagnien, seven Armierungs Kompagnien and one Landsturm Infanterie Bataillon were at work in the Wilhelm Stellung and the Riegel (switch trenches).

Renewed attention to the Flandern I Stellung in May and June 1917.
The preparatory artillery bombardments for the Battle of Messines of late May 1917 made the Germans re-examine the situation in the Salient. On a closer look it was determined that several defensive lines behind the front line did not appear to be as strong as previously thought. Several reasons can be found for this: having realised that multiple defensive lines were necessary, the Germans had started eagerly to build new trench and bunker lines, but this was coordinated by the Gruppen (army corps). After a fair degree of enthusiasm in the beginning, this decreased and labour units were withdrawn and used elsewhere.

Immediately after 7 June 1917 and the opening of the Battle of Messines, which at best could be said not to have gone well for the Germans, they reorganised their troops and command systems. Gruppe (Group) Wijtschate was taken over by Generalkommando IX Reservekorps (IX Reserve Corps staff) under Generalleutnant von Dieffenbach. Gruppe Ypres was handed over on 14 June 1917 to Generalkommando III Bayerisches Armeekorps (III Bavarian Army Corps staff) under Generalleutnant Hermann Freiherr von Stein. Generalkommando XII Reservekorps (XII Reserve Corps staff) under General der Artillerie Hans von Kirchbach, which was relieved from Gruppe Ypres, undertook a new command: Gruppe Gent. This Gruppe Gent was given the responsibility for the defences on the Belgian–Dutch Border in the Etappengebiet (Lines of Communications area) of the Fourth Army as well as the supervision and coordination of the works on the defensive positions behind the Fourth Army front line (that was, in effect, all defensive positions behind the Flandern I Stellung).

The responsibility for the construction and upkeep of the first three positions (the front line, the Albrecht Stellung and the Wilhelm Stellung) rested from this moment with the divisions in the front line. In the case of Gruppe Ypres, each division received the support of one Armierungskompagnie (labour company) for these works: Division Passendale had 3rd Kompagnie Armierungs Bataillon 65 and Division Zonnebeke had 2nd Kompagnie Armierungs Bataillon 35.

Developing the works on the Flandern I Stellung was now in the hands of the Gruppen. In Gruppe Ypres, the Flandern I Stellung and the Houthulst Riegel, running from Houthulst Forest to the Flandern I Stellung, were built under the command of the newly formed 1st Landsturm Infanterie Brigade. This brigade had the following labour units at its disposal: Landsturm Infanterie Bataillon Calw, the staff of Bayerisches Pionier Bataillon 5 with Bayerische Pionier Kompagnie 16 and 17 and Bayerische Reserve Pionier Kompagnie 4, Pionier Kompagnie 336, Pionier Mineur Kompagnie 294, 2nd Kompagnie Armierungs Bataillon 32, 4th Kompagnie Armierungs Bataillon 86, Fuhrpark Kolonne 788 (performing the transportation duties), a hundred Russian prisoners of war and 1,800 voluntary Zivilarbeiter, in all some 4,000 labourers.

An order was issued to 1st Landsturm Infanterie Brigade on 12 June 1917 stating that the Flandern I Stellung had to be ready for use as soon as possible. Of primary importance, all concrete bunkers that were not yet finished but on which work had already started were to be finished as soon as possible. Secondly, barbed wire defences were to be constructed in front of all three lines of the Flandern I Stellung. Where roads passed through the lines, mobile barbed wire obstacles were to be prepared (chevaux de frise and others) so that the gaps could be closed in a very short time. The barbed wire defences in front of the second and third line of the Flandern I Stellung required gaps and were to be built in a checker-board design to allow for counter-attacks. Coming only third in the list of priorities was the digging of real trenches – and this only when there was not enough available building material to build bunkers and barbed wire defences.

When staff from the Gruppe made an inspection of the Flandern I Stellung, it was clear that the position consisted of only one line, which meant that it was not being built according to the rules for defence in depth but rather those for static defence. Gruppe Ypres, therefore, issued an order on 22 June 1917 to change the Flandern I Stellung into a defence in depth position. It was to have three zones: a front zone of three defensive lines with wire entanglements, shelters, command posts and water drainage; a battle zone extending to the Artillerie Schutz Stellung, with wire entanglements, shelters and possibly drainage; and an Artillerie Schutz Stellung, consisting of three defensive lines with wire entanglements, shelters and command posts for company commanders. Importantly, the planners had to take into account the details of infantry companies (which would have 120 men), of whom a sixth were to be deployed in the first line, a third in the second line and half in the third line. In between the lines, machine guns were to be positioned in tactically dominant spots. The Artillerie Schutz Stellung was to be designed along the same principles, i.e. one battalion per regimental sector. Parts of the Bereitschaftsbataillon (support battalion), mainly those armed with machine guns, were to be deployed in the combat zone, the rest in the Artillerie Schutz Stellung. From 25 to 28 June 1917 the Stabsoffizier der Pioniere (the senior engineer officer staff officer) of Gruppe Ypres detached 150 men and several officers to reconnoitre the part of the Flandern I Stellung in its sector. One group investigated the front zone and marked out the trace of the lines, including

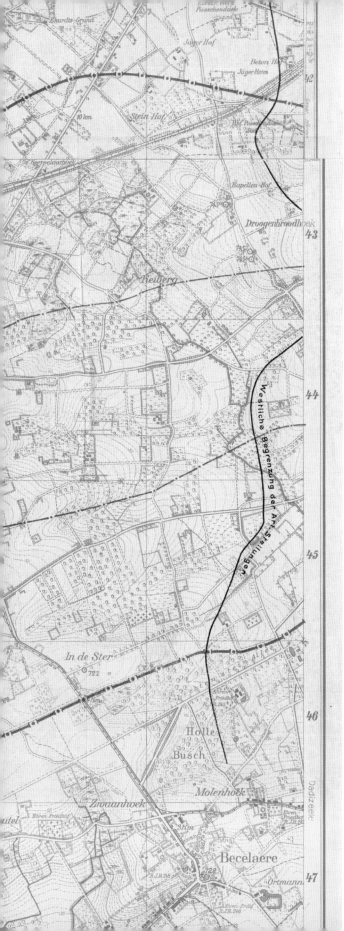

Trench map showing the Flandern I Stellung in Divisional Sector Zonnebeke in June 1917. The rectangles mark bunkers (both shelters and machine gun posts), the circles with a small line sticking out from them are observation posts. Completed works are in blue, the ones still under construction in red. The map clearly shows that the Flandern I Stellung consisted of two lines close to each other without an artillery protective line. The great majority of the completed bunkers were located in the first line. (BayHStA/Abt. IV)

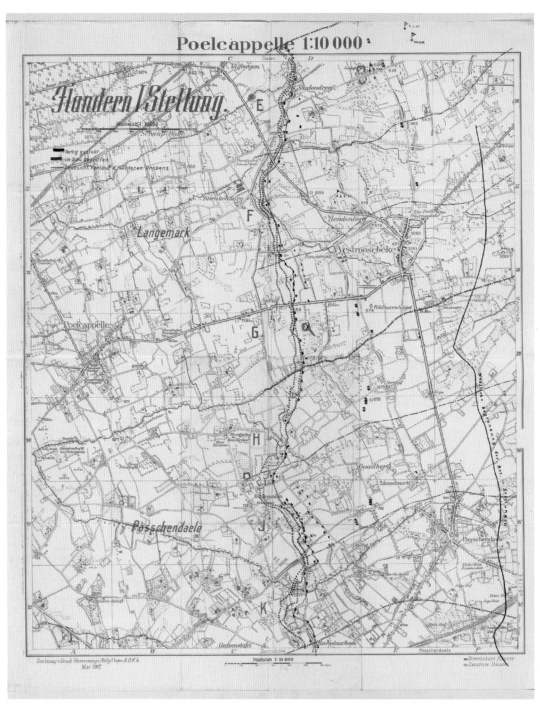

Trench map showing the Flandern I Stellung in the Divisional Sectors Passendale and Langemark in June 1917. The rectangles mark bunkers (both shelters and machine gun posts), the circles with a small line sticking out from them are observation posts. Completed works are in blue, the ones still under construction in red. The map clearly shows that the Flandern I Stellung consisted of two lines close to each other without an artillery protective line. The great majority of the completed bunkers were located in the first line. (BayHStA/Abt. IV)

the places where concrete bunkers were to be built. The second group did the same work for the Artillerie Schutz Stellung. Gruppe Ypres stressed the preference for building the third line of the front zone on the reverse side of a slope, as for all lines of the Artillerie Schutz Stellung. Everything was marked with poles and wooden signs.

Defining responsibilities was not an easy matter. Building the Flandern I Stellung was a matter for the Gruppe; but as the front line divisions were also building bunkers in their rear areas, especially command posts and communication bunkers, disputes arose. To avoid an excessive concentration of bunkers in certain locations and to make sure that all units and formations were building within their own areas, the divisions had to seek authorisation before being allowed to build anything in their rear area beyond the Flandern I Stellung.

The Fourth Army checked the plans of each Gruppe at the end of June 1917 and made numerous points. Armee Oberkommando 4 made various recommendations, among others to have the different lines and positions connected better at the corps boundaries. There were too many bunkers planned for the first line of the Flandern I Stellung, which needed to be addressed, as well as the fact that there was not enough depth in the Flandern I Stellung position. In addition, there was a lack of command posts for the artillery commanders and almost no fortified artillery positions.

The Flandern I Stellung as a standard defence line: from July and September 1917.
Until late July 1917 considerable construction was being undertaken on the Flandern I Stellung, but increasing artillery fire and British advances along the front made it ever harder to continue the work. By mid September 1917, at the latest, responsibility for the Flandern I Stellung was transferred from Gruppen Ypres and Wijtschate to the different front line divisions.

Once the operational control of the Flandern I Stellung was transferred to the front line divisions, no more construction was undertaken on the position. These formations lacked time and labour to devote much attention to this rear position as the continuous attacks on their front line demanded their full concentration. British shelling and aerial observation made work as good as impossible. The 25th Infanterie Division, engaged from 20 September 1917 in the sector around Geluveld, ordered its Reserve Pionier Kompagnie 89 to improve the Artillerie Schutz Stellung and the Flandern I Stellung, but the company could only strengthen the barbed wire entanglements in front of both positions. Continuous artillery fire harassed the work and the engineers had to man the reserve trenches during attacks to prevent a possible break through. Furthermore, carrying ammunition and supplies to the front line was far more urgent and important than building a defence line in the rear.

Early in October 1917 the Flandern I Stellung was captured by the British between Westrozebeke and Beselare. The position consequently lost its status as a strategic defence position and forced the Germans to set about a complete review of their defensive system.

Bunker types.
Unfortunately, no plans of standardised constructions for the Flandern I Stellung have survived in the German archives we consulted. The war diary of Landsturm Infanterie Regiment 39, which worked on the Flandern I Stellung in June and July 1917, mentions such plans, but they cannot be found in the files.

However, surviving bunkers of the Flandern I Stellung give us clues about these standardised bunkers. There appear to have been two prevailing models. The first type was a rectangular

A typical oblong bunker (approximately four metres by eleven metres) of the Flandern I Stellung (1916-1917) and containing three chambers; the one pictured is in Tyne Cot CWGC Cemetery. (*Blieck*)

A typical square bunker (approximately six metres by six metres) of the Flandern I Stellung (1916-1917), containing a single chamber and with loopholes for a machine gun; this bunker is in Groenstraat in Zonnebeke. (*Blieck*)

bunker, measuring approximately four metres by eleven metres, divided into three chambers, which were connecting by narrow openings. There was an option to build a concrete open machine gun position on the side of the bunker. There was usually a small observation slit in the middle of the wall on the enemy side, wider on the inside than on the outside. The second type of standardised bunker was a square construction measuring approximately six metres by six metres, usually equipped with firing-holes. This bunker was obviously a machine gun emplacement.

Switch lines (Riegel).

Riegel, or switch lines, were dug between the different lines and positions. The Germans developed these as they wanted to avoid at all costs an enemy break through at one point in the line and then them building from this to roll up the whole line. The switch lines were built with both tactical and strategic considerations in mind. As more Flandern Stellungen were built and the British and French slowly advanced, new switch lines had to be sited and constructed.

One of the first switch lines that was built was the Tenbrielen Riegel, running from the Wilhelm Stellung west of Zandvoorde to the River Lys at Godshuis, west of Wervik. The exact date when this line was built is unknown, but it can be found on trench maps in December 1916, although only as a line of barbed wire entanglements and some dispersed strong points.

The British preparations for the Battle of Messines in June 1917 added a sense of urgency to the construction of several switch lines, most of which were built by the front line divisions. By the summer of 1917 a significant number of switch lines were in the course of construction, mainly between the front line and the Wilhelm Stellung: Merkem Riegel, Quer Riegel Nord, Quer Riegel Süd, Fortuin Riegel, Wieltje Riegel, Brandenburg Riegel, Grenadier Riegel, Quer Riegel and the Kanal Stellung, the last one also serving as the front line after the British advance south of the Ypres–Comines Canal.

The Tenbrielen Riegel, photographed in May 1917, was constructed according to the book: a continuous fighting trench with wattle-work reinforced walls and here and there a bunker, largely hidden under earth. (Deraeve)

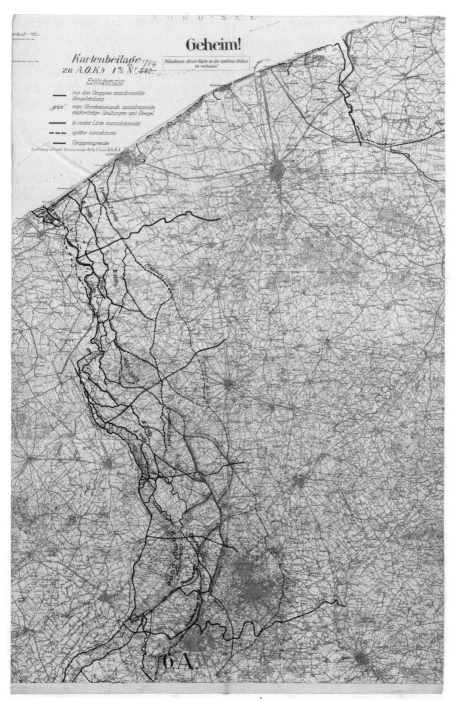

An overview area map, covering the front from the North Sea to just south of Lille, showing different positions and switch lines, as they existed or were planned, in late June 1917. Lines that had been finished or were under construction are in blue, the lines to be constructed by the Gruppen (army corps) are in brown and the lines that were to be constructed by the Army (Gruppe Gent) are green. The prioritised lines are marked by continuous lines, less important lines by dotted lines. The red shaded lines show positions that had become more urgent after the Battle of Messines, earlier that month. (*BayHStA/Abt. IV*)

Some switch lines were also prepared between the Wilhelm Stellung and the Flandern I Stellung. In order to prevent a break-through in the direction of Houthulst Forest, two were constructed: Waldriegel Nord and Waldriegel Süd. The Mittel Riegel covered the area Langemark – Zonnebeke; while the Geluveld Riegel protected the vitally important Gheluvelt Plateau position.

The Geluveld Riegel was under construction from mid May 1917. Bavarian Landsturm Infanterie Bataillon Regensburg (IIIB/14) was transported to the area and billeted in Lager Deimlingseck, a camp, consisting of barracks, in the Nieuwe Kruiseke area, to the southeast of Geluveld, and Lager Koelenberg, a bit further down the Menin Road. The battalion was attached to the 195th Infanterie Division for one purpose only: to build the Geluveld Riegel. The Bavarian soldiers built machine gun emplacements inside ruined farm buildings in the area and expanded the barbed wire entanglements to a width of ten metres. A continuous trench was also dug. To prevent the new works from being discovered immediately, the men started their work day at 2 am. However, intensifying gun fire and aerial bombing seriously hampered construction and the Bavarians were soon commandeered to maintain the front line and second position trenches as these were continually being damaged by heavy shelling. By early June work in the Geluveld Riegel had effectively come to a halt. After the battalion was deployed to man reserve trenches from 7 to 10 June 1917 to stop possible British attacks, it was relieved and moved to the Belgian-Dutch border for garrison duties.

The Bavarians were relieved by Württemberg landsturm soldiers from Landsturm Infanterie Regiment 39. They continued the work on the Geluveld Riegel from mid June 1917. At that point, the work on the continuous trench was abandoned; instead the switch line was to be built according to the prevalent defensive doctrine, with three defensive lines. This meant that two extra bunker lines had to be constructed in front of the current switch line: one line some 250 to 350 metres in front of it and a second line some 150 metres in front of it. The Geluveld Riegel was designed to be able to house two battalions, each holding a 1,100 metres long sector. This implied building 145 concrete bunkers in the front line of the Geluveld Riegel and 145 in the reserve zone. Work progressed only very slowly as the supporting labour force was soon needed elsewhere. Furthermore, unceasing artillery attacks harassed the workers, whilst the Landsturm soldiers were regularly called upon to take up positions in reserve trenches as a British attack was expected at any moment. After 31 July 1917 (ie the opening day of Third Ypres), Landsturm Infanterie Regiment 39 was relieved and further construction work on the Geluveld Riegel was all but halted.

Flandern II Stellung

In late May 1917 a proposal was investigated to build a new strategic defensive position in the sector of Gruppe Ypres. This position was defined as running from the Höhenlinie (ridge line) Passendale-Drogenbroodhoek-Terhand-Koelenberg. After the Battle of Messines, which came to an end in mid June, developing this position was prioritised. The failure of the German Mineure (tunnelling units) to prevent the German lines from being blown up along the Messines Ridge led to their withdrawal from the front line; in reality, mining had reached its high point with the firing of the Messines mines and tunnelling companies – or their equivalents – in all the armies were soon being redeployed to new engineering related tasks. The local Pionier Mineur Kompagnien (tunnelling companies) were withdrawn and grouped to become labour units working on this newly planned defence position, which was in the meantime renamed the Flandern II Stellung. Oberstleutnant Füßlein, formerly commanding the Mineure, and his staff received a new function and thus a new title: Stabsoffizier der Pioniere (Stopi) 62. Stopi 62 oversaw the building of the Flandern II Stellung.

The Fourth Army issued an order about the future construction of the defence positions on 15 June 1917. On that date Gruppe Gent was created. The Generalkommando XII Reservekorps was designated as the staff for this Gruppe and received instructions to coordinate the work on all defence positions in the army area east of the Flandern I Stellung, as well as the Flandern Wotan Riegel in the sector of the Gruppe Lille. Five extra engineer staffs (Stopi) were to be engaged to oversee the work on the sites. At that time ten Armierungs Kompagnien, two and a half Kriegsgefangenen Arbeiter Bataillone (Russian PoW labour battalions), one Park Kompagnie and a Minenwerfer Bataillon were made available as a work force. These labourers were ordered to work on the Flandern I Stellung until the locations of the other defence positions were finalised. The Germans also expected to be able to recruit some 6,000 (Belgian) Zivilarbeiter (civilian labourers). All these units received their orders from Gruppe Gent, but they were all billeted and supplied by the Gruppe in the area in which they were working (mainly Gruppe Ypres and Gruppe Wijtschate). This naturally created significant logistical difficulties.

In early August 1917 all defence positions were re-evaluated by the Fourth Army. Gruppe Gent received explicit instructions to speed up the construction of the Flandern II Stellung, whilst using only the available work force (mainly Armierungs Kompagnien). The Gruppe was instructed to focus on the northern part of this position and the connection towards Houthulst Riegel.

Gruppe Gent understood the importance of the Flandern II Stellung, especially machine gun emplacements, and ordered the construction of betonierte abgespaltene Maschinengewehr Unterstände. Lack of labourers, problems with getting enough building materials to the sites and bad weather seriously slowed down the work. Because of the huge importance of machine guns for defence in depth, the Germans decided to start building simple machine gun posts that were only splittersicher (splinter-proof). To alleviate this weakness, they looked to concealing these machine gun posts: behind hedges, against the rear of slopes or behind ruined buildings. This should have made it almost impossible for the enemy to discover the shelters and would complicate an effective artillery plan. The machine gun crews were only protected against shrapnel; but the main goal was to provide cover for the machine guns and their related equipment (ammunition, spare barrels, water etc.) against rain and mud. These shelters, built using sheets of corrugated iron, were not built in the same locations where the concrete bunkers were planned, but at some distance away. This allowed for the concrete bunkers to be built at a future date. To make it easier for the relieving units, a small marker was placed where the machine gun should be positioned.

In early September 1917 the progress of the work on the different bunker lines was once more evaluated. At that point, the line of the Flandern II Stellung was fixed, whilst the barbed wire entanglements in front of it were practically completed. The control of the Flandern II Stellung north of the line Moorslede-Drogenbroodhoek was then transferred to the front line formations, who were from then on responsible for its further construction. South of this line Gruppe Gent remained in control. Meanwhile, the Fourth Army urged Gruppe Gent to start building concrete bunkers, even if a lot of its labour force (Armierungs Kompagnien) was being shifted towards the Flandern III Stellung.

It is very doubtful whether a lot of work was in fact accomplished on the rest of the Flandern II Stellung before it in turn was transferred to the front line formations. Gruppe Gent issued an order to build more concrete bunkers on 10 September 1917; Oberstleutnant Füßlein responded two days later, saying that he had passed on the order to his work force, emphasising

Overview map, from the summer of 1917, of the positions and switches to the east and northeast of Ypres, extending from the front line to the Flandern III Stellung. (*BayHStA/Abt. IV*)

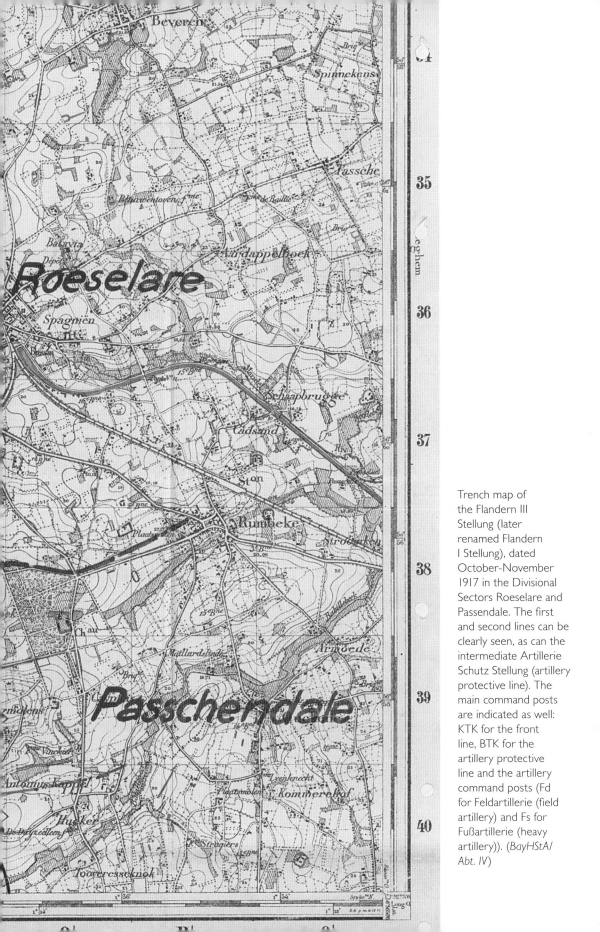

Trench map of the Flandern III Stellung (later renamed Flandern I Stellung), dated October-November 1917 in the Divisional Sectors Roeselare and Passendale. The first and second lines can be clearly seen, as can the intermediate Artillerie Schutz Stellung (artillery protective line). The main command posts are indicated as well: KTK for the front line, BTK for the artillery protective line and the artillery command posts (Fd for Feldartillerie (field artillery) and Fs for Fußartillerie (heavy artillery)). (BayHStA/ Abt. IV)

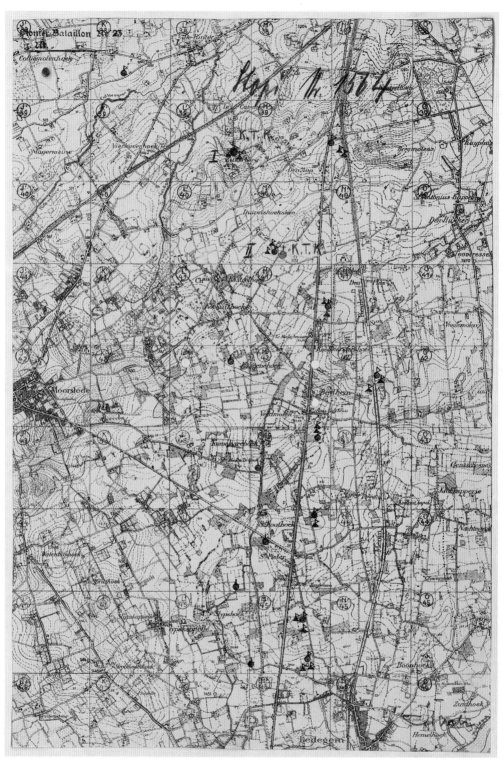

Overview map showing all the important command posts of the Flandern I Stellung between Roeselare and Ledegem (sector of Pionier Bataillon 23 as Baustab rückwärtiger Stellungen). (*BayHStA/Abt. IV*)

As major Allied attacks against the Fourth Army stopped in November 1917, the whole defensive system was once more re-evaluated. The classifications of summer 1917 were no longer relevant as the situation on the ground had changed completely. The Flandern I Stellung had been pierced from Westrozebeke to Reutel, as had the Flandern II Stellung near Passendale. A new scheme was necessary. The former Flandern I Stellung and Flandern II Stellung were renamed. The defensive position formed by the former Flandern I Stellung from the coast to Zande – third defence line from Zande to Werken – Diksmuide-Roeselare-Riegel – former Flandern III Stellung from Roeselare to the Ledegem-Wervik-Riegel was officially renamed Flandern I Stellung in an army order dated 26 November 1917.

Several Riegel (switch lines) were incorporated into the new Flandern I Stellung: Mariakerke Riegel, Koekelare Riegel, Kortemark Riegel (from the Hauptwiderstandslinie to the Artillerie Schutz Stellung), Roeselare Riegel (ditto), Moorslede Riegel (ditto), Winkel Riegel (ditto) and the Menen-Riegel (which was in fact the former Flandern II Stellung from the Ledegem Riegel to the Lys Riegel). Constructing the Flandern I Stellung to the Artillerie Schutz Stellung, including the switch lines, was delegated to the Gruppen. Each Gruppe received a Pionier Bataillon under command as Baustab rückwärtiger Stellungen to conduct the works.

The Flandern I Stellung consisted of a front line and an Artillerie Schutz Stellung, in each of which a limited number of concrete bunkers were to be built. The accompanying orders were issued in December 1917. Gruppe Ypres considered that thirty men should be sufficient to build one bunker. The Baustab rückwärtiger Stellungen of the corps reported in late January 1918 that 2,575 men were needed to build or finish eighty-four bunkers in three divisional sectors.

As far as can be determined from the available sources, the construction of the (new) Flandern I Stellung was finished in early 1918; all the planned bunkers had been built by that time.

The Flandern IV Stellung (NB! From 26 November 1917 on: Flandern II Stellung).

The Heeresgruppe Kronprinz Rupprecht von Bayern (Army Group Crown Prince Rupprecht of Bavaria) ordered the Fourth Army in late June 1917 to reconnoitre defence positions even further to the rear. The first line selected was the Flandern IV Stellung, running from Oostende via Torhout, Izegem, west of Kortrijk and Moeskroen to Wattrelos, connecting west of Toufflers to the Wotan III Stellung of the Sixth Army. The second position was the Flandern V Stellung, running from Blankenberge over Brugge, west of Tielt and east of Kortrijk to Roubaix, where it connected to the Flandern IV Stellung. A Sluis-Brügge Stellung was to be built parallel to the coastline, connecting to the Flandern V Stellung near Brugge. Three possible switch lines were to be investigated. The first was the Diksmuide-Roeselare Riegel, a connection between the front line north of Diksmuide and the Flandern IV Stellung, which was a continuation of the Vladslo Riegel and Werken Riegel, running from Werken, over Kortemark, Gits and Beveren to Ardooie. The second was the Lys Riegel, connecting the Flandern I Stellung to the Flandern V Stellung, running from Linselles over Halluin and Kortrijk to Harelbeke. The third switch line was the Tourcoing Riegel, connecting the Flandern II Stellung with the Flandern IV Stellung, running from Bondues over Neuville to Aalbeke.

The Germans started making the necessary preparations to build the Flandern IV Stellung and its accompanying switch lines in mid October 1917. At that time the Fourth Army ordered Gruppe Gent to reconnoitre the line of the Flandern IV Stellung between Lichtervelde and Gullegem. The accompanying switch lines were to be surveyed at the same time: the Kortemark

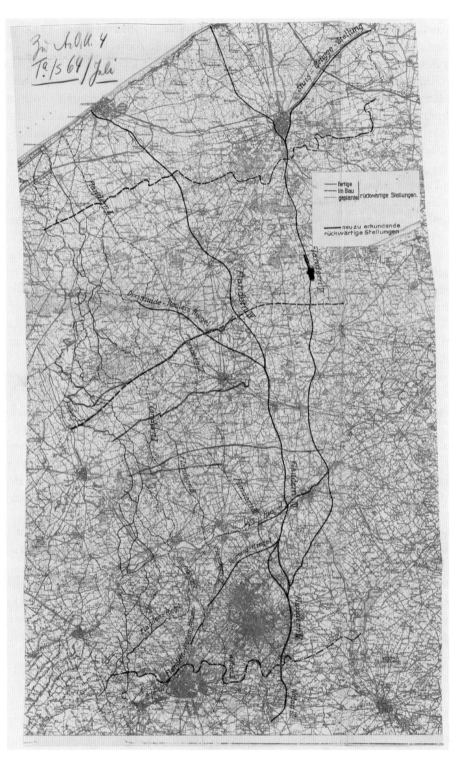

Overview map of the finished and planned positions and switches as they stood in July 1917 showing the planned Flandern IV Stellung and Flandern V Stellung. The brown lines indicate: solid, completed; dashes, in construction; and dotted, planned. (*BayHStA/Abt. IV*)

Riegel (connecting the Flandern IV Stellung to the Werken Riegel near Werken); the Winkel Riegel (connecting the Flandern IV Stellung to the Flandern III Stellung near Ledegem); the Wevelgem Riegel (connecting the Flandern IV Stellung to the Lys Riegel); and the Gullegem Riegel (connecting the Wevelgem Riegel to the Lys Riegel). The Artillerie Schutz Stellung of the Flandern IV Stellung was to be inspected as well. During this survey the exact locations for the different defence lines were to be fixed, as well as the sites of bunkers that needed to be built first and the location of the dumps for materiel, although the building material did not yet need to be transported to these. The route of the narrow-gauge tracks (necessary to transport the building material from the dumps to the building sites) were to be surveyed as well as the billets for the labour force that would be necessary for the work.

All the preparations to start working on the Flandern IV Stellung and its switch lines were in place by mid November 1917. The position was divided into four sectors for the easier management of the work. These sectors were inspected regularly. The four sectors were: (1) Flandern IV Stellung from the northern border of Gruppe Diksmuide to the former border between Gruppen Diksmuide and Houthulst, under the command of Hauptmann Weber; (2) Flandern IV Stellung, including the Kortemark Riegel and the Quer Riegel near Schuddebeurze, in the former corps sector of Gruppe Houthulst, under the command of Stopi 154; (3) Flandern IV Stellung, excluding the Winkel Riegel, in the corps sectors of Gruppe Staden and Gruppe Ypres, under the command of Stopi 40b; (4) Winkel Riegel, Gullegem Riegel, Wevelgem Riegel and Lys Riegel, under the command of Stopi 62. The works were to be started by 15 December 1917. This meant that the Flandern IV Stellung was not completed as planned in the summer of 1917, but only its middle part. This failure can be explained by the changes in the front line. The Allies advanced from October 1917 only in the central part of the Ypres Salient (between Beselare and Houthulst Forest). It was against this bulge that the Germans saw the need to build an extra defensive position in depth.

Because of the reorganisation of the defensive system, the Flandern IV Stellung was renamed Flandern II Stellung on 26 November 1917. Attached to it were some switch lines: Kortemark Riegel, Schuddebeurze Riegel, Roeselare Riegel, Winkel Riegel and Lys Riegel. The construction of the position and its switch lines was the responsibility of Gruppe Nord (Marinekorps) in its sector and Gruppe Gent further south. To speed up the work, the Germans paused the construction of the Holland Stellung along the Belgian-Dutch border and diverted that labour force to the building of the Flandern II Stellung.

The construction of the (new) Flandern II Stellung began in mid December 1917, when its sectors were once more reviewed. Probably under the influence of what was happening on the Eastern Front and the preparations for the major Spring Offensive in the West, a number of labour units were withdrawn from the Flanders front. Stopi 154, Stopi 40b and Stopi 62 continued to oversee the construction of the Flandern II Stellung, but with fewer labour units at their disposal than first promised. Notwithstanding this, the efforts which were put into building the new Flandern II Stellung were remarkable.

At first, the railway network (especially narrow-gauge tracks) was expanded to be able to transport the building material. Extra rolling stock was brought into the area. Before the work commenced, rolling stock and the network in the area Ardooie-Izegem could handle some 300 tonnes of cargo per day. In the area Bissegem-Heule, it could manage about 500 tonnes. The Germans calculated that they could increase this by an extra 900 tonnes per day by adding extra locomotives and wagons. An extra seventy kilometres of narrow-gauge lines (Förderbahnen,

Anlage 1   **406.**

Ausstattung eines ~~Gruppen~~ *Divisions-*Pionierparks

an Sprengminen, Nahkampfmitteln und Baustoffen.

(Einheit ist, soweit nichts anderes angegeben, **Stückzahl.**)

	a) Munition.				d) Unterstands-Baustoffe.		
1.	Sprengminen, ganze schwere	100.	50.	Schurzholz 2	80/120		500
2.	" mittlere	150.	51.	" 3	80/160		500
3.	" leichte	1000.	52.	" 4	120/180		200
4.	Gasminen, leichte	200.	53.	Schurzblechrahmen			
5.	Wurfgranaten	1000.		("Siegfried")			200
6.	Stielhandgranaten	20000.	54.	Wellblechunterstände			
7.	Eierhandgranaten	10000.		("Heinrich")			200
8.	Sicherheitssprengstoff kg	1000.	55.	Bretter qm			5000
9.	Zündladungskörper	50.	56.	Schalbretter qm			5000
10.	Sprengkapseln 8	50.	57.	Bohlen qm			4000
11.	Glühzünder	50.	58.	Kantholz lfdm			4000
12.	Guttaperchazündschnur m	50.	59.	Hurden			2000
13.	Blanker Draht m	500.	60.	Maschendraht, leicht, Rollen			30
14.	Guttapercha-Draht m	500.	61.	" schwer "			30
15.	Glühzündapparate	2.	62.	Eiserne Eisenbahnschwellen			
16.	Leitungsprüfer	2.					
17.	Werkzeugtaschen	4.		e) Sonstiges.			
18.	Leuchtpatronen	20000.					
19.	Signalpatronen Doppelst.rot	2000.	63.	Infanterieschilde			500
20.	" grün	2000.	64.	Laufroste			2000
21.	" schweb.Kug. gelb	2000.	65.	Sandsäcke			200000
22.	Leuchtpistolen	50.	66.	Richtband km			10
			67.	Haspeln			15
	b) Schanzzeug.		68.	Alarmvorrichtungen:			
				a) Torpedopfeifen			30
23.	Spaten	6000.		b) Signalhörner			20
24.	Spatenstiele	500.		c) große Alarmglocken			10
25.	Schaufeln oder entsprechende	2000.		d) Gongs			20
	Zahl Spaten mehr	500.		e) Hupen mit Luftpumpe			20
26.	Kreuzhacken	3600.	69.	Laufgrabenspiegel			100
27.	Kreuzhackenstiele	500.	70.	Karbidlampen			100
28.	Aexte	500.	71.	Karbid kg			100
29.	Axtstiele	200.	72.	Bandeisen Rollen oder Bund			50
30.	Beile	500.	73.	Bauklammern			2000
31.	Sägen (Schrot-)	50.	74.	Nägel t			3
32.	" (Hand-)	100.	75.	Pappnägel kg			50
33.	Schlägel	200.	76.	Dachpappe qm			1000
34.	Schlägelstiele	150.	77.	Schnellbrücken m			200
35.	Hämmer	200.	78.	Förderbahngleis m			1000
36.	Kneifzangen	100.	79.	Drehscheiben			4
37.	Flachzangen	100.	80.	Weichen			4
38.	Drahtscheren, nicht isol.	300.	81.	Laufgrabenpumpen			15
38a.	" " "	30.					
	c) Hindernis-Baustoffe.						
39.	Schraubpfähle	15000					
40.	Winkeleisenpfähle	15000					
41.	Hölzerne Hindernispfähle	15000					
42.	Spanische Reiter	2000					
43.	Stacheldraht t	25					
44.	Glatter Draht 5mm t	5					
45.	" " 2 u.3mm t	5					
46.	Stacheldrahtwalzen	2000					
47.	Dachförm.Hindernis m	3000					
48.	Drahttigel	1000					
49.	Drahtkrampen t	0,2					

The inventory of the contents of a Divisional Pionier Park behind the Flandern IV Stellung (later Flandern II Stellung) during the winter of 1917-1918. (*BayHStA/Abt. IV*)

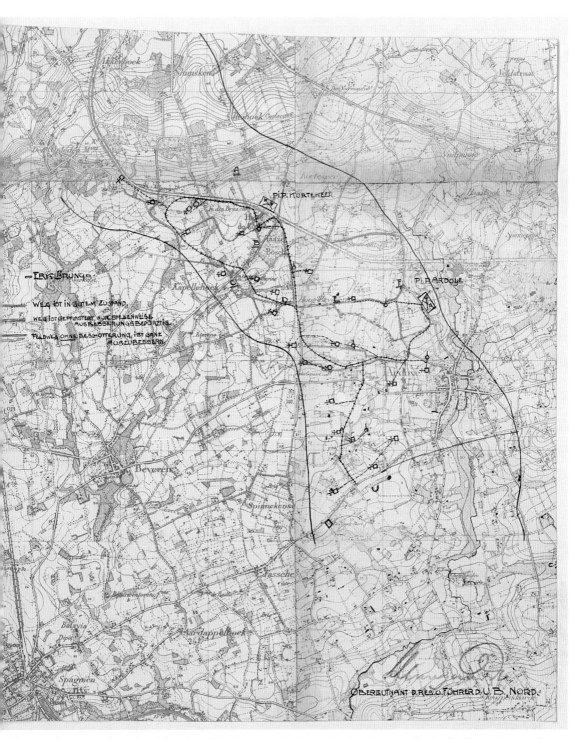

An overview map of the (new) Flandern II Stellung near Ardooie (the location of a Pionier Park), north east of Roeselare, indicating the sites of the planned bunkers. Note that before the Germans could start building the bunkers they had to construct a narrow gauge rail network. (*BayHStA/Abt. IV*)

tramway tracks), using man-powered transport and wagons, were necessary to move all the necessary materials to the building sites.

In late December 1917 orders were issued to fix the sequence of the work. First, command posts for the infantry should be constructed, followed by, secondly, one or two machine gun emplacements in the front line of each regimental sector, which could also be used also as command posts for company commanders. Third came the command posts for the artillery, then observation posts for the artillery, followed by further machine gun emplacements in depth, which were to have as much potential to provide flanking fire as possible. Finally, medical posts were to be built, one for each regimental sector, plus a medical bunker near each Wagenhalteplatz (halting place for ambulance vehicles). Later on, if necessary, Minenwerfer positions could be built. The outline for the two lines of the first position (of the Flandern II Stellung) and the two lines of the Artillerie Schutz Stellung were to be surveyed and fixed during the work. The barbed wire entanglements should also be gradually added during the course of the construction work.

The Flandern II Stellung was constructed in the period January–March 1918 mainly by Armierungs Kompagnien, assisted by Belgian Zivilarbeiter. Because of the strategic developments in March 1918 (in particular the preparations for the Spring Offensive), the position was never finished. There was a regular – and increasing – shortage of building materials, which were now sent to France as the priority, to be used in the preparation for the Spring Offensive there. By April 1918 the work on the Flandern II Stellung was halted completely. After the German 1918 offensives ground to a halt, there was a lack of manpower and building materials to resume the fortification works in the summer and autumn of 1918.

During the Final Offensive of 1918, the Flandern II Stellung was not used to any great degree by the Germans. After they had to give up the Flandern I Stellung in mid October 1918, the German command decided to withdraw to a completely new defensive position, the Lys Stellung and the Gent-Hermann Stellung behind the river Scheldt. Both positions were, effectively, merely lines drawn on a map by German staff officers; neither of them had ever been seriously fortified.

Chapter 3

Who did the Building?

Pioniere – and their tasks.

In the German Army the Corps of Engineers was a highly specialist branch; the field engineers of the German Army were the Pionier Kompagnien (but they were routinely responsible for various activities that were not for the British Royal Engineers, for example), of which there were one or two attached to each infantry division early in the war. Their tasks involved building trenches and shelters in the front line. In addition, they were very active in mine warfare, fought underground, and took a notable part in trench warfare. Hand grenades and Minenwerfer (trench mortars) were specifically engineer weapons early in the war. To support the engineers, many infantry were taught engineering techniques so that they could assist them in building all types of field fortifications. When Hindenburg and Ludendorff took control of the German army in late August 1916, the engineer units were reorganised. Each infantry division was now allotted two Pionier Kompagnien. These were placed under the command of a (divisional) Pionier Bataillon, providing their command and logistical support at divisional headquarters. Some of the former responsibilities of the Pioniere were diverted

Baukommando Flandern in March 1918. German soldiers (Pioniere or Armierungssoldaten) who were deployed to build bunkers on the Flanders front. Note the range of their tools. (*Vancoillie*)

towards new units (e.g. the Minenwerfer Kompagnie). From early 1917 the two Pionier Kompagnien were used mainly to build trenches and other fortifications.

Because of the reorganisation, some of the specialist staff were made redundant. Until early 1917 the German army had some Pionier Regimente, basically units that had their origins in operations involving fortresses and fortification warfare. They were deployed at Army level at the beginning of the war (originally to conduct siege warfare against fortresses; later mainly engaged in mine warfare). These regimental staffs were reorganised into Stabsoffiziere der Pioniere, but extra Stabsoffiziere der Pioniere were raised from scratch as well. Even though the name of this unit (Stabsoffizier der Pioniere or Stopi) can be translated as "staff officer of the engineers", it was a 'staff officer' that comprised several officers, NCOs and men and certainly not just one or two officers. These Stabsoffiziere der Pioniere were allotted to corps staffs (which in turn were often described as 'Gruppen'). The Stopi was responsible for the supply and transportation of engineering material and for all engineer works that were not the responsibility of the divisions. In the case of the Flanders front, the construction and upkeep of the many operational and strategic defence lines, i.e. those beyond the jurisdiction of the front line divisions, was undertaken by these Stopi. They took under command several labour units and the necessary workers to build the lines: independent Pionier Kompagnien, Armierungs Kompganien, Russian and other prisoners of war and Belgian Zivilarbeiter. They also controlled the necessary logistical units that transported the building materials.

Pioniere on the Flanders Front.

Independent engineer units were rare at the beginning of the war, apart from the Pionier Regimente. These Pionier Regimente were originally fortress units and therefore well suited to conduct trench warfare, which can be seen as a type of siege warfare. The Fourth Army was allotted Pionier Regiment 24 (Cologne) and Pionier Regiment 25 (Mainz), with their accompanying Pionier Belagerungs Trains (siege trains) and Park Kompagnien (park companies). Both these latter units were tasked with establishing and managing dumps. The field companies of both regiments were mainly used in underground mine warfare. From 1915 a significant number of Pionier Mineur Kompagnien (tunnelling companies) were raised and several were allotted to Fourth Army, which supervised the underground war in the Salient. For the rest, each division had one or two organic Pionier Kompagnien, which took care of works in the divisional sector.

After the reorganisation of the military engineers in late 1916, the number of engineer units in Fourth Army grew. At Army level a new staff post was created, General der Pioniere Nr. 4, which, among other tasks, commanded engineer units that were under Army control. Again, this was not merely one officer, but comprised a small staff. In June 1917 this 'General of Engineers N° 4' had numerous units at his disposal: five Stopi, two Pionier Bataillone (staffs), nine Pionier Kompagnien (mainly Landsturm companies and companies fit for garrison duty) and seventeen Pionier Mineur Kompagnien.

The number of units further increased during the Third Battle of Ypres, rising to seven Stopi, four Pionier Bataillone (staffs), thirty-two Pionier Kompagnien (of all classifications: Landsturm, Landwehr and fit for garrison duty, but also active and reserve companies) and thirteen Pionier Mineur Kompagnien in October 1917. This clearly illustrates the importance of the engineers during the campaign.

From the summer of 1917 it became increasingly impractical to continue building in or close to the front line. Reserve Pionier Kompagnie 49 (an organic part of the 49th Reserve Division), for instance, tried to complete three concrete bunkers in the Quer Riegel Süd, north-west of Bikschote, in June 1917. A shell that exploded in Dobschützwald (Wood 15), north-west of Pilkem, on 11 June, killed five and wounded a further five Pioniere. The company moved its billets to Poelkapelle; but it was not safe from long range artillery fire there either. The company had to move even further by the end of the month, towards Vijfwege (north-west of Westrozebeke). The engineers had to take a tram each day to travel to Langemark and from there on foot to their building sites near Pilkem. When the working day was finished they had to travel back, all of which took a lot of valuable time. The company was engaged in building bunkers and erecting barbed wire entanglements during its time in the sector.

3rd Kompagnie Pionier Bataillon 11 was an organic engineer company of the 38th Infanterie Division and arrived in June 1917 in Flanders. The division was at first used as an Eingreif Division and the Pioniere were immediately put to work on all kinds of engineering jobs: building foot bridges over streams, reconnoitring and inspecting roads, checking available defence lines and supply dumps in the sector etc. On 20 June 1917 the company received an order instructing them to help in constructing the Gheluvelt Riegel between the Wilhelm Stellung and the Flandern I Stellung and to occupy this line in case of a British attack. This work was halted on 16 July 1917 because of continuous artillery fire and the company was moved to the Flandern I Stellung. Late in July 1917 the 38th Infantry Division took over the divisional sector Zonnebeke from the 17th Infanterie Division and 3rd Kompagnie Pionier Bataillon 11 moved together with its division.

These Pioniere of 3rd Landsturm Pionier Kompagnie des XIX Armeekorps were active in Flanders during the summer of 1917. (*Vancoillie*)

The company was now ordered to improve the barbed wire entanglements in front of the Albrecht Stellung and it built a medical bunker in the sector during this period. Apart from this, the company had to detach some of its men to help manage the Rumpelkammer, a supply dump west of Zonnebeke. As soon as the British offensive started the Pioniere no longer remained active in building duties but had to serve as infantry reserves and to transport ammunitions.

During the Third Battle of Ypres, there was hardly any opportunity to build bunkers or dig trenches for the Pionier Kompagnien of the front line divisions. The only thing that they were able to do was to improve or repair barbed wire defences and construct small shelters, using wood and sheets of corrugated iron of the Heinrich type. Otherwise these units served as emergency infantry reserves and were regularly used to occupy a section of a defence line in the rear to prevent (or counter attack) any possible enemy break in to that line.

Once the level of fighting diminished, from mid November 1917, these Pionier Kompagnien were once more directed to specific tasks, mainly to build or improve defensive works. The 25th Infanterie Division, engaged in November 1917 near Passendale, ordered its organic Reserve Pionier Kompagnie 89 to build Siegfried Unterschlüpfe (shelters built with sheets of Siegfried type corrugated iron) close behind the front line. Concrete work was done near Rumbeke, the small dirt roads in the divisional sector were improved and barbed wire entanglements were erected in front of the Artillerie Schutz Stellung. The company moved to a hutted camp north of Rollegem-Kapelle in December 1917. From there the Pioniere travelled every day to their building sites. They built foot bridges across the Passendalebeek and Heulebeek, constructed concrete command posts and observation posts for the artillery, improved and erected barbed wire defences and built a new divisional observation post in Strooiboomhoek, between Moorslede and Dadizele. To speed up the work, the Pioniere expanded the existing network of narrow-gauge tracks. After a short period of rest in early January 1918, the division was again deployed in the same area. Reserve Pionier Kompagnie 89 was put to work on the barbed wire defences and concrete bunkers of the Moorslede Riegel, a task which it took over from 2nd Kompagnie Pionier Bataillon 8. Concrete bunkers were built and the narrow-gauge network near Colliemolenhoek and Vierkavenhoek was improved. The company had left the Salient by mid February 1918.

The number of engineering units allotted to the Fourth Army decreased gradually from late 1917 (with the ending of the Third Ypres offensive) and declined dramatically from spring 1918. In August 1918, for instance, the Fourth Army only had three Stopi, three Pionier Bataillone (staffs), a full Pionier Bataillon, seven Pionier Kompagnien (mainly Landsturm and fit for garrison duty) and one Pionier Mineur Kompagnie at its disposal at Army level.

An example: 2nd Kompagnie Pionier Bataillon 13.

2nd Kompagnie Pionier Bataillon 13 belonged to the 27th Infanterie Division during the whole of the war. The division was deployed to the Ypres Salient for the first time in early January 1916. On 6 January 1916 the company took over the sector that had previously been in the hands of 1st Kompagnie Pionier Bataillon 15. The billets in Tenbrielen also changed hands. 2nd Kompagnie Pionier Bataillon 13 worked for the 53 Infanterie Brigade in the sector between the Ypres-Comines railway (Höhe 59 – The Caterpillar) and the Ypres-Comines Canal (Bastion – The Bluff). The four main tasks of the company were: building (using ferro-concrete); pumping excess water away; manning Minenwerfer; and special missions under the orders of the division. Two Vizefeldwebel, four Unteroffiziere and fourteen Pioniere were continuously billeted in the Bereitschaftslager, near the canal, as Betonbaukommando. Four Unteroffiziere and thirty-six men of Grenadier Regiment 123 and Infanterie Regiment 124 were detached to it to help with the work. Apart from those men, each of the regiments provided a hundred men to transport building materials, mainly by using the network of Förderbahnen laid in and close behind the front line. The Pumpkommando consisted of twenty-two Pioniere, who were active in the different sub-sectors, operating the electrical pumps and maintaining and repairing the electricity network. One Unteroffizier and twenty-two Pioniere were responsible for the rather primitive Minenwerfer in the sector. Some Pioniere were detached to perform special technical tasks and the rest of the company worked on the second line of the front line position, every day supported by sixty men from each of the infantry regiments. The improvement and upkeep of the front line trenches were a matter for the infantry manning the line. Building and improving the first trench line of the second line was also a task for the infantry.

Numerous bunkers existed in the sector, mostly basic constructions; but there were still many wooden buildings as well. The company took on the task of building newer, stronger troop shelters (using more iron rods in the ferro-concrete, thus making the bunkers stronger) and strengthening the existing wooden huts and shelters by using concrete blocks. Most of the trenches had to be redesigned according to the latest regulations, whilst the walls had to be strengthened using wattle work and/or chicken wire. Niches were dug out from the trench sides for hand grenades, which were now available in large numbers.

The Bereitschaftslager (camp for support troops) next to the Ypres-Comines Canal. Note the wattle-work with which the sides have been reinforced to prevent collapse as a result of rain or frost. Wooden boards have been put on the ground so that the soldiers did not have to walk in the mud. Notice the lock gate in the upper left of the photograph. (*Vancoillie*)

Pioniere building a bunker using concrete blocks. The work area has been camouflaged from aerial view by a canopy of branches. (*Vancoillie*)

The fighting for the Bastion in February and March 1916 caused extensive damage to the trenches in the area and the Pioniere had to put most of their efforts into repairing these. In March 1916 they began this by repairing the destroyed barbed wire defences and then made some deep dugouts that were built into the canal bank in the reserve positions.

Heavy fighting in June 1916 in the sector inevitably left its marks and the company was hard at work once more, repairing trenches and barbed wire entanglements. When there was spare time, extra concrete bunkers were constructed.

The company moved from the Salient, together with its division, in July 1916 to the Somme and returned to Flanders in early September 1916. Once returned, it was active in the sector of Infanterie Regiment 120 near Wijtschate. The company first constructed three concrete bunkers and then dug, improved and repaired trenches in the Ic-Stellung (the second trench line of the front line position).

The company was transferred once again to France in November 1916; but returned once more to Flanders in mid August 1917, when it was in the line near Passendale, together with its parent division. By this time the Battle of Third Ypres had been underway for a little over a fortnight; the fighting was especially heavy in the nearby area of Langemark.

The company was billeted in Kalve, near Passendale, from 20 August. It considered the possibility of excavating some minierte Unterstände (deep dugouts) on the Feldherrenhügel (Zeugeberg, a small hill to the southwest of Westrozebeke). These dugouts were primarily designed as command posts. The works were regularly disturbed because of British attacks, during which the Pioniere had to man trenches. In order to make the task progress more rapidly, the division released the Pioniere on 24 August from their duty as infantry reserves and instructed them to work exclusively on the Stollen (dugouts) on the Feldherrenhügel. The Pioniere worked in two shifts on three dugouts, each having two entrances. However, the next day that order was rescinded and the company was ordered elsewhere. The work on the three dugouts was taken over by 1st Reserve Kompagnie Pionier Bataillon 6. In fact, in those few days much was accomplished: of the Trichterstollen (a deep dugout with the entrance in a shell-hole), eight frames had been installed from the first entrance and nine from the second entrance.

Three and four frames were in place for the entrances to the deep dugout to the west of the Trichterstollen and three and five frames respectively of the entrances of the third deep dugout (near the 'three trees').

The company itself was engaged in the 's Graventafel – Kleinmolen area to work on barbed wire entanglements. From September the Pioniere were used as infantrymen in reserve positions. The company then moved, once more with its parent division, to the Belgian-Dutch border from mid September 1917 to early October 1917 to rest and to reorganise. In early October 1917 it returned to the Ypres Salient, this time in the Staden sector.

Leutnant der Reserve Becker, an officer of 2nd Kompagnie Pionier Bataillon 13, was instructed to identify possible locations in the Artillerie Schutz Stellung of the Flandern I Stellung near Stampkot, to the west of Staden, for two Doppel MG Unterstände (twin machine gun emplacements). The Pioniere themselves were at first employed with extending and improving the barbed wire defences in Houthulst Forest.

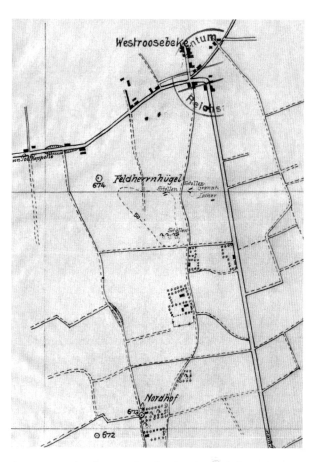

A company sketch map showing locations of deep dug-outs between Westrozebeke and Passendale late August 1917. (HStAS)

Two officers of the company inspected the area on 16 October 1917 to see whether there were suitable places to unload and store building materials and source clean water in order to construct the two concrete bunkers. In the meantime, the approximately 250 men of the company were divided into three groups and worked in shifts. Each group worked for two days, then was relieved by the next group. The Pioniere were thus able to repair and improve 210 metres of barbed wire defences and construct seventy metres of new barbed wire entanglements of some four to five metres depth. During the following days some hundred metres of barbed wire entanglements, approximately five metres wide, were erected daily.

The construction of the two Doppel Maschinengewehr Unterstände started on 18 October. Each bunker was 8.85 metres long and 9.60 metres wide, had a corridor at the back and two chambers measuring three metres long and four metres wide, formed by double elephant shelters (Heinrich type). Large niches were put in the corridor wall, in which machine guns could be stored. The machine guns were to be fired from outside the bunker. All walls and the roof were 1.50 metres thick. Each bunker required no less than forty two different types of pre-bent iron rods, measuring from 0.50 to 9.40 metres in length. In total, 2,983 rods were needed, with a total length of 10,251.15 metres!

Barbed wire entanglements in Houthulst Forest during the winter of 1917-1918. (*Schmieschek*)

Before the Germans started building the northern bunker on 18 October, they erected some form of camouflaging construction over the building site. The southern bunker was built inside an existing farm building, which was gutted and from which the back wall was partially removed and then supported to avoid it collapsing. The roof was adapted and enlarged so that the bunker would be totally hidden inside the building. Some Pioniere started laying new narrow-gauge tracks to bring up the building material. Another part of the company was still working on the barbed wire defences in Houthulst Forest, until that work (or at least that carried out by members of the unit) was stopped on 23 October 1917.

From 19 October the building material was transported to Stampkot and from there to the building sites. The construction pits were dug, but a storm then destroyed most of the camouflage, so that it had to be redone. By the end of the month the pits were 1.40 and 1.60 metres deep respectively and most of the building materials were on site. Several direct hits on the narrow-gauge network slowed down the supply of materials. The iron rods were bent to the correct measurements in Pionier Park Sint-Jozef.

Both pits had to be excavated until they were 1.90 metres deep; then the Pioniere started the concrete works. First, the iron rods for the foundation plate were put in place, after which they could start pouring concrete. When the base was ready the walls were built up. The bunkers were not completed when the company was relieved from its sector, together with its parent division, on 13 November 1917. This is interesting to note – with getting on for four weeks spent on building them, using considerable manpower, these bunkers were still incomplete. This is a reflection of construction difficulties – probably as much a consequence of poor weather as anything else. The relieving unit continued to work on both bunkers but changed the design. This unit, which had come from the Eastern Front and, apparently unaware of the ban on big slits/apertures on the forward face of bunkers in Flanders, now included a huge slit in the centre of the front wall of each of the bunkers. They were probably never completely finished. The south bunker was removed after the Second World War, whilst the north bunker is today used by the owner as storage.

After 2nd Kompagnie Pionier Bataillon 13 left the Ypres Salient in November 1917 it never returned.

A firing slit was not in the original plans for this Doppel MG Unterstand near Stampkot. The machine guns were supposed to be kept inside the bunker and were to be taken out and deployed near the bunker or on top of its roof during enemy attacks. The unit which came after 2nd Kompagnie Pionier Bataillon 13 came from the Eastern Front and was unaccustomed to the conditions and building regulations on the Western Front and changed the original plans of the bunker. (*Blieck*)

2nd Kompagnie Pionier Bataillon 13 started constructing two similar bunkers near Stampkot (Staden); one of them has survived. This bunker was designed as a Doppel MG Unterstand. (*Blieck*)

An example: 3rd Landwehr Pionier Kompagnie des XIII Armeekorps.

3rd Landwehr Pionier Kompagnie des XIII Armeekorps arrived by train in Ledegem on 9 October 1917. Its men were temporarily billeted in a tented camp near Beitem while they were working on the Artillerie Schutz Stellung of the Flandern II Stellung in the divisional area, Sector C of Gruppe Ypres. The company soon moved to a hutted camp in Ledegem, which was improved by the men themselves.

From 13 October 1917, three platoons of the company started constructing concrete bunkers: two near Strooiboomhoek (between Moorslede and Dadizele); two near Slypskapelle; and two close to the crossroads of the road from Slypskapelle to Ledegem and the road from Menen to Roeselare. On 15 October, 3rd Landwehr Pionier Kompagnie des XIII Armeekorps was made bodenständiges Beton Bau Kommando der Eingreif Division C der Gruppe Ypres (sector concrete building command of Eingreif Division C of Gruppe Ypres). It was subordinated to the Baustab rückwärtiger Stellungen (which was in the hands of Pionier Bataillon 23). The two bunkers near Strooiboomhoek were outside this sector and so were handed over to another unit. The men who had been working there were transferred to improve the hutted camp near Ledegem but were also soon constructing a Divisionsgefechtsstand (divisional battle headquarters) south of Sint-Pieter (Lord Farm on British trench maps). Two platoons worked on these four bunkers from 6 am to 12 noon. In the afternoons they worked on the huts of the camp in Ledegem, where the third platoon was employed full time. The priority for the company, however, lay in building command posts.

The building sites were hidden from aerial and other observation by placing camouflage nets over them. Huts were then put up near the building site, where the workers could rest, eat and find shelter against the elements. Construction pits were then dug, along with suitable drainage. To support their work, men were detached from the Eingreif Division in the sector. The building material was transported from the Pionier Parks in Ledegem, Izegem and Roeselare. On 23 October 1917, at last, concrete pouring could start for the foundations of the bunkers near Slypskapelle and, on 27 October, the first concrete was poured for the Divisionsgefechtsstand.

The work was reorganised from 1 November. 3rd Landwehr Pionier Kompagnie des XIII Armeekorps stopped work on three of the five bunkers on which it had been working until then and took on new building projects, so that now it was working on ten bunkers in total, of which two had already been begun. The company receives instructions to use the numbers U 251 to U 300 to refer to the bunkers (U = Unterstand). All of these constructions were to be built as Einheitsunterstände, except for the two bunkers on which work had already been started (U 252 and U 261).

U 251:   Regimentsgefechtsstand (regimental battle headquarters) at Schouthoek. This bunker exists today, just north of the farm in Groene Jagerstraat 2 in Ledegem (Marks Farm).

U 252:   Originally this was to be a Divisionsgefechtsstand (divisional battle headquarters), but it was later redesignated to be a Regimentsgefechtsstand (regimental battle headquarters). This bunker exists today, just east of the farm in Provinciebaan 104 in Ledegem (Lord Farm).

U 253:   Regimentsgefechtsstand between the Menen – Roeselare road and the Menen-Roeselare railway line. This bunker no longer exists; it stood to the west of the current Nijverheidslaan in Ledegem (Bud's Farm).

Unterstand 252, adjacent to the farm at Provinciebaan 104 in Ledegem. This bunker was originally designed as a Divisionsgefechtsstand (divisional battle headquarters). (*Blieck*)

U 255: Untergruppenstand at Schouthoek. This bunker exists today, just south of the farm in Groene Jagerstraat 2 in Ledegem (Marks Farm).

U 256: Untergruppenstand. This bunker no longer exists; it stood just to the south of Unterstand 252 (near Kut Copse and Phil's Farm).

U 257: Untergruppenstand. This bunker exists today; it stands just west of the farm in Provinciebaan 104 in Ledegem (Lord Farm) but it cannot be visited.

U 258: Untergruppenstand. This bunker no longer exists; it stood just to the southwest of Unterstand 253, north of Fabriekslaan in Ledegem (Hunk Houses).

U 259: Untergruppenstand. This bunker no longer exists; it stood to the immediate southeast of Unterstand 253, west of Nijverheidslaan in Ledegem (Bud's Farm).

U 260: Bereitschaftstruppen Kommandeurstand (BTK – support units command post). This bunker no longer exists; it was close to the south of the house in Heerweg 2 in Ledegem (south of Craft Cottage).

U 261: Bereitschaftstruppen Kommandeurstand (BTK – support units command post). This bunker no longer exists; it stood just south of the farm in Slypsstraat 12 in Ledegem (Cherub Farm). This bunker was first planned as a Brigade Gefechtsstand, measuring 13.40 by 7.30 metres, with three chambers, a corridor at the back and an observation cupola.

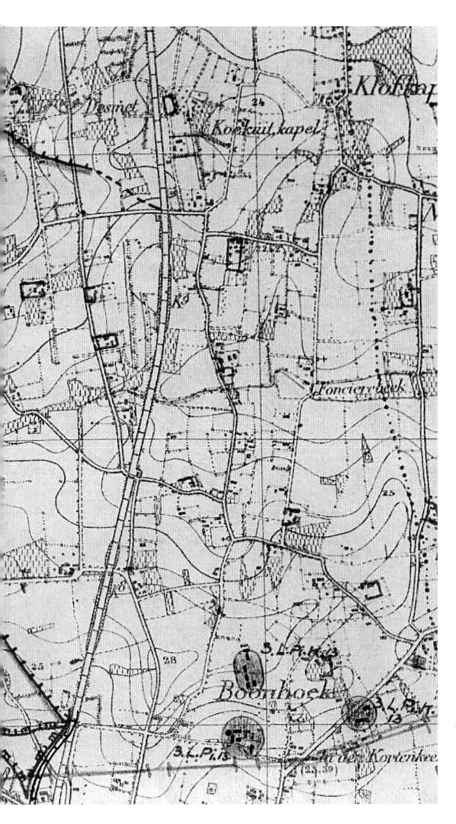

Overview map of an area north of Ledegem, from late 1917, showing the bunkers under construction by 3rd Landwehr Pionier Kompagnie des XIII Armeekorps. (*HStAS*)

Unterstand 255 alongside Groene Jagerstraat in Ledegem. This is a typical Einheitsunterstand with sloped roof. (*Blieck*)

Rear view of Unterstand 255 along Groene Jagerstraat in Ledegem. There are two entrances with steps in between so that the bunker could be used as a parapet. The Germans could deploy a machine gun at this position or were able to observe the area from it. (*Blieck*)

To speed up the work, the Eingreif Divisionen in the sector and the Armierungs Kompagnien daily detached some 200 to 300 men to assist the Pioniere. From 1 November 1917, concrete pouring recommenced for both bunkers that had been started earlier. Preparatory work had to be done first for the other bunkers (narrow-gauge tracks, camouflaging, huts, digging construction pits etc.) before concrete could be poured. The foundations for bunkers U 252 and U 261 were ready by 5 November and work started for the formwork of the walls and positioning the iron rods. Only in mid November could the pouring of concrete commence for the base plates for the new bunkers. By the end of that month none of the bunkers were completely finished, but they were pouring concrete for the walls of U 252 and U 261 at that point. A shell exploded near U 255 on 2 December and wounded three Pioniere and two of the detached workers, but the building site itself was not hit. 3rd Landwehr Pionier Kompagnie des XIII Armeekorps was relieved on 4 December 1917 by 3rd Kompagnie Pionier Bataillon 23. The company moved to the north to work on the Flandern II Stellung. The bunkers near Ledegem were completed by the relieving unit.

Fighting units.

Overview.

Fortification works in the front line itself were usually undertaken by the fighting units themselves. It was, of course, very difficult to get and maintain extra workers into the front line because of the shelling and there was only limited available space in the trenches.

The first tasks that were undertaken in the front line were the building of fighting and communication trenches. During intensive fighting around Ypres in late October and much of November 1914 few trenches were dug by the German units in the area. During these first days of combat in the Salient area, it was usual to withdraw a short distance at nightfall to sleep, while the forward positions were protected by sentries, just as in previous wars. This method of defence was soon found to be inadequate and the first, very primitive, trenches were dug. Often the ditches along roads and fields were deepened for this purpose. The goal of the Germans at this point in the war was to attack and break through, so the German command did not see why they should waste time by building elaborate field fortifications, as these required a lot of trouble and effort, which could be better expended in the relentless attacks that characterised the fighting in the Salient at this time. There were other reasons why no defensive works were built, which included the lack of equipment (shovels, spades, axes etc.) in most of the newly raised units and the precipitate training these units had undergone, in which there was no time (nor tools) to build practice trenches.

As soon as the front stabilised, German troops were initially ordered to dig in wherever they were at that time. The voluntary giving up of hard won terrain was never considered, even if this would have made defence easier. At best, the front line was downgraded to a lightly defended outpost line, behind which the main fighting trench was dug at a more suitable location. Landwehr Infanterie Regiment 77, for instance, suffered severe casualties due to the fact that their sector near Wallemolen, between Passendale and Poelkapelle, was situated on a forward slope and towards a number of streams. Not only did the Allies (in this case the French) have excellent observation into the German trenches, but the water caused permanent problems. The regiment therefore converted the front line into a line of manned outposts and built a new main fighting trench some 600 to 800 metres to the rear of this outpost line.

In German units (as was the case for the British and the French), a trench routine was gradually established. One battalion occupied the front line (Kampfbataillon – battalion in line), one battalion was in reserve in the second line (Bereitschaftsbataillon – support battalion) and one battalion was resting some kilometres behind the front line (Ruhebataillon – resting battalion). As far as working on the defences was concerned, this meant that the Kampfbataillon maintained and developed the front line trenches, the Bereitschaftsbataillon the reserve trenches and the communication trenches and transported building material to the front line, while the Ruhebataillon built or improved the rest camps and billets. This last battalion was occasionally called up to help with the transportation of building material and with the construction of positions further in the rear. This basic routine was, with variations according to circumstances, followed until the end of the war.

From 1914 until late 1916 most of the German units in the Ypres Salient were organically connected: ie they belonged to bigger formations. Army corps, composed of two permanent divisions, were appointed a sector, which they had to hold, defend and fortify. After the reorganisation of infantry divisions in the German order of battle (essentially this involved reducing a division from twelve battalions to nine and began in 1915), surplus divisions not connected to an army corps (sometimes called 'flying divisions') become available from 1915. This, and the heavy strains endured by divisions during the major battles of 1916, led to the norm of a German army corps staff remaining in a particular sector for a longer period of time, which had under command divisions which were no longer connected to the military area from which the army corps originated (Korpsbezirk) or which were not a part of the peace time composition of the army corps. The Germans followed this procedure in order to bring more continuity (and therefore efficiency) in their front line. Even though the divisions in the front line changed, the tasks remained the same because the higher echelon (i.e. the army corps) remained the same and was usually present in the area for a long period of time, so that its staff knew the area very well and was able to apply the same guiding lines as regards its sector of responsibility to its incoming units and formations. This policy was particularly effective for the elaborate defensive system that characterised the Salient area for most of the war. Seeing the benefit of this system of command and control, the highest level of command in the German army (Oberste Heeresleitung) issued new guidelines in late 1916 that applied to the whole length of the Western Front, thereby providing those most desirable military virtues of standardisation and continuity. Before this, a relief in a sector could lead to a fundamentally different way of holding the line and of constructing defensive works, resulting in a waste of (increasingly valuable and scarce) materiel and labour.

Incessant shelling and the heavy and persistent fighting during the Third Battle of Ypres, between them stretching from late May to mid November 1917, demanded the complete attention of the fighting units, making it impossible for them to dig trenches or build concrete bunkers. The evolution in defence tactics, implemented as a consequence of lessons learnt, such as fighting from non continuous positions and defence in depth, gave fighting units the false impression that putting effort into building a strong front line was no longer worthwhile.

Gruppe Wijtschate (Generalkommando IX Reservekorps) issued an order on 17 October 1917 that emphasised once more the need to have numerous fortified shelters in the front zone. Its staff pointed to the fact that every day many men were sitting around idle (although it is doubtful that these soldiers felt in any way under occupied!) in their billets behind the front line, even for a few hours. These men could be put to more useful purposes by building concrete works in their immediate surroundings. Not only could new concrete bunkers be built, but it would be very beneficial to fortify existing cellars by using ferro-concrete, something which could be quite easily done. The recommended ideal locations for this type of work were the scattered buildings situated relatively close behind the front line.

One of the divisions to respond to this order was the 1st Bayerische Reserve Division, which created Betontrupps from the men who were detached full-time to the billets behind the front line for a variety of duties. Each infantry regiment was ordered to raise two Betontrupps, comprising one NCO and ten men. To each Trupp two Pioniere were detached from the divisional engineers; they provided technical assistance for any such work. The goal was to exchange the men in the Betontrupps regularly for others who were permanently detached to rear area duties, thereby extending the expertise in a particular formation or unit.

In late 1917, after the complete dislocation of the line as a consequence of the advances made by the Allies during Third Ypres, it was essential to prepare the front line for the coming winter and, especially, to make improvements to the living conditions in it. However, preparations for new offensives in the spring of 1918 and the accompanying hope that the war would soon be finished because of these, took away much of the incentive for such improvement. During 1918, the Germans had high hopes – or they did until July – that one final offensive in Flanders (code-name Hagen) would break through the Allied lines and allow them to push on to the Channel ports, thus rendering all this extra work on the defences useless. When the Allies turned the tables in the summer of 1918 (in the French sector in late July, in the British in early August) and most of the German units for Hagen were hastily sent to France, it was too late to start building up a new, elaborate defensive system. The German army was exhausted, disappointed and war-weary; whilst the rampaging Spanish flu epidemic, following four years of war, wrought havoc amongst the German forces. The strength and will-power to build new defences in the autumn of 1918 almost from scratch was all but completely gone among the undermanned units of the Ypres Salient.

An example: Infanterie Regiment 126 (October 1914 – December 1915).

Zwarteleen: November – December 1914.
The 8th Royal Württemberg Infanterie Regiment 126 'Großherzog Friedrich von Baden' arrived in late October 1914 in Flanders as a part of the 30th Infanterie Division. It took part in the fighting near Geluveld, Zandvoorde and Klein-Zillebeke. At that stage there was hardly any opportunity of building trenches or field fortifications. After the bloody German attacks were stopped in mid November 1914, the severely damaged regiment held hastily dug positions near Zwarteleen, between Hill 60 and the Saubucht, a marshy area near what the British were later to call Mount Sorrel. This sector consisted of nothing more sophisticated than a front line trench and a communication trench. The orders were clear, however: the Germans were to stay and become the masters of No Man's Land and the enemy was to

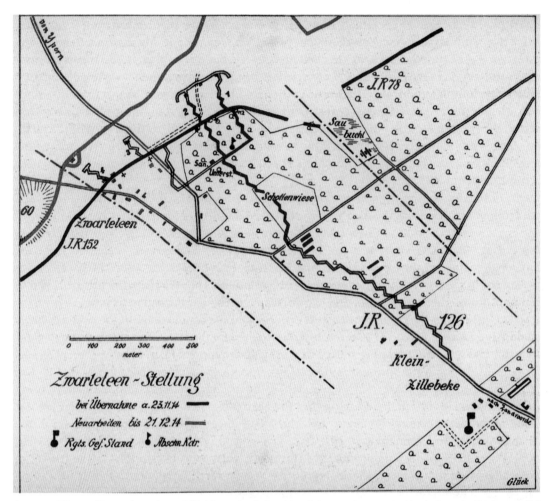

A map of Sector Zwarteleen (note Hill 60 on the left edge of the map), occupied by Infanterie Regiment 126 from 23 November to 21 December 1914. (*Infanterie Regiment 126*)

be kept under pressure at all times by the use of methods such as sap trenches (ie pushing trenches into No Man's Land from their trenches) and hand grenades. At the same time the position was to be fortified by any means available, barbed wire entanglements were to be erected to protect the front line and adequate shelters were to be built to quarter reserve troops. Even resting troops were given no respite: practice trenches were to be dug so that the men could train there for coming attacks.

The few trenches that were available that early winter were shallow, filled with mud and often knee deep, or worse, in water. No traverses had been dug, so that the trenches were vulnerable to flanking fire; in this case, for instance, from the direction of Hill 60 (which the French held for some weeks after the battle died down). The high ground water level and the impermeable nature of the subsoil (i.e. the blue clay) quickly turned the ground into a swamp. Apart from these difficulties, there was a severe lack of building material and tools to carry out essential works. Barbed wire entanglements were at best minimal and the few shelters that had been built were not even splinter-proof nor did they offer anything like adequate protection against the seemingly never-ending rain. The communication trench was only partly finished; and what had been 'completed' was invariably flooded and dug with walls that were too steep, meaning that they collapsed because of the rain. To make matters worse, the poor condition of the narrow dirt roads (in reality they were not much better before the war) made it almost impossible to bring up building material.

Notwithstanding all of these factors, the regiment worked very hard to improve their sector. The trenches were gradually deepened and water and mud was pumped or scooped out. The breastworks were strengthened and steel 'sniper' plates and wooden trench frames put in place. The two sap trenches that had been started were lengthened and connected by a trench. Two more sap trenches were dug in the direction of some houses, with the aim of incorporating them into the defensive system. Improved barbed wire defences were erected, particularly at the heads of the sap trenches. The supply roads were significantly improved. As the Germans now had better fighting trenches, they soon became masters of No Man's Land. Near Klein-Zillebeke, close to the battle headquarters of the regiment, shelters were built. However, enemy artillery fire and the weather ('frost and thaw' was every bit as damaging to trench walls as the rain) frequently undid much of the hard work. The regiment, much reduced by the heavy fighting of the late autumn, did not win the fight against the weather. Painfully dug fortified trenches collapsed after heavy rainfall and soldiers more often than not stood knee-deep in mud in spite of all their efforts. The French – at this time there were no British troops in the Salient – bombarded the German trenches in mid December 1914 with

The primitive battle headquarters of Infanterie Regiment 126 near Klein Zillebeke, photographed at the end of 1914. (*Infanterie Regiment 126*)

trench mortars and artillery in preparation for the attacks that they launched at this time, which destroyed all work done in the sector. Infanterie Regiment 126 was relieved from the Zwarteleen Sector on 22 December 1914.

Groenenburg: December 1914 – May 1915.
After a very short period of rest, Infanterie Regiment 126 was sent back to the front line, this time in the Groenenburg Sector. The trenches here were somewhat better than the ones near Zwarteleen (it would be difficult to be otherwise) as they suffered less from ground water. The supply lines could not be directly observed by the enemy and therefore attracted less attention. A new, welcome, feature was the availability of 'winter' huts for the resting battalion of the regiment, near Doornkapel (Chapelle d'Epines), between Zandvoorde and Kruiseke. A hutted camp was built here, well protected against Allied aerial observation. The huts were comfortably equipped with coke stoves, lamps, water basins, plank beds and straw. Over time they were made more comfortable, mainly by making use of furniture that was taken from abandoned buildings nearby. A canteen was constructed and several field kitchens installed. All of this building and improvement work demanded considerable energy, but the rewards were great and, once these were ready, resting troops could recover in the camp from the hard time that they had endured in the front line trenches.

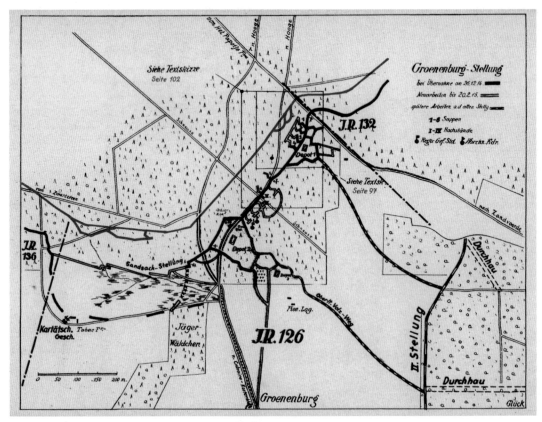

Sector Groenenburg (Shrewsbury Forest to the British), as occupied by Infanterie Regiment 126 from 26 December 1914 to 20 February 1915. (*Infanterie Regiment 126*)

However, the main concern of Infanterie Regiment 126 remained the improvement of the front line trenches. An essential first task was to improve water drainage, which then allowed for the digging of deeper trenches. Parapets were strengthened and traverses were added to the fighting trenches. More 'sniper' plates were positioned. No Man's Land, which in this sector was mainly woodland, was cleared to give a clearer field of fire. The trench walls were strengthened by using brushwood and wattle to avoid collapses. With the help of the engineers, communication trenches were dug and barbed wire entanglements were placed. The comfort of the troops was also taken into consideration; each company sector was provided with a coffee kitchen, where a hot cup of coffee could be got at any time of the day or night. The shelters were equipped with heating and the straw was changed regularly. Latrines were built as well, and they were regularly disinfected (latrine duty was a common punishment for minor offences). In the hutted camp near Doornkapel, a water purification system was installed to ensure a good supply of healthy drinking water.

Losses sustained during the fighting in October and November 1914 were gradually made up by new drafts, so the regiment could take up extra work. More saps were dug and even observation posts (wooden towers). Part of the regimental sector lay in marshy ground, and so surface trenches (i.e. breastworks) had to be built up by the use of numerous sandbags. The marsh itself was denied to enemy surprise attacks by entanglements and flanking trenches were dug in order that the defenders might be prepared for all contingencies. For the first time the Germans put duck-boards on the trench floors (the Germans used the term Knüppelrosten, wooden racks), which made the trenches much easier to pass along, whilst it was somewhat easier to drain the water from the trenches (with the addition of sumps). Increased troop numbers meant that they needed more shelters; new stretches of trench were dug ten metres behind the front line trench. Basic shelters were built into the side of these new trenches. These short lengths of trench were then soon linked up to form a continuous second trench line. Fourth Army (under whose command the division fell) issued orders on 19 January 1915 that several parallel trenches, to be used as shelter during heavy bombardments, were to be dug. By late January 1915 the sector of Infanterie Regiment 126 was well fortified and built by the standards of that time.

German Sandsackstellung (sand bag position/breastworks) to the left and the British trenches to the right inside Shrewsbury Forest, near Zandvoorde, in 1915. (*Infanterie Regiment 126*)

As the surface work was now well in hand, in February and March 1915 the Germans in the sector started engaging in an underground war, which in turn required a huge amount of materiel. The Allies would, of course, develop underground warfare as well. However, the Germans soon became the masters of winning the mine craters that were the result of the blowing of mines, turning these very swiftly into small fortifications by using sandbags and timber and then sapping back to connect them to their front line trench system.

Above: Medical aid post in the sector of Infanterie Regiment 126 in the spring of 1915. (*Infanterie Regiment 126*)

Left: German soldiers observing the British trenches using primitive trench periscopes. (*Infanterie Regiment 126*)

Above: Soldiers of Infanterie Regiment 126 set about reinforcing a British mine crater immediately after its capture. (*Infanterie Regiment 126*)

Right: A shelter of the Bereitschaftslager Waldheim. (*Infanterie Regiment 126*)

The work of the artillery gradually destroyed the large wood in which the front line was situated, which improved the Allied observation of the German trenches. The need to get improved protection against shell fire, only achievable by improving the quality and strength of shelters, became increasingly evident. The existing shelters, which offered at the most minimal cover against shrapnel, had to be improved so that they would offer protection against direct hits as well. From April 1915, the German army made rails and railway sleepers available to front line units, along with the means and raw material to make concrete. Entanglements in front of the front line were improved by using 'Frisian riders' and barbed wire concertinas. A new hutted camp was built to the northwest of Zandvoorde for the Bereitschaftsbataillon, named Bereitschaftslager Waldheim.

Doppelhöhe 60: May – June 1915.
Early in May 1915 the British (who had returned to the Salient in February/March 1915) withdrew some distance following German successes to the northeast of Ypres (including the recapture of all of Hill 60) during the Second Battle of Ypres and took up new positions on the Doppelhöhe 60 (Tor Top). The Germans followed up and dug in along a wood edge, parallel

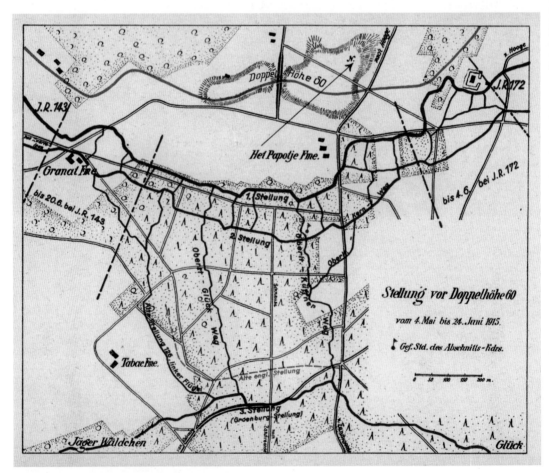

Sector Doppelhöhe 60 (Mount Sorrel), as occupied by Infanterie Regiment 126 from 4 May to 24 June 1915. Note the clear 2nd Stellung, second line, whilst the original front line (see map p 162) has been made into a third defence line. (*Infanterie Regiment 126*)

to the current Pappotstraat. At first Infanterie Regiment 126 suffered casualties from gun fire but, as soon as the shelling decreased in intensity, new trenches were dug. When designing and digging these the regiment took into account its experiences from the previous months and the lessons that had been learnt. The infantry immediately made traverses in the trenches, shelters were constructed at the most suitable places and, particularly, the need for good water drainage was taken into account before the work got underway. Positioning defensive obstacles was a job that was mainly left to the Pioniere. The Ruhebataillon provided the labour to dig the communication trenches. Everything went smoothly because there was now a sufficient supply of building material, which was transported by making use of narrow-gauge tracks that had been laid very close to the front line system.

The defensive system also was developed in depth. Generalkommando XV Armeekorps' orders of 18 May 1915 required the digging of a second trench line, approximately a hundred metres behind the front line trench. This second trench line was to be used for shelter if the front line trench came under heavy shelling; whilst it could accommodate reserves and have them close to the front line in case of emergencies. Numerous communication trenches were dug between both trench lines to allow swift movement between both lines. This 900 metres long second trench line was ready on 22 May 1915; each of the four company sectors now had three communication trenches between the lines. General der Infanterie von Deimling visited the sector soon after and commended the regiment and the men on their excellent work. In honour of several officers that were involved in the building of some of these trenches, these were named after them. Thus Oberleutnant Kern Weg, Oberleutnant Küffner Weg and Oberleutnant Volz Weg got their names. One of the communication trenches had double the standard width to facilitate the transport of supplies and wounded and was called Oberst Glück Weg after the regimental commander. The former front line (Groenenburgstellung) was remodelled as a third defensive trench line and Armierungstruppen started working on a fourth defensive trench line. Neither of these latter trench lines should be confused with the concept of elastic defence (which was only introduced some time later), but more with the need to be prepared for emergencies and a possible enemy break through. In effect it was a front line system – and succeeding lines of trenches in a system became a standard feature in the war, particularly from mid 1916. Hence the importance of understanding that First, Second Line etc refers to defence trench systems and not to the front line as such and certainly not to a single trench line. In late June 1915, Infanterie Regiment 126 was relieved in front of Doppelhöhe 60; it could be proud of the well constructed and maintained sector that it passed on to its successor.

The Volz Weg (Volz Road or Way), a communication trench named after Oberleutnant Volz of Infanterie Regiment 126. (*Infanterie Regiment 126*)

Left: The Küffner Weg (Küffner Road or Way), a communication trench named after Oberleutnant Küffner of Infanterie Regiment 126. (*Infanterie Regiment 126*)

Below: A German trench destroyed by artillery fire in the Hooge Sector. (*Infanterie Regiment 126*)

Hooge: June – December 1915.

Infanterie Regiment 126 moved to the Hooge Sector, which ran from just south of the Menin Road to the Bellewaardebeek. When they arrived they found that the condition of the trenches in this sector were abysmal. Continuous fighting since May 1915 had left its mark on the state of the defences. Shell proof shelters were non-existent, apart from one command post for the sector commander on Höhe 55, the highest point of the area, on the Zandberg, just south of a bend in the Menin Road. The trenches in the sector were shallow and the men often had to stand up to their knees in mud and water. The second trench line was unusable as it did not offer a sufficient field of fire. The communication trenches between the front lines and the second line were, in effect, non-existent and the only supply trench to the rear was the Meisengasse. The whole sector sloped down towards the enemy lines, thus offering them a perfect view of all the trenches. The difficulties in building a defensive system here could be summarised as one of geology: clay-like soil and high ground water level. Rain could only slowly seep into the soil and thus digging trenches down into it was almost impossible, as aquiferous layers brought water down from higher areas, quickly turning trenches into small streams. The Germans had once more to revert to building breastworks and parados using sandbags. The area near Bellewaardevijver (Bellewaarde Lake, part of the grounds of Hooge Chateau) was also very troublesome. A dam on the western side created very considerable water pressure on the trenches in the immediate surroundings.

Infanterie Regiment 126 was supported by two engineer companies to undertake improvements and they set about undertaking these as soon as they arrived. The engineers started by repairing and extending the barbed wire entanglements and then constructing fortified observation posts, ammunition dumps and shelters. They also took on responsibility for the drainage works.

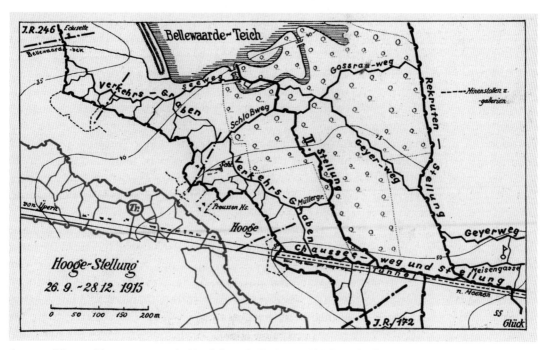

A map of Sector Hooge, as occupied by Infanterie Regiment 126 from 26 September to 28 December 1915; notice the 'Tr', behind the British lines (in red), which indicates a mine crater. (*Infanterie Regiment 126*)

The infantry set about constructing trenches, breastworks and building splinter-proof dugouts. They also brought up the building material and assisted the engineers wherever and whenever necessary. The troops in the front line trenches were only engaged in building, improving and the upkeep of their own trenches and could not be used elsewhere. The improvements advanced slowly, mainly because large parts of the sector could be taken under flanking fire. Thus, all too often, whatever got done during the night, at the cost of much sweat, got destroyed almost immediately during the day. Mine warfare continued in all its fury as well, which in turn required significant manpower.

Labour was used at first to improve the usual routine of delivery of food, ammunition, building material etc., and the removal of the wounded. The command post of the sector commander had to be moved as a matter of urgency as it was attracting artillery fire. A second communication trench, one and a half kilometres long, was dug north of the Meisengasse. Oberleutnant Volz was responsible for selecting its line, but the trench was later named after the Grabenoffizier (the officer in charge of building and upkeep of the trenches in the regimental sector), Leutnant Geyer. Leutnant Geyer was wounded during the construction of this trench, on 11 July 1915; and died of his wounds on 14 August 1915 in hospital in Hannover. To speed up the work, an Armierungskompagnie was brought in to do most of the digging. The new command post was finished rapidly and a medical aid post was dug along the Meisengasse. Bad weather and shelling continued to harass the smooth progress of the work. Trench walls occasionally collapsed, largely because the walls had too steep an incline, which was the way German soldiers had been taught to do such work in peace time. Construction materials were transported by narrow-gauge trains to the Pionier Park Veldhoek and from there by using manpower and wagons to the trenches at the front.

Most of this hard work was destroyed in the course of the unusually heavy fighting in the Hooge Sector in July and August 1915. Almost all of the trenches and shelters were completely ruined. The British fired a mine on 19 July under the trenches near Hooge and seemingly endless attacks and counter-attacks followed for several weeks. Infanterie Regiment 126 was relieved early in August 1915.

The Regiment returned to the sector on 26 September 1915. There had been heavy fighting the previous day (a British diversionary attack, associated with the opening of the Battle of Loos), but a relative calm now returned to the area. To prevent a British break through in this part of the front, Generalkommando XV Armeekorps ordered a thorough rebuilding and reworking of the defensive system. In the meantime there was a more pressing problem: a solution had to be found for the high water table issue. The Germans found a regular way to lower the water level of the Bellewaardevijver by one to two metres by channelling the water flow away under the German trenches towards the lower British held area. At the same time, autumn weather brought more rain and thus more ground water.

It was clear that digging trenches, reinforcing trench walls and water drainage all had to be done simultaneously. All trenches were from now on constructed with a small incline in the floor; at the bottom of the trench a wooden gutter was built. On top of this wooden duck boards were placed to enable easy movement and to stop the gutters being destroyed by walking directly on them. At the lowest lying places the water was diverted using further drainage; or a big hole was dug to hold the water, which could then be scooped or pumped away. The ability to lower the water level of the Bellewaardevijver was extremely useful, as most of the drained water could be diverted towards the pond. The trench walls were reinforced using wooden boards or wattle, reinforced by beams at certain places, especially where the water pressure was very strong.

The building material was brought up from the Pionier Hauptpark to the smaller Pionier Park at Veldhoek, to the west of Geluveld. Russian prisoners of war and Belgian civilian labourers were active behind the lines making the wattle-work to reinforce the trench walls. Infanterie Regiment 126's sector had a total of some seven kilometres of trenches, for which fourteen kilometres of wattle was needed. Logistics were a nightmare. Apart from the wattle, all other building material had to be transported to the front line trenches – the final stages of which inevitably had to be done by human muscle power: timber supports for the tunnellers and for supporting dugouts; barbed wire to build a triple entanglement in front of the different trench lines (themselves totalling three kilometres); and building material for all kinds of shelters and dugouts. Several narrow-gauge trains left Veldhoek every night pulling twelve small railway wagons towards the front line over dangerously exposed tracks. The British were well aware of this traffic and tried to disturb the Germans with shelling (of course the same procedure was applied on the other side of the wire).

Constructing new shelters sufficiently strong enough to withstand shells was a slow process. The main reason for the delay was the fact that work in the front line trenches could only be done during the night. There were technical issues as well that slowed things down. Building the roof of a bunker or reinforced dugout was far from easy: first a layer of rails or (iron) railway sleepers or steel plates, on top of this a twenty centimetres layer of sandbags, then another layer of rails, sleepers or plates and on top another layer of sandbags. The first bunkers were built, mostly in groups of four, including a command post, a machine gun post, an observation post and a troop shelter.

The most remarkable construction in this sector was, however, Hoogetunnel. It was built to solve the problem of keeping the communication trenches, especially the Meisengasse, in this sector in a usable shape. Collapsing walls and shelling frequently disrupted supplies to the front. At first the Germans looked at the idea of building a new communication trench just to the south of the Meisengasse, on the north side of the Menin Road; however, in the autumn of 1915 it was decided to build a tunnel – in effect a subway – under the Menin Road. A Tunnelbaukommando was immediately formed from members of Infantry Regiments 105, 126, 132 and 172 and put under the command of Leutnant Lorenz of 4th Kompagnie Pionier Bataillon 22. Work started on 3 October 1915. From the Meisengasse and the Chausseestellung, every hundred metres a tunnel was dug towards the centre of the Menin Road. As soon as the point was reached, connecting tunnels were dug from one to the other along the planned length. Digging was done day and night in three shifts of seven hours, with half an hour breaks in between. The western end of the tunnel was prioritised as the German lines here were in full view of the enemy and thus a

An interior view of Hooge Tunnel, what the British would call a subway, built under the Menin Road and providing secure access to the Front Line. (*Infanterie Regiment 126*)

subway was particularly welcome here. Twelve teams of four men were at any one time operating, in effect, non-stop. Once the western part was competed, the tunnellers continued eastwards. The gallery – or subway – was approximately two metres high and 1.60 metres wide at the bottom and 1.20 metres at the top. It was electrically lit. The tunnel advanced at approximately eighty metres per ten days, enabling the Germans to finish the 800 metres long tunnel by Christmas. The tunnel was considerably extended in 1916 and finally measured 1,500 metres, running from 't Kantientje (near Veldhoek, west of Geluveld) to a point just past the bend in the Menin Road to the west of the Zandberg (Clapham Junction), at which point it connected to the trenches of the Hooge Sector.

Infanterie Regiment 126 left the Hooge Sector in late December 1915. From September to Christmas 1915 it had got through an enormous amount of materiel: 880,000 sandbags, 13,750 thick boards and spars, 9,000 metres of barbed wire spirals, 7,820 pieces of wattle–work and fascines, 6,725 beams and 1,085 rails. In addition to this impressive list there was a weekly requirement of 300,000 kg of gravel and 150,000 kg of cement. Hoogetunnel alone had required no less than 5,798 wooden props.

An example: Reserve Feldartillerie Regiment 51 (October 1914 – July 1916).

The First Battle of Ypres and the winter of 1914-1915.
Reserve Feldartillerie Regiment 51 was deployed in Flanders from mid October 1914 and it participated in the fighting at Roeselare, Westrozebeke, Poelkapelle and Langemark. Only when the Battle of First Ypres had come to a stalemated halt could attention be given to the construction of shelters and fortified positions. The gunners started work on shelters for troops and officers, telephone posts and kitchens from mid November 1914. These were not splinter proof and were built using beams and doors from nearby houses. The order was issued to reinforce the defence lines at the end of 1914, which meant that the gunners had to prepare different positions, protected by barbed wire, so that the batteries could switch their locations regularly. In reality, these artillery positions were nothing more than rapidly built sheds on top of and around which was strewn construction waste as camouflage. The priority for any available time in the winter of 1914-1915 was largely devoted to training drafts in the arts of the artillery, as experienced men were very scarce in the regiment after the fighting of October and November 1914.

A gun position of Reserve Feldartillerie Regiment 51, hidden between some ruined farm buildings during the winter of 1914-1915. (*Reserve Feldartillerie Regiment 51*)

After Second Ypres (the gas attack) and beyond: 1915-1916.
Reserve Feldartillerie Regiment 51 was involved in the gas attacks and fighting in the Salient in April and May 1915 and thus there was not time to build or improve their positions. The first orders to construct fortified artillery position appeared in July 1915, i.e. only after a period of rest and training for the men of the regiment. The General der Fußartillerie (general of foot artillery, in this case the senior gunner staff officer) of Fourth Army decreed that there should be artillery positions for each of the infantry defence lines. This meant that each battery had a main position and a reserve position behind the first and second defence line and the same behind the second infantry defence position. These reserve position could also be used if extra artillery units were deployed to the sector. An observation post was included for each position, which had to be able to function even during heavy shelling. These observation posts were not to be positioned too close together, nor on sites that were known to enemy observers. Because of the increasing use of aerial observation, all observation posts were to be well camouflaged. The importance of extra observation posts, further away from the front line, was stressed; if possible these were to be built in trees or as newly built (but camouflaged) observation towers.

The regiment worked continuously building all these battery positions in July and August 1915. The building material was partly provided by the gunners themselves by cutting down trees in the immediate area; but much was transported via the Pionier Parks: railway sleepers, stakes, sheets of corrugated iron, boards and beams. Observation posts were built in the different trench lines and on two heights, Hill 35 and Hill 32. Wooden signs at the posts made clear to which battery the post belonged. The gunners were very busy, with little time left for other tasks; the specified work was finished by 1 September 1915.

A gun position of Reserve Feldartillerie Regiment 51, built inside a farm building in the spring of 1915. (*Reserve Feldartillerie Regiment 51*)

A gun position of Reserve Feldartillerie Regiment 51 in the spring of 1915. (*Reserve Feldartillerie Regiment 51*)

Water, once more, was the main enemy of the gunners in the winter of 1915-1916. They struggled to keep their main and reserve positions dry and had no spare time to build main and reserve positions behind the second and third defence line. Their dugouts still only gave protection against rain and shrapnel and not against high explosive shells. Very few observation posts were built using ferro-concrete. The oldest of these were built with walls and roofs that were too thin and would require replacement at some stage. Observation posts built later had observation slits; but these were made so large that artillery shells could pass through them. An observation post of 8th Batterie was hit by an 18-pounder shell (ie a small calibre shell) that left a thirty centimetre hole in the sixty centimetre thick ferro-concrete wall.

The regiment continued diligently to build all types of fortifications in the spring of 1916, mainly observation posts and ammunition bunkers. However, they seemed to lack technical expertise, as several of these concrete bunkers were destroyed by direct hits.

On 15 March 1916 Fourth Army ordered XXVI Reservekorps to start building artillery positions for eighty heavy and twenty six light batteries, including accompanying observation posts. The 51st Reserve Division, to which Reserve Feldartillerie Regiment 51 belonged, was ordered to build forty five heavy and eighteen light battery positions and seventy two observation posts. Reserve Feldartillerie Regiment 51 created a Baubüro (building staff), put under the direction of Leutnant der Reserve Baumann. Artillery officers were sent out to reconnoitre possible locations for the batteries, preferably offering some protection against aerial observation. A standard model was designed for the observation posts. After all the locations were pinpointed, the necessary building material required was calculated. They estimated a need for a hundred wagons of cement, 250 wagons of gravel, 120 tonnes of rails and some 64,000 wooden props. The building material was transported using standard-gauge tracks to Langemark, Keerselare, Sint-Juliaan and Zonnebeke. There it was unloaded and the material transported by logistics units to the building sites. Three companies of infantry assisted in the building of the observation posts, one and a half companies of infantry with building the heavy battery positions and another company of infantry in constructing the light battery positions. The work progressed slowly at first but, after the supervision was tightened, the rate of work sped up. After two weeks the detached infantry was withdrawn and in late April 1916 all works

Gunners of Reserve Feldartillerie Regiment 51 building concrete artillery positions near Frezenberg in the summer of 1916; note the track that has been laid to make the bringing up of materials more practical. (*Reserve Feldartillerie Regiment 51*)

were halted. By then sixteen positions for light batteries and a large number of heavy battery positions were finished as well as some observation posts. The whole operation was probably nothing more than a diversion to make the allies believe that something big was planned near Ypres. It is notable that the Battle of Verdun had commenced in February and Falkenhayn – uniquely amongst senior German commanders and quite erroneously – seemed to think that the British would launch an offensive in the Arras area to relieve the pressure on their French

A completed command post near Frezenberg during the summer of 1916. The command post has its own telephone exchange, clearly indicated by the 'F' over the entrance. (*Reserve Feldartillerie Regiment 51*)

allies; he planned to rebuff this with a massive counter attack. It seems at least possible that he thought that work like this on the Salient would pin them in position.

The regiment now turned its attention to reinforcing and developing its own positions, upgrading both troop shelters and ammunition bunkers. By mid May 1916 one observation post, six troop shelters and seven ammunition bunkers were under construction and a considerable number had been finished. The observation posts were now built using ferro-concrete, with a roof, front and side walls measuring at least eighty centimetres. Most posts no longer had an observation slit. Thus, even though some of the concrete bunkers received direct hits, they were no longer destroyed. Consequently, the ammunition supply situation improved because sufficient shells could now be safely stored in ammunition bunkers close to the gun positions. Reserve Feldartillerie Regiment 51 left the Ypres Salient in October 1916, leaving behind a well fortified artillery position for its successor regiments.

An example: 17th Reserve Division and 185th Infanterie Division (October 1916 – April 1917).

17th Reserve Division: October 1916 – January 1917.
The 17th Reserve Division was relieved on the Somme in October 1916 and by the end of the month it found itself in the Ypres Salient, in the Passendale divisional sector, subdivided from north to south into regimental sectors Hummel, Wieltje and Verlorenhoek, between the Ypres-Roeselare railway and the Ypres-Langemark road.

The defensive system that the division took over was fairly well developed. The front line consisted of two trench lines, perhaps too close together, with a third trench line further to

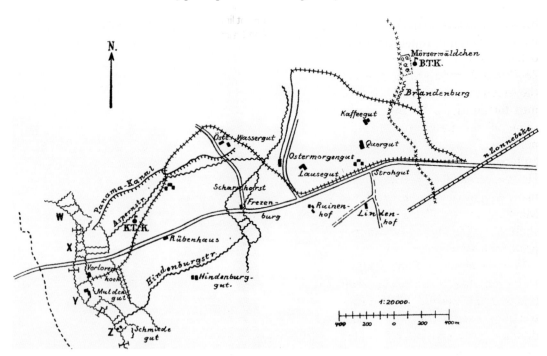

A map of Infanterie Regiment 163's sector (17th Reserve Division) during the winter of 1916-1917. (*Infanterie Regiment 163*). Frezenburg lies roughly in the middle of it, on the Zonnebeke-Ypres road. Note the 'Panama Kanal', upper left of the map.

the rear. Several communication trenches had been dug to connect these trench lines. Most of the trenches were built above ground as breastworks using sandbags because of the high ground water level. These defensive works were weak and could be easily destroyed by shelling. The strength of the front line came from a number of dispersed concrete bunkers, built with concrete blocks. These bunkers could not withstand heavy shelling, but they offered a lot more protection than the shelters in the trenches. Heavy and often persistent rainfall created huge problems in the front line, even though some drainage ditches had been dug. The Germans suspected that the British had dammed the drainage in the northern sector (held by Reserve Infanterie Regiment 76). In the southern sector, a water course had been built to collect and divert all superfluous water towards the Hanebeek. This was called the 'Panama Kanal' after its famous namesake – who says that the Germans do not have a sense of humour? But even this arrangement could not handle the flow of water in the autumn and winter of 1916-1917. This led, not infrequently, to men wading in water up to their waists in the trenches and the permanent presence of water in the concrete bunkers.

The second defence line was located in the area Frezenberg- Fortuin – Sint-Juliaan – Pilkem. Even though it existed as a continuous trench line, some places had been reinforced into strong points with multiple trenches – what the British called redoubts. These positions were given the names of notable German military personalities, such as Scharnhorst near Frezenberg or Graf Haeseler and Herzog Albrecht near Sint-Juliaan. Remarkably for this stage in the war, this sector had, therefore, defence in depth, complete with strongpoints. A continuous third defence line was non–existent at the time in the divisional Passendale Sector; there were only scattered strong points, such as the Werke Wittenberg and Brandenburg before Zonnebeke. Strong points had also been built between the defence lines, for instance Höhe 28 (Plum Farm); whilst many of the solitary farms had been turned into fortifications. In and around some of the farms a substantial number of concrete bunkers were built, such as Kaserne Blücher and Haeseler near Sint-Juliaan or the many dugouts near Frezenberg. Most units were billeted in wooden shelters, offering only limited protection against shrapnel.

Some communication trenches had been dug between the front line and the Second Line. These trenches were very wide and drainage gutters had been included under the duck boards. Some of these communication trenches, however, were under direct British

The 'Panama Kanal' was built in 1915 to drain water away from the German front line towards the Hanebeek. Aspernstrasse ran south of and parallel to it. (*Vancoillie*)

Two German officers posing next to the Panama Kanal. A gutter, draining rain water towards the canal, is visible on the left hand side. (*Vancoillie*)

observation, so camouflage nets were placed above the trenches. Corduroy tracks (ie roadways constructed with halved logs) had been built as well, as otherwise men and wagons would sink into the mud. Away from these tracks, almost invisible trip wire entanglements using plain iron wire were hidden in the area between the front line and the second defence line. A dense network of narrow-gauge tracks were laid in the rear areas in order to bring up building material and supplies as close to the construction sites and front line as possible.

The reserve battalions were billeted a distance from the front, partly in the buildings of villages like Moorslede, partly in hutted camps, for instance in the woods near Westrozebeke.

The Ypres front was relatively quiet in late 1916, which made working on the trenches and bunkers possible, even during the day. Infanterie Regiment 162 used the time to reinforce as many cellars of the houses in Sint-Juliaan as possible with ferro-concrete, thus making them safe for use as shelters.

The construction of concrete bunkers was emphasised in order to provide as many shell proof shelters as possible for the infantry. One Pionier Kompagnie was detached to Infanterie Regiment 163 especially for this purpose; but more manpower was needed for the work. The reserve battalion had to deploy a substantial number of its men to help with the construction of these reinforced dugouts. As winter approached the speed of the work had to be increased. The infantry helped make the concrete, transported the building material, improved the railway network and developed the barbed wire entanglements in front of the different defence lines. In addition, they had to dig new trenches, improve existing trenches and repair abandoned shelters. A specially formed Bau Kompagnie of the regiment was billeted in the Maurerhof (Springfield), near Zonnebeke, and worked on improving trenches and helping to maintain the drainage system.

The Aspernstrasse (Aspern refers to a family name in Northern Germany), a communication trench in the sector of Infanterie Regiment 163. (*Vancoillie*)

A makeshift road/track, made from wooden boards, in the sector of Infanterie Regiment 163. As the ground in Flanders was notoriously very wet and muddy, plank roads were built to ease the way for traffic. (*Vancoillie*)

German officers inspecting progress in the construction of a kitchen bunker near Frezenberg, late 1916. (*Vancoillie*)

A special bunker, a concrete kitchen bunker near Ostermorgengut (Low Farm), was completed during this period. It was very well located and almost invisible to enemy observation. Once handed over, on 2 December 1916, four field kitchens (for the four companies of the front line battalion) were installed and it immediately came into use. The kitchens were sufficiently spacious, had plenty of day light in the chambers and had been well designed for the purpose. Even during heavy shelling and severe front line fighting, the chimneys kept smoking and the kettles simmering. For the soldiers at the front, therefore, these kitchens provided morale-boosting warm food and a continuous supply of hot coffee.

185th Infanterie Division: January – February 1917.
The 185th Infanterie Division relieved the 17th Reserve Division in the Salient in late January 1917, though many men were detached from the latter and stayed behind to help in developing the defences. After the relief, all the Bau Kompagnien of the 17th Reserve Division remained in the sector to support the 185th.

In early 1917 the different defence lines were renamed: the second defence line became the Albrecht Stellung and the third defence line the Wilhelm Stellung. Continuous heavy frost prevented most of the usual problems with ground water; but it also halted any construction work involving concrete.

In the northern regimental sector (Hummel), Reserve Infanterie Regiment 28 faced problems, particularly with drainage and the high water table. The front line was protected by well built barbed wire entanglements, but the trenches suffered from ground water. Both the first trench of the first defence line and the communication trench, with shelters, close behind the first trench, were regularly shelled and badly damaged. The second trench of the first defence line, the A Linie, was positioned too far behind the front line and, because of the swampy ground, a good interaction (for example, the option of launching a counter-attack) with the front line was impossible. The trenches were built on a forward slope, i.e. towards the enemy, and thus could be observed and shelled accurately. Luckily for the division, a number of strong concrete bunkers had been built in this area.

The Bereitschaftsbataillon was located only partially in the Albrecht Stellung; some of its men were responsible for the strong points in front of this line, while the others sheltered in the many Kasernen (ferro–concrete barracks) of the Albrecht Stellung. A small number of men of the Bereitschaftsbataillon occupied the Wilhelm Stellung, the third defence line, which lay further back. Men in the Albrecht Stellung in particular were often temporarily detached to the Pionier Park in the regimental sector or to help building concrete bunkers and assist in the repair of barbed wire entanglements and trenches after they had been shelled.

Infanterie Regiment 161 occupied the central sector, Wieltje. The front line consisted of a first trench, some 300 to 500 metres from the British trenches, a second trench, north of

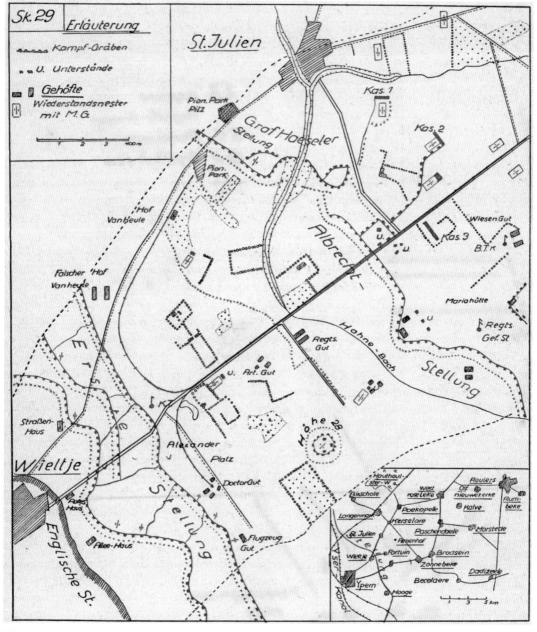

Sector Wieltje, as occupied by Infanterie Regiment 161 (185th Infanterie Division) in early 1917. The map shows fighting trenches (Kampf-Graben) (*Infanterie Regiment 161*)

the Ypres – Poelkapelle road and a third trench lay parallel to the front line some 200 metres further back. The Albrecht Stellung was located one and a half kilometre behind the front line. Its three Kasernen (concrete barracks) were formidable constructions. One and a half kilometres further to the rear, soldiers worked hard to improve the Wilhelm Stellung.

Strong points existed between the different lines, mostly concrete bunkers surrounded by barbed wire and occupied by machine gun crews. At the time of arrival of the regiment, nine of those posts existed or were under construction. The BTK (Bereitschafts Truppen Kommandeur) and Regimentsgefechtsstand were based just behind the Albrecht Stellung. The KTK (Kampftruppen Kommandeur) was in a concrete bunker just north of the Ypres-Poelkapelle road and close to the front line. This was not an ideal spot: it placed him too close to the front and too far from his reserves (located in the Kasernen of the Albrecht Stellung). Infanterie Regiment 161 raised its own Infanterie Pionier Kompagnie of 150 men, billeted in Almenhof (Otto Farm), near Zonnebeke. Its sole task was to improve the fortifications in the regimental sector.

Leutnant Herminghaus, Infanterie Regiment 161, described the different defence lines in the sector:

> The company is billeted in the Albrecht Stellung, for some in small concrete bunkers, suitable for 3-4 men, for some in large concrete bunkers, which are very strong and which are suitable for a platoon (50 to 60 men). These large dugouts [sic] are vaulted constructions with elephant shelters inside. I am billeted in Kaserne 3 'Graf Haeseler'. A trench, containing a thick layer of ice, is running just in front of the bunker. The ice makes it impossible to close the door. All trench walls are covered with wooden boards or wattle-work and duck-boards are placed on the trench floor. The cold weather creates an overall calm in the sector and the men are unable to do building work. The company moves to the front line a few days later. There, everything is destroyed. A concrete troop shelter has been turned on its side after an artillery bombardment. The trenches are completely ravaged and any bunker is being turned into a strong point. During a meeting of the officers with the battalion commander, the latter explained that continuous trenches are no longer required. The defence should take place in and around the bunkers, each surrounded by barbed wire. A small group can defend itself in all directions from such a strong point in the event of an enemy attack.

Infanterie Regiment 65 replaced Infanterie Regiment 163 in the southern sector, named Verlorenhoek, and found the same typical defensive: the front line – the Albrecht Stellung – and the Wilhelm Stellung, with dispersed strong points between the lines. There was also an Infanterie Pionier Kompagnie employed to improve the sector. The Wilhelm Stellung consisted of nothing more than some dispersed strong points such as Brandenburg (Bremen Redoubt) and Wittenberg, each behind a double barbed wire entanglement.

The persistent British shelling succeeded in destroying several bunkers, however: in February 1917 five bunkers were destroyed in the sector of Infanterie Regiment 65 and several bunker dugouts were smashed in the sector of Infanterie Regiment 161.

The infantry, almost needless to say, were as busy digging and building as the Pionier Kompagnien of the division. 10th Kompagnie Pionier Bataillon 28 built concrete bunkers close behind the front line as well as tank traps on the Zonnebeke-Ypres road. However, most of its effort was put into maintaining and repairing narrow-gauge tracks connecting the Pionier Park in Zonnebeke and the front line. These tracks were used to transport building material, using wagons that were pushed (and pulled) by manpower.

German soldiers pushing wagons along the narrow gauge track on the road from Zonnebeke to Ypres. (*Vancoillie*)

17th Reserve Division: February – March 1917.

The 17th Reserve Division returned to sector Passendale in February 1917. Infanterie Regiment 162, in the central sector, Wieltje, complained after the relief that the front line trenches were in a bad state (this was a constant refrain of relieving units on both sides of the wire) and that bunkers without any protection or inter-connection were scattered within the sector. The barbed wire entanglements were rebuilt and the narrow-gauge network had to be repaired. The reserve battalion had to be brought up to work on the construction of bunkers and strong points in the Wilhelm and Flandern Stellung. Progress was slow: conserving materials had become a major concern, with orders issued frequently during this time from on high calling for ever more economical use of sandbags, barbed wire, concrete and all other building material, as well as tools.

185th Infanterie Division: March – April 1917.

The 185th Infanterie Division relieved the 17th Reserve-Division in late March 1917. Its regiments returned to their former sectors.

Reserve Infanterie Regiment 28, again in the northern-most sector, Hummel, were able to work more than hitherto on improving the trenches and bunkers as lasting misty weather hid everything from the enemy's eyes. The weather, however, created extra stress as it was feared that it provided ideal conditions for surprise attacks. Since the days remained foggy until noon, the men improved and built bunkers and strongpoints well into daylight hours under the cover of the low clouds and thus without enemy interference. On the other hand, damp weather and soggy ground cancelled out some of these advantages.

When Infanterie Regiment 161 returned to the central sector Wieltje it was very happy to see that its predecessor has done a more than decent job on the defences. Near the bunker of the

A large bunker under construction inside a ruined farm near Frezenberg. Note the narrow gauge tracks in the foreground, used to bring the vast quantities of building material that were required to the construction site. (*Vancoillie*)

KTK (nick-named Salon-Vatican after the first letters of the company sectors S to V), a new large dugout had been constructed in which the regimental staff officers was accommodated. The regimental Infanterie Pionier Kompagnie, based in Almenhof during the time in the sector, expanded to 232 men.

The 185th Infanterie Division left the sector Passendale in mid April 1917.

Armierungstruppen.

Background.

Units were raised to perform a number of works: improving fortifications and building trenches; destroying houses around the fortresses to have a clear field of fire; removing obstructing trees etc. in order to bring the German border fortresses into a state of defence. These units were called Armierungstruppen (literally: armament troops). The men serving in these units were Landsturmpflichtig (required to serve in the Landsturm), both with and without previous military service. As the trench war was fought outside Germany's borders and the German fortresses did not play an active role in the war, the Armierungstruppen were sent to the war zone and put to work digging trenches and building field fortifications in the rear areas up to the Second Line. The units were soon organised into Armierungs Bataillone, which were then usually detached to different Armies. The Armies then allocated the companies of the battalion to different Corps. The men were known as 'Schipper', a slang word that both refers to the blue peacetime uniform that they wore at the beginning of the war and to their main occupation of shovelling. They were unarmed. From late 1915 on the men gradually adopted the standard field grey uniforms.

217 Armierungs Bataillone (generally translated as labour battalions) were raised during the war and were usually deployed on a company basis; the battalion HQs were often used as a directing and coordinating staff over several companies of different battalions in a particular divisional or corps sector. They formed the back-bone of the military workforce in the Operationsgebiet (zone of the field army) and were used for all kinds of tasks, such as: the building and upkeep of roads and railroads; loading and unloading of trains, ships and lorries; digging trenches, huts and bunkers; assisting in the management of dumps etc. A significant task for these men was providing a large proportion of the workforce assigned to building concrete constructions. Some of the Armierungs Kompagnien were very specialised and were used for specific tasks. Consequently, some of them were renamed to reflect this; for example, there were Straßenbau Kompagnien (road-construction companies) and Parkkompagnien (park companies, which established and managed dumps).

Armierungstruppen in the Ypres Salient.

The first Armierungstruppen arrived in Flanders in the summer of 1915. The front line by then had once more stabilised after the Second Battle of Ypres and several corps and divisions had been deployed to other sectors. The Ypres Salient became a relatively calm sector, in which no large operations were planned. As there were fewer fighting units present, there was a need to find labour other than infantry and other front line soldiers to improve the defensive system.

In July 1915, the Bayerisches Armierungs Bataillon 1, with four companies, was the first labour battalion allocated to Fourth Army in Flanders. At about the same time, Armierungs Bataillon 124 was allocated to the Marinekorps, stationed along the Flanders' coast, to build and improve coastal fortifications.

1st Kompagnie Bayerisches Armierungs Bataillon 1 was allocated to XV Armeekorps (sector Menin Road to the Ypres-Comines Canal) and then split between the 30th and 39th Infanterie Division on 22 July 1915. 2nd Kompagnie was detached to XXIII Reservekorps (northern Ypres Salient) on 24 July 1915 and 3rd Kompagnie moved on 30 July 1915 from France to Poelkapelle and was put at the disposal of the 52nd Reserve Division (XXVI Reservekorps). 4th Kompagnie was finally moved to Oostende on 1 August 1915 and there allocated to the 2nd Marine Division. From this date

Armierungssoldat Josef Schmid, a 25 year old farm worker, a member of 4th Kompagnie Bayerisches Armierungs Bataillon 1. This unit worked in the sector of XXVI Reservekorps in Flanders in the spring of 1916. (*Vancoillie*)

onwards the battalion was fully engaged within Fourth Army's area and all the companies set about digging trenches and improving field fortifications.

The distribution of the companies changed soon after. 1st Kompagnie was given exclusively to the 39th Infanterie Division on 9 August; and on the same day 2nd Kompagnie was transferred to the 30th Infanterie Division. 4th Kompagnie moved to the area of Poelkapelle and Langemark on 12 August; under the command of the 51st Reserve Division, its job was to build a second defence line in the sector. The battalion (approximately 2,000 men strong) was thus fully engaged in the sectors of XV Armeekorps and XXVI Reservekorps, with one company allocated per divisional sector. When XIII Armeekorps relieved XV Armeekorps between Hooge and the Ypres–Comines Canal, it also took over both the Armierungs Kompagnien working there at the time.

The Bavarian companies remained in the Salient until mid July 1916 and were working on different defensive lines behind the front line up to the third defence line (Wilhelm Stellung). Several of its members became casualties during this period. The battalion was transferred to the Somme in July 1916.

Fourth Army had the following Armierungs Kompagnien at its disposal in the summer of 1916 (from north to south): Armierungs Bataillon 124 and 4th Kompagnie Armierungs Bataillon 48 in the Marinekorps; Armierungs Bataillon 33 (HQ, 1st, 3rd and 4th companies) with the 4th and 5th Ersatz Division (Korps Werder); 2nd and 5th Kompagnie Armierungs Bataillon 33 with XXVI Reservekorps; Armierungs-Bataillon 27 (HQ, 1st and 3rd companies) with XIII Armeekorps; and Armierungs Bataillon 35 (HQ, 2nd, 3rd and 4th companies) with XXIII Reservekorps. These labour units stayed more or less in place until the summer of 1917.

The Battle of Messines, in June 1917, and the British preparations for the Third Battle of Ypres immediately provoked an increase in the number of Armierungs Kompagnien. By the

Members of 33rd Kompagnie Armierungs Bataillon 33, quartered in Einsdijk, enjoying a band concert. (*Vancoillie*)

Armierungssoldaten of 2nd Kompagnie Armierungs Bataillon 33 in the spring of 1916. They were deployed at the time in XIII Armeekorps' sector, southeast of Ypres. (*Vancoillie*)

Men of 1st Kompagnie Armierungs Bataillon 78 queuing for their meal from the Gulaschkanone (soldiers' slang for field kitchen) in November 1917. This unit was working for Gruppe Wijtschate at this time. (*Vancoillie*)

end of the month, no less than nine Armierungs Bataillone (in total twenty eight companies) and thirty Armierungs Kompagnien were allocated to Fourth Army. By 12 August 1917, this had increased so that the Army had fifteen Armierungs Bataillone (thirty nine companies) and thirty three independent Armierungs Kompagnien at its disposal. By 17 October 1917 this had further increased; the Army now had control over fifteen battalions (thirty nine companies) and forty five independent companies.

After Third Ypres, during 1918, the number of labour units in Fourth Army did not decline as much as the number of fighting units, a sign of their significance in Flanders. In August 1918, Fourth Army had ten Armierungs Bataillone (HQs), six Armierungs Bataillone with a total of thirteen companies, thirty Armierungs Kompanien and four Straßenbau Kompagnien. In addition, the Army also had thirteen Militär Gefangenen Kompagnien (military prisoner company) at its disposal. These units were composed of German military prisoners (soldiers convicted for a wide range of infringements, from petty crimes to cowardice); their function was similar to the work of Armierungs Kompagnien.

An example: 2nd Kompagnie Armierungs Bataillon 131.

2nd Kompagnie Armierungs Bataillon 131 arrived at Ledegem Station on 13 September 1916. Fifty five NCOs and men were sent to the Pionier Park in Ledegem to work there; sixty three went to Molenhoek, in Beselare, where they were placed under command of 1st Kompagnie Pionier Regiment 24; twenty five NCOs and men went to Geluwe and were placed under the command of 2nd Kompagnie Pionier Regiment 24; and twenty seven NCOs and men were sent to Terhand (Geluwe), where they are assigned to Pionier Kompagnie 304. The administrative headquarters of the labour company was also established in Terhand. The unit was dependent on the various companies for its daily assignments; but administratively it came under the command of Armierungs Bataillon 27 HQ in Menen, commanded by Hauptmann Schulz. This dispersal of men over several units and locations and the unusual, potentially conflicting, command structure was typical for most labour units from late 1916.

The company was granted a week's 'rest' and time to familiarise itself with new Front before it was put to work. At Pionier Park Ledegem, all types of building materials and tools had to be unloaded, reloaded or stored; the men billeted in Molenhoek and Terhand dug trenches for the 4th Ersatz Division astride the Menin Road; while the men from Geluwe worked at the Pionier Park Veldhoek, near Geluveld, and assisted in building the second defence line in the area. Five Armierungssoldaten were sent from Ledegem to the ammunition dump, named Westhoek, in what is now Oliekotstraat in Dadizele. They were placed under command of an engineer NCO to help with the supply of engineering related ordnance – Minenwerfer, hand grenades, explosives etc. Most of the basic labouring here was done by Russian PoWs.

The weather could make work on the trench lines very difficult and often impossible. For example, during the night of 17-18 October 1916 the Armierungssoldaten from Molenhoek moved on foot to the area between Frezenberg and Zonnebeke to construct trenches there. Once they arrived there, however, they were immediately sent back to their billets as the pouring rain had transformed the ground into gooey mud, making digging simply impossible. The men were completely sodden by the time that they returned to their quarters in Beselare (and were, doubtless, utterly fed up).

Two NCOs and twenty-four men arrived on 24 October 1916 as replacements for 2nd Kompagnie Armierungs Bataillon 131. They were all given a gas mask in Beselare and then distributed across the different detachments. On the same day a new task was given to the unit: an Unteroffizier (corporal) and eight men, billeted in Geluwe, were detached to work on the training ground at Nachtegaal, on the Menin Road between Geluveld and Geluwe.

The weather was very rainy and windy in late October and early November 1916, which turned the roads into a very bad state. This complicated the work of the men. Hardly surprisingly, at the same time the health of the men working outside suffered as a consequence of the bad weather; a number of Armierungssoldaten had to be sent down the line to hospitals in Geluwe and Ledegem.

On 28 November 1916, 2nd Kompagnie Armierungs Bataillon drew up an overview of its tasks on the relief of the 4th Ersatz Division by the 207th Infanterie Division. The company commander, Hauptmann Fetzer, was billeted at that time in Dadizele, together with his orderly. An Offizier-Stellvertreter (acting officer – there were increasing numbers of these in the German army as the war went on, unlike, say, in the British army, which was much more relaxed about commissioning from the ranks) and sixty-three NCOs and men were billeted in Terhand. They were responsible for the administration of the company, though some of these men worked on the trenches under the command of 2nd Kompagnie Pionier Regiment 24 and a few men worked in Pionier Park Westhoek (Dadizele). Some Armierungssoldaten were permanently accommodated at Pionier Park Westhoek, where amongst other things they had telephone duties, kept an eye on the Russian PoWs there and prepared material for collection. Sixty-four NCOs and men were quartered at Molenhoek. They worked on the trenches, mainly in the area Frezenberg-Zonnebeke. Some men from Molenhoek, however, were detached to work on the high tension electricity network in the area. The sixty-eight NCOs and men stationed in Geluwe marched every day to a section of the Wilhelm Stellung south of the Menin Road to construct concrete bunkers. Some of these men remained at Pionier Park Veldhoek, whence building materials for the line were distributed. At Pionier Park Veldhoek, four men were permanently employed in bending iron rods for the concrete bunkers to exact requirements, while three others attended to telephone duties. Nineteen NCOs and men were stationed at Pionier Park Ledegem. They loaded and unloaded supplies and supervised the Belgian workers. Six Armierungssoldaten were quartered at Pionier Park In de Ster (Beselare), where they loaded and unloaded supplies. Finally, two men were billeted at Pionier Park Nachtegaal (Geluwe), where they prepared supplies for collection. All of this dispersal of manpower, engaged in multiple and disparate tasks, must have been an administrative nightmare for Hauptmann Fetzer.

The Pionier Park at In de Ster became ever more significant and was expanded accordingly. Around New Year 1917 a standard gauge rail connection was opened from Zonnebeke to this Pionier Park. Nine Armierungssoldaten of 2nd Kompagnie Armierungs Bataillon 131 were 'permanently' detached to the Pionier Park on 29 December 1916 to unload train wagons.

Sixteen men, stationed at Molenhoek, moved on 1 February 1917 to Geluwe in order to build a concrete bunker near Veldhoek (a kilometre or so west of Geluveld) and were placed under the command of the Pionier Versuchs Kompagnie.

Men quartered in Geluwe and who had been employed on the Flandern Stellung near the Menin Road, mainly in guarding Belgian civilian labourers at work in the area, received a new job on 3 February 1917. They were to build extra narrow-gauge tracks between Veldhoek and the second defence line. Wagons, loaded with building material, would be transported, powered by manpower, using these tracks. The men involved moved from Geluwe to Terhand and Dadizele.

On 22 February 1917 the weather improved and a thaw set in, which made digging easier and allowed for the recommencement of building concrete constructions. However, the warmer weather had a fairly disastrous effect on the state of the roads in the Ypres Salient. Foggy weather had the advantage of grounding enemy spotter aircraft, leaving the Germans to work more or less unhindered by shells. The Armierungssoldaten worked zealously on the Albrecht Stellung and Wilhelm Stellung near Veldhoek (Geluveld) and close to Polygon Wood. Reinforced dugouts were built and drainage ditches dug.

Some men were detached on 28 March 1917 to help run the narrow-gauge network. On the same day one Unteroffizier and thirteen men, amongst a group which had been detached to regimental sector Aachen to build concrete bunkers, returned to the company. However, most of that group stayed where they were and were used to improve the trenches locally.

It was decided in the spring of 1917 that 2nd Kompagnie Armierungs Bataillon 131 was billeted too close to the front line; therefore six Armierungssoldaten were tasked to build four new huts near Vijfwegen, south of Dadizele, in April 1917. The building material was delivered to the site on 2 April 1917 but, because of bad weather, actual construction only started on 4 April. By 7 April the structural work of the first hut was finished, the windows could be fitted and the first beds moved in.

On 8 April 1917 sixteen men, working near Zonnebeke to build and maintain the high tension electricity network, were moved to Vijfwegen, where they undertook a similar assignment. The ruins of an electricity cabin built by the Germans during the war still stands near Vijfwegen.

The remainder of the building material for the huts near Vijfwegen was delivered on 11 April 1917. By 13 April the second hut had been finished and on 21 April the third was ready as well.

The crossroads at Vijfwegen, south of Dadizele, in the autumn of 1917. 2nd Kompagnie Armierungs Bataillon 131 was at that time building an extensive hutted camp just to the east of the crossroads (see map). (*Vancoillie*)

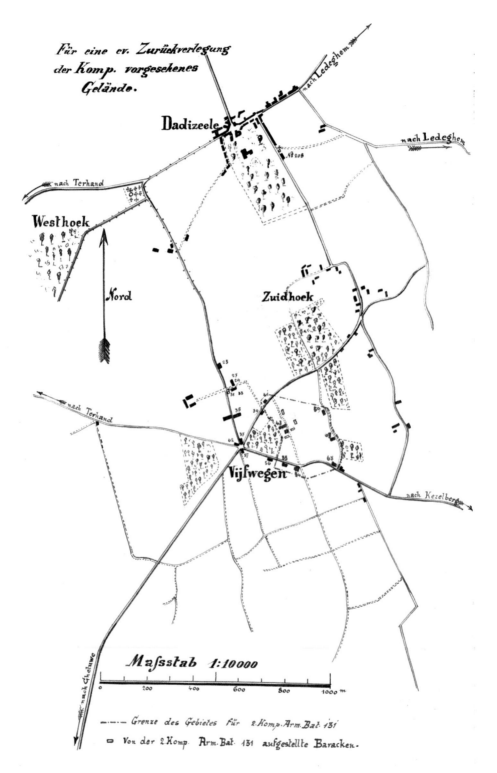

A map of the hutted camp near Vijfwegen that was built by 2nd Kompagnie Armierungs Bataillon 131, indicating the camp boundary and the location of some of the buildings. (*HStAS*)

Most of the necessary interior fittings (mainly furniture) were also delivered by then. Soon afterwards bricks and tiles were provided, so that the huts could be made weather proof. The fourth and final hut was finally completed on 7 May; this one even had a tiled gable roof. The hutted camp was eventually taken over by another unit on 31 May 1917.

When the 207th Infanterie Division was relieved by the 195th Infanterie Division, a full overview was made of the employment of the 223 men of 2nd Kompagnie Armierungs Bataillon 131. The men were engaged in no fewer than fifteen different assignments: sixty men were working on several ammunition and pioneer dumps in the area, ninety men were working on several defensive lines in different sectors, ten men were active with military railways, sixteen worked on the electricity network, five were detached to telephone units in Gent, four were building barracks near Vijfwegen, one soldier was working in Halluin (northern France) in a technical workshop, eleven men were on leave or sick and sixteen were doing administrative work for the company. The 223 men were quartered in no less than thirteen different locations.

The Armierungssoldaten that set off from their quarters to their work early on 7 June 1917 soon had to return to their billets. The British shelling in support of their attack in the Wijtschate Salient made it impossible to do any work. It was clear the next day, however, that the building sites and workplaces of the company had survived the shelling more or less unscathed, so that work could be continued. However, the Armierungssoldaten were now employed more and more in building concrete bunkers as a result of an anticipated major British attack.

For example, one Unteroffizier and twenty men were detached to build a light signal bunker near Geluveld church on 11 June 1917. The next day, another fifteen men were assigned to build a command post behind the Wilhelm Stellung south of Geluveld. Both work parties left their billets in Terhand at 11pm and marched some six kilometres to the building sites. They had returned by 7am to their quarters. The men building the command post near Geluveld were supervised by Pionier Kompagnie 237 from the 18th June. They worked in two shifts: one from 5 to 11am and the other from 11am to 4.30pm. Both groups at work near Geluveld continued to build the command post and the light signal bunker over the following days.

After the 119th Infanterie Division was relieved by the 6th Bayerische Reserve Division on 16 July, 2 Kompagnie Armierungs Bataillon 131 remained in the same sector. The ever increasing shelling of the area made working conditions more and more difficult. The maintenance of the narrow-gauge network west of Veldhoek was a particularly thankless job, as (seemingly inevitably) the tracks were destroyed as soon as they were repaired. In the meantime, the men who were billetted at Molenhoek had to move to Terhand, as their quarters near Beselare were under constant shelling.

The company at this time had three working parties in the divisional sector. The first party consisted of two groups of one Unteroffizier, one Gefreiter and sixteen men. They left at 0.15am from Terhand and were employed carrying building material between 2 to 5.30am to the Königsburg (King's Fortress), a command post near the former ice house in Herenthage Wood (near Kantintje Cabaret); and in building shelters from 6 to 10 am near Polderhoek Chateau. The working party was back at Terhand by noon. This party had a 'double crew', as each group was only employed every other day. The second working party consisted of two groups of one Unteroffizier and ten men; and, again, each 'crew' was only engaged every other day. They left at 3.15am from Terhand and worked from 5am to 3pm building a command post south of Polygon Wood. This party was back in

Terhand by 5pm. The third working party left at 7.15am, and was employed in building a command post at Molenhoek, near Beselare, from 8am to 4pm. They returned to Terhand by 5.30pm.

When Terhand came under shell fire, the company moved to Dadizele to find safer billets. However, work at the construction sites was seriously hampered by increased shelling. The men had to stop working regularly and, whenever the shelling became too intense, it frequently became impossible to reach the sites when the roads were under fire.

Work assignments changed again for the company on 29 July 1917. Three command posts had to be completed: the one south of Polygon Wood; a command post behind the Flandern Stellung near Reutelhoek; and the command post at Molenhoek. The Armierungssoldaten had to work on site for eight hours a day, which meant that they were away from their billets for between ten and twelve hours a day. The men had to work every day of the week from now; and all this under difficult circumstances. When the Allied offensive started on 31 July 1917, all current work was halted. 2nd Kompagnie Armierungs Bataillon 131 moved to Klephoek (east of Dadizele, on the road from Menen to Roeselare) and later to a hutted camp near Ter Kommeren, to the west of Moorsele. Here they were out of reach of all but the biggest British guns. The assignments for the company changed and were now, usually, focused on logistic support and the maintenance of the electricity network in the area.

These ruins of a German electricity installation can still be seen today close to Vijfwegen, near Dadizele. Members of 2nd Kompagnie Armierungs Bataillon 131 were detached to work on the electricity grid. (*Vancoillie*)

Prisoners of War.

The Germans used many prisoners of war as labourers in Flanders. From the end of 1915 at the latest, several thousand Russian prisoners were at work behind the front line. They were given a wide variety of assignments but were mostly working in the logistical chain: loading and unloading all sorts of material, building and maintaining traffic infrastructure, labouring on agricultural and forestry activities, etc. These prisoners of war were grouped into units approximately 2,000 men strong: Kriegsgefangenen Arbeiter Bataillone (Prisoner of War Work Battalions), each guarded by a company of Landsturm. They were billeted in hutted camps surrounded by barbed wire fences.

Some of these Russian PoWs were billeted in Sleihage (between Roeselare and Staden) from late 1915. They belonged to Kriegsgefangen Arbeiter Bataillon 10 and were guarded by 1st Kompagnie Landsturm Infanterie Ersatz Bataillon Kassel 2 (XI/6).

The Fourth Army was given Kriegsgefangenen Arbeiter Bataillon 29 in late December 1915. It consisted of some 2,000 Russian prisoners, who were then dispersed over the different army corps: 250 Russians to XV Armeekorps (detrained in Wervik and quartered in Ten Brielen and Laag-Vlaanderen, both near Wervik); 500 Russians to XXVII Reservekorps (detrained in Ledegem and housed in Ledegem (150), Terhand (175), Molenhoek (100) and Moorslede (75)); 500 Russians to XXVI Reservekorps (detrained in Roeselare and quartered in Sleihage (250) and Westrozebeke (250)); 500 Russians to XXIII Reservekorps (detrained in Torhout and billeted in Pierkenshoek, near Houthulst (400), and Zarren (100)); and 250 Russians to the Marinekorps (half of them housed in Brugge and half in Oostende). The Russian prisoners were then sent from these camps to the Arbeitskommandos in the neighbourhood. The Bayerische Bewachungs Kompagnie des Kriegsgefangenen Arbeiter Bataillons 29 (a company detached

Russian PoWs of Kriegsgefangenen Arbeiter Bataillon 29 engaged in roadworks southeast of Ypres in the spring of 1916. German guards keep a close eye on their prisoners. (*Vancoillie*)

Russian PoWs of Kriegsgefangenen Arbeiter Bataillon 29 with their guards near Langemark. The prisoners all wore an armband with "XXIX" (referring to their battalion number) and a small oval identity disc on which their battalion number was engraved. (*Deraeve*)

from the Bayerische Landsturm Infanterie Ersatz Bataillon Zweibrücken Kaiserslautern IIB/12) was responsible for guarding the prisoners.

From 1916 many Russians were employed in building defensive works in the Salient, mainly digging trenches but also transporting building material. The Russian prisoners of war were treated badly and their ration allowance was small. They had to work eight hours a day on weekdays, four hours on Saturdays and were 'free' on Sundays. They received a daily ration of 400 grams of bread, 175 grams of fresh meat and 500 grams of potatoes (although there was an allowance of a kilogram of potatoes twice a week). After Hindenburg and Ludendorff took over in August 1916, there was a stricter supervision of the treatment of these Russian prisoners and their situation improved. The Germans realised that healthier and better-treated prisoners worked better. For example, from August 1916, the prisoners of war were weighed every month to give a general idea of their health, whilst camps were regularly inspected to get rid of the worst abuses. Nevertheless, the average weight of a Russian prisoner of war in Flanders fell from 65.06 kilos in August 1916 to 63.30 kilos in December 1916.

Because of the troublesome food situation in Germany (decreasing harvest yields and minimal food imports because of the Allied blockade), the rations for the Russian prisoners were further reduced in early 1917 to a daily ration of 400 grams of bread, 300 grams of potatoes, a hundred grams of fresh meat, eighty grams of Dauerfleisch (preserved meat) and eighty grams of rice at noon. Meat was only available five days a week. In addition, forty grams of lard was supplied every ten days and ten portions of a hundred grams of conserved meat were issued a month. It is no wonder that the average weight of a PoW further steadily decreased, to 58.3 kilos in August 1917. A limited improvement in the rations in the summer of 1917 led to a small increase in the average weight.

The first 500 Italian PoWs arrived in the Fourth Army area in late November 1917. They were quartered at Bosmolens, near Izegem. The Germans captured thousands of Italians prisoners in the late autumn of 1917 during their offensive in northern Italy at Caporetto and these men were put to work. The Italians were used to work on traffic infrastructure, but also in constructing the (new) Flandern I Stellung near Zilverberg, south of Roeselare. The number of Italian PoWs slowly increased. They were sent by different PoW camps in Germany to Fourth Army. Italiener Kommando I and Italiener Kommando XII were deployed in Flanders by late March 1918. These Italians were also guarded by the Bayerische Bewachungs Kompagnie des Kriegsgefangenen Arbeiter Bataillons 29, which now had some 5,400 prisoners to watch over.

According to the Peace of Brest Litovsk, signed on 3 March 1918 between Germany and Soviet Russia, all Russian PoWs were to be returned to Russia. This meant, inevitably, that Germany lost much of its cheap – and, more importantly, available – labour force; they were replaced over time by Italian PoWs and later by British, French and Portuguese prisoners as well. The signing of the peace treaty led to strikes and discontent among the Russian prisoners in April 1918. They demanded to return home as soon as possible. The last Russian prisoners of war, from Kriegsgefangenen Arbeiter Bataillon 29, were returned to Germany on 19 June 1918. In the meantime, Kommandos (detachments) of prisoners of war of other nationalities took over the place of the Russians. The Bavarian company previously guarding the Russian prisoners officially took over guard duties for the Italiener Kommando I on 20 June 1918, i.e. the day after the last Russian PoWs returned to Germany.

British and French PoWs were used as labourers from April 1918; however, there was stricter supervision to ensure that they were kept sufficiently far from the front line to comply with the Geneva Conventions. These prisoners were captured during the Spring Offensives and were immediately transferred to these work detachments instead of first being sent to PoW camps

Italian PoWs working on a road in Flanders in early 1918. The Italians gradually replaced Russian PoWs (as a consequence of the armistice and then peace with Soviet Russia) from late 1917 on. (*Vancoillie*)

British PoWs were used to work well behind the German front line from April 1918, mainly to build and maintain roads and railroads. (*Vancoillie*)

in Germany. Fourth Army listed 2,549 British, 5,477 French and 179 Portuguese PoWs in its labour force on 1 June 1918. The largest proportion worked on road and railroad construction or in Pionier Parks. The relative low number of British labour prisoners was due to the fact that the Fourth Army exchanged 3,159 British PoWs for Flemish Zivilarbeiter (forced civilian labourers) with Militär Eisenbahn Direktion 3 in France in April 1918. This was done in a bid to appease the Flemish population and to build more support for the Flamenpolitik (the pro-German Flemish policy) of the German government.

Civilian labourers.

1914 – mid 1916.

Civilians were used as labourers in the service of the German army from the earliest days of the German occupation. Civilians living close to the front line were forced to dig trenches; others helped to clear up the battlefield, bury animal cadavers and even gather in fallen soldiers for burial. Farmers and wagon drivers were requisitioned, together with their vehicle(s) and draft animals, to transport all types of supplies for the army.

Of course, it went wider than this. For example, a steel wire factory, Bekaert, in Zwevegem, near Kortrijk, was already producing barbed wire at the outbreak of the war. When the Germans occupied the factory they confiscated the existing stock of barbed wire for use at the front. The Belgian factory workers went on strike in June 1915, not willing to produce barbed wire which was being used against their own countrymen in the trenches along the

Belgian children and youngsters are used by the Germans to clear the fields and meadows close behind the front of all sorts of war debris and salvage, but were used for agricultural work as well. (*Vancoillie*)

Photographed in January 1915, these Belgian civilians were used by the Germans to improve the roads near Beitem (south of Roeselare). (*Reserve Jäger Bataillon 26*)

Yser. The mayor was taken hostage by the Germans in an attempt to convince the workers to start working again; whilst the Etappenkommandant of Kortrijk (comparable to a Town Major in the occupied area), von dem Knesebeck, issued a public notice, stating that the civilians had to go to work again, including making barbed wire. The notice advised the labourers that they could not be charged with treason after the war as they were doing their work under coercion.

There were strikes and refusal to work elsewhere in the German occupied area in the Ypres region. In Bissegem, west of Kortrijk, a dispute broke out in 1915 because the civilians

During the first years of the war, civilians in the Operationsgebiete (zones of the field army) of France and Belgium were mainly used to make sections of wattle-work. These were then used to reinforce trench walls. (*Vancoillie*)

were forced to make wattle mats. Taking some of the village dignitaries hostage did not solve the situation, so the Germans imprisoned all the civilians refusing to work. After the Ortskommandant (local commandant) threatened to execute some of these men there was a half-hearted return to work.

The use of civilians as labourers in the service of the German army remained limited until mid 1916. This was in large measure due to the fact that civilians could only be employed within the confines of their own commune because of military regulations restricting movement within the zone of the field army.

Mid 1916 – mid 1917.

The Germans took far-reaching measures in the Etappengebiet in October 1916. A law was promulgated that every able bodied man was to be forced to work in the war industry; and the Germans used this law to round up unemployed men in the Etappengebiete of Belgium and northern France. These men were then examined to see if they were capable of work. Whole districts were sealed off and raids organised to ensure that all those eligible were present at the checks. The workers that resulted were grouped into Zivil Arbeiter Bataillone (ZAB, civilian labourer battalions) and predominantly sent to France to work in the German military rear areas, where they built roads, railroads and bunkers, dug trenches, did forestry work, quarried stone, etc. All of the ZABs were, therefore, directly supporting the German war effort. The workers were generally very badly treated. Most of the men signed a contract in due course (in reality, they had no other choice), which improved their work and living conditions somewhat. Most of the workers were gradually sent back from the ZABs to the occupied territories in Belgium and were replaced by PoWs. However, Fourth Army tried to get these Zivilarbeiter back in late 1917, as they were then sorely in need of labourers to build the (new) Flandern I Stellung and Flandern II Stellung. There was also a political imperative: they also wanted the men back to gain support for the Flamenpolitik, a German policy designed to benefit from the cultural split in Belgium between the Flemish and French speaking areas.

Another approach was required in the Operationsgebiet in Flanders (at that time approximately the area to the west of the line Brugge-Roeselare-Kortrijk). The Germans wanted to avoid transporting Belgians working for the German war effort any great distance as to do so threatened to increase the potential for espionage.

XXVI Reservekorps, then holding the north-eastern part of the Ypres Salient, in July 1916 issued an elaborate regulation that laid down the principles for putting civilians to work for the German army within the Corps area. Remarkably, only people domiciled within the corps area could work within it. Recruiting workers from the Etappengebiet of Fourth Army or from the Operationsgebiet of other army corps was strictly forbidden; this in order to prevent too much travelling around. The Ortskommandanturen inside the corps area were ordered to prepare lists of possible labourers. Units that needed workers were to contact the Ortskommandanturen, which would then recruit the necessary men. The Ortskommandanturen then issued the necessary Reisescheine (travel documents) for the workers; within the Operationsgebiet, inhabitants were forbidden to leave the territory of the village – Ortskommandantur – where they lived. The labourers could travel by their own means to their workplace except if it was located in the areas cleared of the local civilian population, close to the front line. In the latter case, troops were detached to guard and accompany the workers. Early in the morning, trains from Roeselare, Hooglede, Staden and Torhout left in the direction of the front line to bring the

Belgian civilians making barbed wire barricades at the Pionier Park in Koekelare. (Deraeve)

workers to their workplaces. Trains then returned them in the evening. Workers who lived too far away could opt to be billeted in hutted camps in Roeselare, Hooglede, Sleihage, Moorslede or Passendale. Men who took this option were transported there on Monday morning and were returned home by train on Saturday.

The rules for Belgian workers differed from one army corps to another. An official inquiry into the matter by Fourth Army in the autumn of 1916 revealed that some of the Corps did not compel civilians to work for the German army, while others did. The work that the civilian labourers performed also differed. Some Corps only used civilian workers within the area of the Ortskommandantur where they lived and to do a variety of minor tasks.

The civilians in the Operationsgebiet were put under ever more pressure to work for the German army from the autumn of 1916. The international laws of war forbade the use of forced labour close to the front line or in serving the war industry, so the Germans tried to convince the men to sign a contract as voluntary labourer (freie Arbeiter). Belgian civilians could then be used as voluntary workers to build bunkers, work on ammunition dumps, build barbed wire entanglements, etc.

From late 1916, several hundred of these 'free workers' from the Operationsgebiet were assigned to build the Flandern Stellung. They received at least five francs per day as unskilled labourer or seven francs if they were skilled. Some money was deducted from their wages for food (if they were fed by the army) or for their accommodation in a hutted camp.

Belgian labourers erecting barbed wire entanglements in front of one of the defence lines in the Ypres Salient. (Vancoillie)

Belgian labourers at work building a narrow gauge track in the Ypres Salient. (*Vancoillie*)

From the summer of 1917.

A number of German staff officers came together early in July 1917 to discuss the possibility of recruiting 30,000 so-called freie Stellungsarbeiter to develop the defence lines of Fourth Army. As civilians could not be forced to work close to the front line, ie within reach of enemy artillery, and as they could not be forced to work directly for the German war effort, they needed civilians to volunteer for this kind of work. In order to seduce enough Belgians to sign a work contract, the Germans decided to pay relatively high wages to these labourers. This consisted of: a high daily rate; a one-off payment of fifty francs cash to the family of the workers on signing the contract; an extra monthly payment of ten francs to the wife of the worker; five francs for each child under the age of 14; a free delivery of coal to the family of a married worker (worth 17.50 francs) during the period October to March and 7.50 francs from April to September; free medical care for the family of a married worker through the Belgian Red Cross; and a hundred francs cash to the family of the worker if he signed a new contract when the previous contract ended. If a labourer was rendered unfit for work during his contract, there was compensation on offer of up to 2,000 francs.

The basic daily rate for a civilian labourer who worked for the German war effort was five francs for an unskilled labourer and seven francs for a skilled labourer. A pay rise of one franc per month was permitted up to a maximum daily rate of twelve francs if the worker was doing very well or if he had certain responsibilities. If the labourer was working close to his home, he received his daily ration via the local food committee, as for all other civilians. If he was housed in a camp, he had to pay a daily fee of 2.50 francs for food and accommodation. All free labourers received leave at least every two weeks. This leave had to be sufficiently long to enable them to spend at least twenty four hours at home.

Belgian labourers dragging a roller, used in roadworks. (*Deraeve*)

This liberal remuneration was not sufficient inducement, however, to recruit the number of labourers the Germans wanted. The Germans expected in early July 1917 to be able to recruit 30,000 labourers; by 30 July they had only 8,870 Belgian labourers available to build the Flandern I Stellung and Flandern II Stellung. Because of intense shelling, working on the Flandern I Stellung was no longer possible for these workers, who were put on to work on the Flandern II Stellung.

Unlike the forced labourers from the Etappengebiet, the free labourers were not grouped into battalions; they were mostly sent to hutted camps spread all over the German army's rear areas. The Belgian free workers were then dispatched from these camps and sent to whichever German labour unit was in need of them. The camps were inspected monthly to ensure that living conditions were adequate.

However, the living conditions did not always live up to expectations. Some camp commanders did not respect the agreements that had been promised to the Belgians. This led to some Belgian civilian labourers not returning to work after their leave. In one such case, over thirty civilians from Etappenkommandantur Oudenaarde stayed away after their leave ended. The Etappenkommandant, Rittmeister Backhausen, was immediately called to give an explanation. He ordered the labourers to be interviewed and it seems that there were various reasons why the men had not returned. Workers from the camps in Moorsele, Tourcoing, Beitem and Roncq said that they received a loaf of bread only every five days. When they took their leave every two to three weeks, as agreed, they were forced to bring bread from home in order to have enough to eat. This lack of sufficient food was enough to make them stay away. The fact that some were only granted leave after five weeks caused difficulties: it had been impossible to change their clothes for five weeks; whilst their wives and families got into financial difficulty as the men did not return home with their wages. Workers billeted in the camp at Hooglede

ANWERBUNG
VON FREIWILLIGEN ARBEITERN

Zum Bau von Häusern, Baracken, Wegen, Eisenbahnen, sowie sonstigen Erd-, Maůer-, Holz- arbeiten werden freiwillige Arbeiter eingestellt.

Lohn mindestens 4 Fr. täglich neben freier Verpflegüng ünd Unterkünft.

Postverkehr mit den Angehörigen gestattet. Urlaub in beschränkten Umfange zülässig.

Meldüngen werden jederzeit bei der Kommandantůr entgegen genommen.

Der Kommandant.

AANWERVING
VAN VRIJWILLIGE WERKLIEDEN

Voor het bouwen van huizen, barakken, spoor- wegen en straten evenals andere aard-, metsel- en houtwerken worden vrijwillige werklieden ge- zocht.

Dagloon ten minste 4 Fr. en logement met verpleging.

Postverkeer met de familie en aanverwanten mag geschieden. Verlof in beperkten omvang gepermitteerd.

Meldingen worden tot ieder tijd aangenomen bij de Kommandantuur.

De Kommandant.

Recruitment notice for voluntary labourers, as displayed all over the Operationsgebiet from late 1916. Note the very favourable pay and conditions offered (in comparison to normal conditions in those days). The text does not mention building defence lines, although many of these labourers were engaged in building bunkers and erecting barbed wire entanglements. (*HStAS*)

received enough food; but they had to work under artillery fire and did not want to return to work. Some workers from the camp at Moorsele complained that they were under strict guard, just like prisoners, even though they were considered to be free workers. Some workers stated that they were willing to go to the camp at Tourcoing, over the border in northern France, as the living conditions were better there. The Etappen Inspektion forwarded a letter to all the relevant units, making several pointed remarks, along with an urgent instruction to take better note of the men's work and living conditions, especially necessary given the shortage of labour.

A further problem in engaging a very large number of Belgian workers lay in the provision of adequate supervision. The Germans calculated that they needed one Armierungs Kompagnie per 1,000 workers to manage their employment and one Fuhrpark Kolonne to transport building material. As there was a shortage of such German support units, they found that they could not recruit more Belgian workers.

Gruppe Gent, responsible for building the rear defence lines, had some 9,000, mainly Belgian, free workers at its disposal in early October 1917. It wanted more. In answer to the call for assistance, the Gruppe was promised a thousand extra labourers by the General Gouvernement Belgien.

Accidents were frequent, whilst the increasingly bad weather inflicted further suffering on the workers. As the front line moved eastwards some of the camps came within reach of long range British artillery. The German authorities tried to obviate this problem by building new camps further away from the front line. The contracts stated that Belgian workers should not be working under artillery fire; so, when this happened, the men sometimes stopped work.

However, notwithstanding all these problems, the number of Belgian free labourers increased. A lot of the men in German occupied territory were attracted by the generous pay, especially when there was hardly any other work available locally. The Belgians tried to work as little as possible in order to appease their consciences and to avoid helping the German war effort too much. The Germans continually complained about the fact that the Belgian workers smoked and talked far too much when they were supposed to be working. There were some instances when workers performed small acts of sabotage.

In early December 1917, that is after Third Ypres had closed, the Belgians were mainly used as auxiliary workers, engaged in the building of the revised defence lines: earthworks; excavation; construction and maintenance of railroad networks; building of barbed wire entanglements; and supporting ferro–concrete construction. The bringing up and mixing of the concrete was done by German soldiers as they did not trust the Belgians to do this properly. The loading and unloading of building material was one of the principal tasks for Belgian labourers, who were usually deployed in large groups to reduce the need for guards. Belgian workers of Gruppe Gent used 400 tonnes of building material per week at this time. They should have been able to use double this amount but, because of logistic difficulties, only 400 tonnes were available to them. The total amount of material transported to the area added up to some 3,000 tonnes per week. The Germans calculated that twenty-five workers should be able to process thirty to forty cubic metres of concrete per day; one worker should be able to build ten metres of barbed wire entanglements per day or dig out 0.75 cubic metres of earth.

Belgian labourers photographed in a camp near Sint Pieter (north of Ledegem). These men were engaged primarily to work on the Flandern I Stellung, but they were also used to build and maintain roads and railroads. (*Deraeve*)

Belgian labourers, from Bissegem, employed to work in road construction in the Kezelberg area (near Dadizele and Ledegem). (*Debrouwere*)

The construction of the (new) Flandern I Stellung and Flandern II Stellung was well under way on 27 December 1917; on that day some 30,000 workers were involved in their construction, of whom just over half was made up of Belgian free labourers. An official census by Fourth Army on 15 January 1918 listed 19,629 Belgian workers at work in the different Flandern Stellungen; whilst 1,323 of them were building fortifications for Gruppe Nord (Marinekorps Flandern).

The high wages for the 'free' labourers active in building defence lines created problems early in 1918. The Belgians earned eight to ten francs per day and, in addition, received support for their families on top of their wage. Belgian companies that were still active in the German occupied area paid, at most, only 5.60 francs per day, without any support for families, as the workers lived in their own homes. This led to a shortage of skilled labourers in these factories; the men often preferred working for the Germans as they were better paid.

Given the lack of sources, very little is known about Belgian civilian labourers from spring 1918, after work on the defence lines was halted. What records exist suggest that most Belgian labourers were primarily engaged in making and maintaining roads in the summer of 1918.

Chapter 4

Defence materials: Origin and Transportation

Types of materials.

Ferro-concrete.

One of the most persistent myths relating to the bunkers of the First World War is the presumption that Portland Cement, which was certainly used extensively by the Germans, would have been produced in Britain. This cement, it is alleged, would then have been exported to the Dutch and they then sold it to Germany. The use of the name Portland Cement was still widely in use in Germany during the First World War; but it has nothing to do with the manufacturer of the cement. It was a generic term that referred to the colour of the dried, end result, which looks very similar to the well known and admired Portland stone (durable, it was the favoured material for the memorials and headstones of the Imperial War Graves Commission after the war). Germany, naturally, had numerous cement factories at its disposal at the outbreak of the war. These factories exported their produce all over the globe. At the outbreak of war, however, the demand for and production of cement collapsed for three main reasons: because large civil works were halted or postponed for the duration; because both factory workers and construction workers were called up for service; and because the Allied blockade prevented Germany from exporting its cement as before. The production of cement fell to twenty to twenty-five percent of its pre-war level. Yet even this limited production was enough for Germany to continue to export some its production to neutral neighbouring countries, such as the Netherlands and Denmark. In addition, Germany captured cement factories in Belgium and northern France during the advance of 1914 and a certain level of production was maintained in these. The Germans established six military cement factories (Militär Zementfabriken), supervised by the military element of the General Gouvernement Belgien. Among these, almost certainly, was the Cannon Brand Artificial Portland Cement Works at Burcht, near Antwerp, and the cement factories around Tournai.

The first problems with Great Britain involving the cement issue began in 1915 and became increasingly acrimonious in 1916. The Germans transported building material (sand, gravel and cement) by coastal shipping from Germany through the Netherlands to occupied Belgium. Officially, this building material was to be used to repair civil infrastructure: the harbour of Gent, the embankments of the river Scheldt and countless bridges and roads that were destroyed earlier in the war. Great Britain filed official protests against what was happening but could not do much about it. British engineers took samples of concrete from several captured German bunkers after the Battle of Messines and during the Third Battle of Ypres to establish the provenance of the building materials used. It seems that none of the materials were imported from Britain.

However, returned British PoWs reported the alleged presence of British cement bags behind the German front line; whilst cement bags were found in captured German trenches

Logo of the Cannon Brand Artificial Portland Cement Works from Burcht (near Antwerp). This factory fell into German hands in the summer of 1914 and the Germans kept the factory operational. The cement which was produced here was used, amongst other things, for building bunkers and fortifications. (*MMP.1917*)

bearing the brand name 'APC'; numerous memoirs of the war make this allegation. British soldiers believed that this abbreviation referred to the British Associated Portland Cement Company. The British press published these stories and created what amounted to public hysteria over the issue. The firm had to defend itself against the allegations of exporting cement to Germany via the Netherlands. It soon became clear that 'APC' in fact related to the Cannon Brand Artificial Portland Cement Works in Antwerp, a factory in German hands since 1914.

A sudden increase in demand for British cement from the Netherlands in 1917 can also be explained. This was caused by a change in German trade policy, which sought to get a higher price for German cement. As Germany almost had a monopoly on the Dutch cement market, they temporarily blocked the export of cement to the Netherlands to try and get a higher price for their product. The Netherlands at that time were engaged in developing their flood defence works, which required huge volumes of cement. Consequently, they turned to the United Kingdom to source their cement, even though it was considerably more expensive. The whole cement matter was investigated by a British parliamentary committee, which published its report in the spring of 1918. It concluded that no German front line bunkers were built with British cement that had been delivered to Germany via the Netherlands.

The affair led to increased tension on the (German controlled) Belgian–Dutch border in early November 1917 (note, this when it was quite evident how significant a role concrete defences were now playing in German defences on the Western Front during and after the Third Battle of Ypres). The Germans sent extra troops to the border after rumours spread that the British would send an ultimatum to the Netherlands concerning gravel and cement transports via the Dutch waterways. Because of this increased tension with the British in late 1917, the Dutch reinforced their military presence, particularly in the regions of Walcheren and Zeeland. The Germans considered that a British landing in these areas was a real possibility, leading them to send extra divisions to the border to be in a position to stall a British advance from their rear. New intelligence gathered through a variety of channels proved less alarming and by the end of November 1917 a number of units and formations were withdrawn from the border area.

Sand and gravel, two other essential ingredients of concrete, were both available in sufficient quantities within Germany and the occupied territories. Together with cement, these materials were transported using waterways and/or the railroad network to Fourth Army area. Quarries in Belgium and northern France were exploited, under German supervision, their product destined for military use. The workers were mainly Belgian and French civilians (forced or voluntary); but prisoners of war were also employed.

Fourth Army's demand for cement from late 1916 was on a colossal scale and greatly exceeded the demands for this material from other German Armies on the Western Front. Fourth Army used even more cement than was supplied for the construction of the Hindenburg Line during the same period (the last quarter of 1916 to the first quarter of 1917). In the first three first quarters of 1917 the Fourth Army required more than 50,000 tonnes of cement per month; by comparison: building the Siegfried Stellung (Hindenburg Line) from mid October 1916 to mid March 1917 'only' needed 175,000 tonnes of cement in total. The Army's demand diminished from the second quarter of 1918 to approximately 10,000 tonnes of cement per month. The scale of this needs to be appreciated: a freight train wagon at that time could carry up to ten tonnes; whilst a freight locomotive could pull about twenty-five wagons. Thus the transportation of cement alone, if transported solely by train, would require seven complete freight trains daily! The use of sand and gravel, both also needed for concrete, was even bigger, though could usually be sourced closer to Fourth Army's front.

At a meeting in late November 1917 staff officers of Fourth Army estimated that they would require 9,000 tonnes of gravel and sand and 1,570 tonnes of cement weekly for the construction of the Flandern II Stellung. To relieve the very considerable strain on the rail network, which of course also had to transport troops and ammunition of all types, they planned to make as much use as possible of the extensive inland waterways network in Flanders.

An advanced dump for building materials. In the centre of the photograph concrete blocks are visible and to the right are barrels. Cement was usually transported and stored in bags; but barrels were sometimes used. (*Deraeve*)

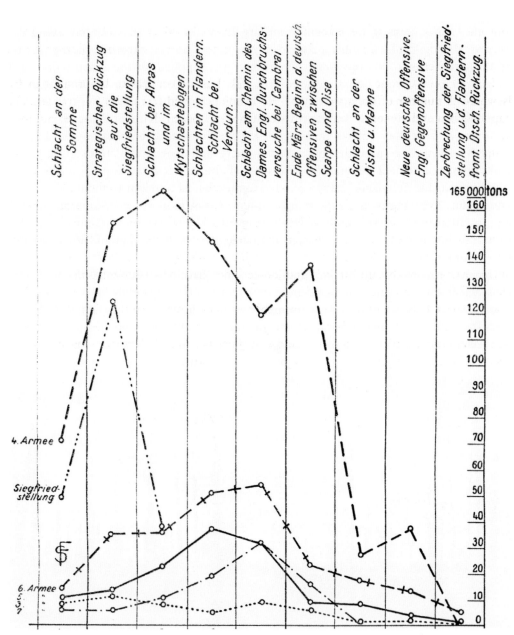

A graph illustrating the use of cement by the different German Armies on the Western Front (the indication of major military events is given the top of the graph, starting with the Battle of the Somme). Note that the cement usage of the German Fourth Army dwarfs that of all other Armies – even that allocated to the construction of the Siegfried Stellung (Hindenburg Line). Note the dramatic drop in usage after the opening of the German Spring offensive in March 1918. (Seeßelberg)

Timber.

Most of the timber that the Germans needed for military construction came from the forward area during the first years of the war. Beams were retrieved from destroyed buildings near the front line, whilst doors and window frames were dragged to their trenches to be used there. Trees were felled from the numerous woods in the Ypres Salient for use in building log cabins and the first shelters.

These sources became scarce very quickly and thus timber had to be brought in from elsewhere. A number of units were deployed in the occupied territories (Operationsgebiet, Etappengebiet and General Gouvernement Belgien) to make full use of the trees and forests that were in them. As a matter of policy, timber was taken as much as possible from the occupied territories to spare Germany's own forestry resources and to minimise the pressure on the overburdened German railway network. Belgium's forestry, however, was only of limited use to the Germans because it was not suitable as building timber. The Germans had to resort to felling trees alongside roads and in parks, more suitable to be cut as boards. Even so, the Germans had more or less exhausted most of the larger woods in occupied Belgium by the end of the war with their insatiable appetite for timber and wood. Foresters and employees of the German forestry agencies were sent to occupied Belgium to take control over its forests and timber production. They had local labourers and prisoners of war available for the work.

Some wooded areas within the Etappengebiet of Fourth Army were exploited to the limit. Near Torhout, sixty-two Russian prisoners of war made charcoal, cut trees and fabricated wattle sections in Munkebossen and Lakebossen. They belonged to Kriegsgefangenen Arbeiter Bataillon 29 and were guarded by twelve Bavarian Landsturm soldiers.

Civilians at work under German supervision in a saw mill in Wervicq Sud. (*Deraeve*)

A wood workshop in Halluin, where timber was processed into all types of requirements for the military – furniture, coffins, sentry boxes, etc. (*Vancoillie*)

290

Several saw mills and factories existed pre-war to process timber. Most of these were taken over by the German military. In Halluin, just over the French border, close to Menen, several military technical works were installed, among which was a carpentry plant, where furniture was made to equip the numerous huts that were being built as billets. Seventy soldiers and two hundred civilians were employed in these works in the spring of 1916. By the end of 1917 this number had grown exponentially. In and around Gent, several firms, employing thousands of workers, made parts for the Genter Baracken.

Exact figures about the use of timber for the German war effort are not to be found as a considerable amount of it was taken from the immediate area. Gruppe Gent estimated in November 1917 that just building the Flandern II Stellung required not less than 170 wagons (of ten tonnes) of timber from Germany every week. At least by that stage in the war huge numbers of pit props and timbering were no longer being required for the war underground; the Germans invariably timbered the whole length of their tunnels, or at least the most important ones – essential in Flanders, not necessary in chalk area further south – but they still often did so there as well.

Steel and iron

General comment.
Steel and iron were necessary in many different forms for front line construction: rails for normal and narrow-gauge lines to allow for the increasing demands on transport, naturally; but it was also needed in the construction of shell-proof dugouts. Countless kilometres of barbed wire and thousands of pickets were necessary to erect barbed wire entanglements. Then there were the millions of nails, thousands of work tools, iron rods to be used in the ferro-concrete, iron sheets in different forms etc. The amount of steel and iron that was used is staggering.

Barbed wire.
Belgium had several factories that produced barbed wire at the outbreak of the war, such as Tréfilerie Leon Bekaert in Zwevegem (to the east of Kortrijk), the Clouterie et Tréfilerie des Flandres in Gentbrugge (near Gent) and a factory in Ruisbroek (near Brussels). Bekaert had a pre war yearly production of about 7,000 tonnes of barbed wire; however, it has to be kept in mind that the specifications for barbed wire for military as opposed to civil purposes soon became very different. The Germans took over control of these firms shortly after the invasion. They kept up and increased production of barbed wire using Belgian labourers, most of whom were still available. Many of these Belgian workers soon tried to sabotage production or went on strike. In Zwevegem, for example, the Germans initially reacted to these issues by bringing in troops to oversee production. Later, German workers and prisoners of war were used to ensure production. Thus twenty five Russian prisoners from Kriegsgefangenen Arbeiter Bataillon 29 were sent to Gentbrugge in March 1916. They worked in the barbed wire factory and were guarded by one Unteroffizier and three men. When the end of the war approached and the Germans had to withdraw from much of occupied Belgium, all the production machinery was dismantled and transported to Germany to prevent a swift restart of production after liberation.

German soldiers making Drahtwalzen (barbed wire coils) in the Pionier Park of XV Armeekorps in Wervik. (*Deraeve*)

Apart from producing barbed wire, later in the war the Germans requisitioned nearly all available barbed wire in the controlled zones of Operationsgebiet, Etappengebiet and General Gouvernement Belgien, most of which, naturally, was designed for use in meadow fencing and keeping in livestock. In Kortrijk, the first notices about this were posted in March 1917, requiring all farmers to bring in their barbed wire stocks in rolls of twenty-five metres. The General Gouvernement Belgien was not spared either; in Spa, for instance, all barbed wire was requisitioned on 28 April 1917; shortly afterwards this was extended to smooth wire. The commune tried to fob the Germans off and reacted to the order at a very low pace; so the German authorities sent men to Spa to administer the process and oversaw the gathering in of the wire themselves. By late June 1917 they had requisitioned 9,360 kilograms of barbed wire and 2,886 kilograms of smooth wire.

The total usage of barbed wire by the German army during the First World War has been estimated at 600,000 tonnes, at a total value of 330 million marks. The weekly usage of barbed wire was 2,000 tonnes (200 train wagons) in July 1915, 3,000 tonnes in August 1915, reaching a high point of some 7,000 tonnes per week in July 1916 during the Battle of the Somme; after this the usage slowly declined, largely a reflection of the changes in both defensive and offensive methods.

As for most other building materials, Fourth Army had the biggest appetite for barbed wire of all the Armies for much of the war. During 1917 it required approximately 105,000 tonnes; for the whole year, whilst total production by the German war industrial machine came to only some 200,000 tonnes. A large proportion of this barbed wire production came from factories in occupied Belgium and by requisitioning it in the occupied territories.

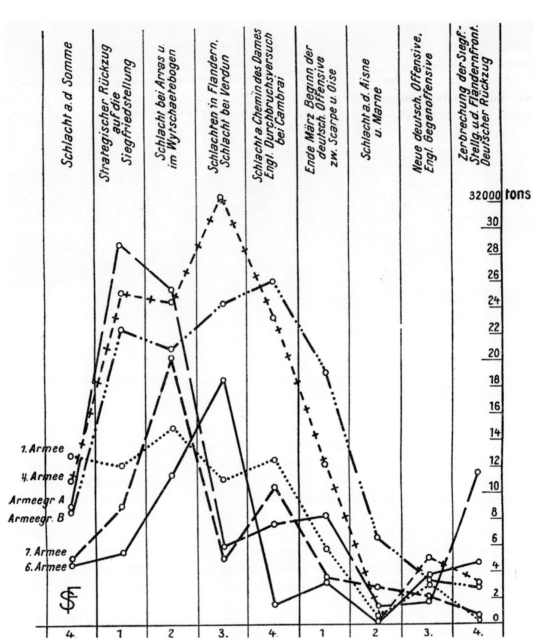

A graph illustrating the use of barbed wire by the different German Armies on the Western Front. The usage of the German Fourth Army is indicated by the +-+- line. (*Seeßelberg*)

Iron in construction.

Iron, a huge amount of it, was essential for all kinds of military construction. Building a standard concrete bunker required a few tonnes of iron: in the form of iron rods to reinforce the ferro-concrete but also in rails, iron reinforcing beams etc. At first, the Germans made much use of recycled railway track in the construction of bunkers. However, this led to unanticipated problems in the structural strength of these bunkers, as the binding between the concrete and the rusty iron was often not good. In any case, the stocks of used rails were soon exhausted, whilst new rails were better devoted to expanding and repairing the railway network, so inevitably iron beams were used more and more as the war went on.

The amount of iron that was needed for the rail networks, both normal and narrow gauge, was enormous. In addition, iron and steel were needed for sheets of corrugated iron for shelters and bunkers, metal tools, nails by the millions as well as barbed wire, rods, pickets etc. Germany

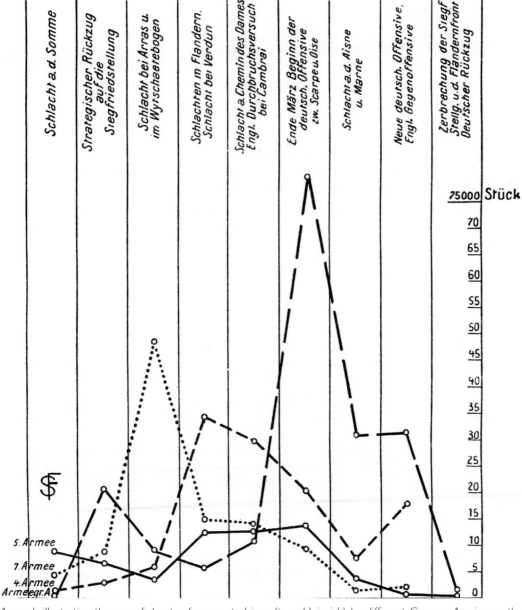

A graph illustrating the use of sheets of corrugated iron (type Heinrich) by different German Armies on the Western Front. The usage of the German Fourth Army is indicated by the ---- line. Note its considerably higher than average usage in the second half of 1917. (Seeßelberg)

had a formidably large metal industry at the outbreak of the war and there was an important metal producing capability in the occupied territories. The problem lay in the lack of ore. Iron ore available in German Lorraine was rich in phosphor and relatively poor in iron, which pre-war forced the import of most of its iron ore. Iron ore for the war industry could still be imported from Sweden once hostilities broke out, but the supply coming from Spain, France and other countries fell away sharply, either because the country concerned was at war with Germany or because the imported ore had to run the gauntlet of the British naval blockade. Germany called on all its citizens and industries to use all metal very sparingly and began a massive recycling scheme, first by voluntary donations of metal in Germany and later by forced requisition of it both in Germany and in the occupied territories.

One of these metal products that was requisitioned in the occupied territories was tram rails. As early as 7 August 1915 1,475 metres of tram rails in Kortrijk were pulled up. In due course, several local tram lines in Fourth Army's sector, which were of little or no use to the German military, were broken up and the rails used to expand the military network.

Sheets of corrugated iron.
The German army had used sheets of corrugated iron before the war to build huts on their training grounds. Indeed, a military manual of 1893 described the method for connecting two sheets of corrugated iron and using several of these to build huts. However, as with many other materials, the arrival of Hindenburg and Ludendorff as directors of Germany's war effort in late August 1916 led to the systematic mobilisation of German industrial and economic resources, indicating that the war had to be recognised as one of matériel. The production of elephant sheets grew massively; consequently Fourth Army, which had been receiving only a limited and inadequate supply of iron sheets, was now much better supplied. During the first half-year of 1917 the demand for these sheets of corrugated iron, type 'Heinrich', was still limited (some 10,000 double sheets delivered), but demand rose swiftly because of the destruction of many shelters during the Third Battle of Ypres. During the third quarter of 1917, 35,000 double sheets of corrugated iron were delivered to the Army; and 30,000 in the last quarter of 1917. The Germans in the later stages of the war made increasing use of smaller sheets of corrugated iron, known as 'Siegfried'.

Transportation.

These huge quantities of building materials had to be transported from the places where they were produced to dumps near the front; and then from these dumps to the building sites – or at least as close to them as possible. The Germans in Flanders used railways, roads and waterways. Each means of transportation had its own specific needs, units to run and maintain them, advantages and disadvantages.

Railroads.

The standard gauge network – an overview.
Transporting building material by railroad was logistically a difficult task. The railroad network was the principal means of transporting anything any great distance, so naturally included troops, supplies (food – and this not only for men but for the thousands of horses and mules

employed at the front – and equipment) and, of course, staggering amounts of ammunition that had to be transported by the same means at the same time. Fortunately for the Germans, Belgium was an industrialised country with a particularly large railway network, both standard and narrow gauge. The Germans made good use of this network and even expanded it. The presence of this dense railway infrastructure, both here and in northern France, was of vital importance to the German war effort – and, conversely, a huge headache for the Allied armies, as the British and French armies jostled for access to lines and limited railway stock.

To organise this vast rail network, the Germans created in Brussels the Militär General Direktion Brüssel, which supervised and controlled all rail traffic in the General Gouvernement Belgien and the Etappengebiete of northern France. Subordinated to this organisation was the Militär Eisenbahn Direktion 1 in Lille, which in turn controlled the railways in the areas of Fourth and Sixth Armies. Both levels of command had several military railroad units at their disposal as well as civilian personnel, German, Belgian and French.

Eighteen full trains travelled to Fourth Army's area in Flanders every week in January 1916. Two of these were loaded with engineering material, seven loaded with building material for trench construction, and two with building material for road construction. The balance was for everything else. This was during a rather quiet period at the front.

According to calculated figures by the staff, a division on the Western Front in 1916, during a calm period in its sector of up to twenty kilometres deep, needed a daily supply of four to ten wagons of engineer material (fifty-one to a hundred tonnes), three to five wagons of timber (twenty-eight to forty-six tonnes), five to ten wagons of gravel and pebble for road construction (sixty to ninety-five tonnes) and five to ten wagons of building material for trench line construction and maintenance (sixty-five to 130 tonnes).

Staden Station during the war and under German management. Note the name of the station in the lantern of the lamp posts, shown clearly in the one at the bottom left of the photograph. (*Deraeve*)

In 1916 the General Staff published a manual giving the average tons deadweight per wagon of ten tonnes in order for transportation to be planned more efficiently. For example, if a wagon was loaded with tools, it could hold no fewer than, respectively: 6,000 spades, 3,000 shovels, 2,000 heavy pickaxes, 4,000 light pickaxes, 6,000 axes, 3,500 heavy wire cutters or 5,000 light wire cutters. If a wagon was loaded with wire, there was space for 200 rolls of smooth wire or 400 rolls of standard barbed wire. Each roll comprised some 200 metres of wire. 3,000 wooden stakes, 3,000 screw pickets, 2,000 pointed iron pickets or 1,500 iron pickets with attached footplate could fit on one wagon. Mallets were needed to drive wooden stakes into the ground, of which 1,500 could be transported using one wagon. Thirty earth drilling machines could be accommodated on one wagon or eight hand fans (for use in underground warfare), including eighty metres of fixed tubing and twenty metres of bendable tubing.

If a wagon was loaded with 'Heinrich' sheets of corrugated iron, then a hundred sheets fitted in a wagon, along with the necessary parts to connect two elephant plates. 500 rolls of roofing felt of one metre width and ten metres length could be loaded on one wagon; or 300 rolls of fifteen metres length. Depending on the size of the sandbags, forty to sixty thousand of these could be loaded on one wagon.

If the wagon was loaded with cement for concrete construction, 200 bags of fifty kilograms could go on one wagon; or 250 bags of 40 kilograms; or fifty-five barrels of 180 kilograms. One wagon load provided six cubic metres of cement. Finally, a wagon could carry either six cubic metres of gravel or 5.5 cubic metres of cobbles.

The Third Battle of Ypres: the railway statistics.
The achievements of the German railroad organisation during the Third Battle of Ypres are astonishing. Apart from the fact that the Fourth Army expanded to some 800,000 soldiers and 200,000 horses and mules, demanding a gigantic supply effort just to feed every man and supply fodder to every animal, battle-weary and exhausted troops had to be relieved, wounded evacuated and fresh troops brought in. Between 15 June and 15 November 1917 approximately 40,000 wagon loads of ammunition came to its area by rail. In October 1917, Fourth Army required every day, just to supply its troops, fifty-two full freight trains, in this case each of thirty-five wagons (compared to the standard twenty-five). These trains ran to destination stations as close as was prudent behind the front line. Troop transports moved in and out of these stations at the same time. A total averaging 1,400 wagons were unloaded every day in these stations in November 1917. The work had to be done under difficult circumstances, as many of the stations came under long-range artillery fire or aerial bombing regularly. From 15 June to 15 November 1917, 242,185 wagons were unloaded in stations in the area held by Fourth Army, of which 41,100 were loaded with engineering material and 79,146 with building material.

In order to be able to cope with the increasing amount of railroad traffic, the existing railroad network was expanded from June 1917. Because of the loss of territory as a result of the fighting in the Salient area in 1917, certain lines became unusable, such as the Roeselare-Ypres line west of Moorslede, the so-called Herzog Albrecht Bahn (Duke Albert Railway), named after the GOC Fourth Army until early 1917, which ran into Houthulst Forest, as well as the line from Menen to Comines. The line from Kortrijk to Menen was doubled from one to two tracks; other lines were also doubled, new connections between existing lines were built and extra stations were built or brought into use, all to be able to cope with traffic flow.

Railroads were of vital importance in the German logistics chain. The line from Ypres to Roeselare, destroyed west of Moorslede during the Third Battle of Ypres, was repaired by the Germans after their advance in the spring of 1918 and once more put to use again. (*Deraeve*)

Rail lines and stations were, naturally, a favoured target for shelling. The photograph shows the result of shelling on Vijfwegen Station (near Staden) in 1916. Note the huge stocks of timber and wattle-work in the background. (*Deraeve*)

The construction of the (new) Flandern I Stellung and Flandern II Stellung in late 1917 once more raised the need to transport enormous quantities of building materials. The Germans had to upgrade the railroad network in the area involved. There were no changes for Gruppe Nord (Marinekorps Flandern), but elsewhere new stations were built or existing ones expanded. Thus, building material for the Flandern II Stellung in Gruppe Diksmuide's sector was to be transported to the stations of Zedelgem and Elsenbeke (in Sint-Henricus, west of Lichtervelde). The stations at Ardooie, Kortekeer (northwest of Ardooie) and Lichtervelde were important for Gruppe Staden. Gruppe Ypres made as much use of the waterways in its sector as possible. Gruppe Wijtschate mainly used the stations at Bissegem and Heule, but also made good use of the River Lys, which ran through its sector, to bring up building materials.

The narrow gauge network.
In 1914 Belgium had a dense network of narrow gauge railway (or tram) lines (buurtspoorwegen or local tramways), designed for trams that transported both people and freight. These lines were taken over by the Germans and put almost exclusively to military use, especially close to the front line. Soldiers were transported by these trams to their reserve positions, which gave them good access to the front and vice versa. Gradually, this network was improved and trans-shipment stops, between standard gauge and narrow gauge rolling stock or between waterways and narrow gauge trains, were built and large dumps established, where freight could be temporarily stored or immediately transferred by one means of transportation to another. Examples of such dumps are Ledegem, Menen Coucou and Bissegem.

Freight was then transported from these large dumps to smaller dumps (Pionier Parks) closer to the front line. Steam or petrol engines were usually used for this. As many of these engines produced both smoke and noise, such transports happened mostly during the hours of darkness.

Troops (sometimes) and supplies (more often) were transported to the front line in narrow gauge wagons pulled by small engines (this one is called 'Frieda'). (*Deraeve*)

Two narrow gauge trains in Poelkapelle. Given the early stage in the history of the car, there were numerous pre war narrow gauge lines; the military of both sides made extensive use of this means of transport, which was relatively easy to construct and maintain. (*Deraeve*)

Narrow gauge tracks near Wijtschate. An advanced dump, tucked away between houses, can be seen to the left of the right hand track. (*Deraeve*)

P. Park = Veldhoek.

Pionier Park Veldhoek, west of Geluveld. Wooden planks and boards to be taken from the dump to the front line are being loaded onto wagons, which would then be pushed by man or horse power to the trenches near Hooge. (*Deraeve*)

German soldiers loading and unloading horse drawn wagons with wooden boards and sheets of corrugated iron in Herenthage Wood, on the Menin Road. (*Vancoillie*)

Specialised units ran these narrow gauge networks. Eisenbahn Betriebs Kompagnien were responsible for running the lines, whilst construction and maintenance was chiefly done by Eisenbahn Bau Kompagnien and, later, also by Eisenbahn Hilfs Kompagnien. Prisoners of war, military prisoners and civilians were engaged to help build and maintain the network. Overall supervision within the sector was in the hands of Kodeis 4 (Kommandeur der Eisenbahntruppen bei der 4. Armee, Commander of Railway Troops, Fourth Army).

The final leg of the transportation, from the Pionier Park to the building site, was done as often as possible by narrow gauge rail as well, Förderbahnen. Freight was carried mostly in single, relatively small, wagons that were pulled (or pushed) by manpower and occasionally by mule.

Roads.

Cooperation with the Westfälische Bauindustrie A.G.
Narrow gauge lines did not always exist for the transportation of goods from the Pionier Parks to building sites. Closer to the front line and in places where there was no narrow gauge network, transport had to be done over normal roads. However, apart from the main roads, which were paved with cobblestones, almost all roads were unpaved. Many of them were unusable when the weather was bad, especially for heavier traffic. The Germans paved and improved a lot of these roads from late 1914 and, as needed, constructed new roads.

The German army brought in a partner, a private company, to cope with this problem, as it lacked the necessary technically equipped units to build decent roads. Baudirektion 4 (the works department staff within Fourth Army, responsible for the building and maintenance of roads) signed a contract on 15 January 1915 with Westfälische Bauindustrie A.G. from Haspe, in Westphalia. The company took responsibility for all road construction works within the Fourth Army area (both Etappengebiet and Operationsgebiet) and provided 1,200 (German civilian) workers, some twenty foremen, four to six supervisors, along with the necessary machinery and tools. A worker received a daily salary of 6.70 marks, a foreman 8.70 marks and a supervisor twelve marks (by comparison: a private soldier in the field only received 0.53 marks per day, while the most junior officer got approximately ten marks per day). This inequality in pay rates between soldiers and workers led to a wage cut of one mark for workers and foremen in May 1916.

However, because of increasing wages in Germany, the company reported in March 1917 that it could no longer recruit workers any more who were willing to work near the front line for the wages agreed upon in 1916. Replacing the German workers by Belgian civilians or Russian prisoners of war was said to be impossible, either because the works were militarily sensitive or because the work sites were within reach of enemy artillery. Even replacing the German civilian workers by German soldiers, Straßenbau Kompagnien or Armierungs Kompagnien, was not a realistic option as there were not enough such technical units available at that time. The company suggested that the only option was to agree upon new (and higher) wages.

Fourth Army was not taking that option: on 5 April 1917 it sent most German civilian workers home and ended the contract with Westfälische Bauindustrie A.G. Some of the foremen and supervisors were required to stay longer to oversee the Belgian civilian labourers who were brought in to replace the German workers. The remaining Germans were forced into military service or vaterländischer Hilfsdienst (patriotic auxiliary service), which left them doing the same job for the wage of a private soldier.

German workers in the service of Baudirektion 4, as can be seen from their armbands. They built roads in the Ypres Salient for Westfälische Bau-Industrie A. G. (*Vancoillie*)

Straßenbau Kompagnien.

Each Army was given one Straßenbau Abteilung (road construction detachment) in October 1914. This unit worked under the command of the Baudirektion and carried out road works in the Operationsgebiet and Etappengebiet. These detachments were transformed into Straßenbau Kompagnien in early 1915. Fourth Army had at its disposal its organic Straßenbau Kompagnie 4; but, in addition, was allocated Straßenbau Kompagnie 23.

As the need for decent roads to transport troops, building material and ammunition and the necessity to repair the roads after artillery bombardments grew enormously from the summer of 1917, the number of Straßenbau Kompagnien available was increased to seven by August 1917. The need for such units in the Army, with the technical skills to build roads, remained high right through to the end of the war. There were still four Straßenbau Kompagnien, for example, attached to Fourth Army in August 1918.

The main tasks for this type of unit lay in improving roads (usually paving – and sometimes widening – them) and taking care of the maintenance. This latter assignment was very important from mid 1917, as shell holes in the roads had to be filled up as soon as possible to bring the road back into use. A significant number of new roads were built as well, mainly roads that bypassed potential choke points. These bypass roads moved traffic from village centres, where traffic jams could quickly arise and which could be very dangerous if spotted by enemy observers and subsequently shelled. Many of these roads were retained after the war and incorporated into the post war road system and continue to exist.

Roadside drainage ditches were regularly cleared so that surface rain water could be removed efficiently and thus keep the roads from turning into quagmires. Straßenbau Kompagnie were often assigned extra labour in the form of Armierungssoldaten, infantry, newly arrived recruits (who got

A group photograph of Straßenbau Kompagnie 4 (Road Construction Company 4) taken in Flanders in the autumn of 1917. (*Vancoillie*)

German soldiers filling potholes. A truck has brought up the rubble with which to work on repairing the roads. (*Vancoillie*)

accustomed to the realities of the front line, with all its dangers, in this way), prisoners of war and Belgian civilians to enable them to keep up with the many tasks of their job and to help in loading and unloading the building materials that they needed. The number of auxiliary workers, therefore, in any one unit was often much higher than the established strength of a Straßenbau Kompagnie.

Logistic units transported building materials for the Straßenbau Kompagnien, mainly Fuhrpark Kolonnen (supply parks, using horse drawn vehicles) and Armee Kraftwagen Kolonnen (Army motorised transport columns, using lorries). They were allocated by higher command according to necessity.

Waterways.

In the fighting of the summer and autumn of 1914 many of the bridges crossing rivers and canals were destroyed or badly damaged, which initially made the waterways of limited use to the Germans as debris blocked much of the traffic. The waterways were duly cleared and placed under the responsibility of the Etappen Inspektionen and the General Gouvernement Belgien from 1915. As the railroad network approached its carrying capacity in 1916, the waterways were put under the general supervision of the Militär Kanal Direktion in Brussels (Inland Water Transport Directorate), which controlled several Kanalbetriebs Ämter (Waterway Operating Traffic Offices). Such offices were established in Gent and Lille and they controlled all water transport in their areas. The waterways were initially extremely important for the transportation of food for the local population (via the Commission for Relief in Belgium), but they became gradually more important for the transportation of building material, troops and other supplies as well. Most rivers and canals in Fourth Army sector were navigable for shipping/barges of up to 500 to 600 tonnes.

Numerous ships from Germany loaded with building materials passed through Dutch waterways. The German ships used the complex canal network and navigable rivers in the Netherlands to navigate from the Rhine to Gent or Antwerp and from there moved to inland harbours in Flanders. They were loaded with sand, gravel and cement for the construction of bunkers and mined dugouts. The British estimated that in March 1916 about sixty ships reached the Lys harbours of Menen and Kortrijk via the Netherlands and were unloaded there. By September 1916 this figure had risen to 300 craft. This led to the bad tempered diplomatic row between Britain and the Netherlands mentioned earlier in this chapter; but the Germans supplied the necessary documentation to prove that all building materials were used to rebuild the civil infrastructure that had been destroyed in 1914.

Levels of traffic on the Belgian waterways increased greatly during 1917, largely to transport the necessary building material for bunker lines, particularly supplies for the (new) Flandern I and Flandern II Stellung, construction of which started in November 1917. Almost all the building material used in the Ypres and Wijtschate corps sectors was brought in by ship. The inland harbour of Izegem, for example, was vital for Corps Sector Ypres. Gruppe Gent built new quays and installed an extra harbour crane to provide enough trans-shipping capacity. This allowed daily processing of up to 400 tonnes of building material for Gruppe Ypres (to improve and build the front line, communication lines and the Flandern I Stellung) and 200 to 250 tonnes of building material for Gruppe Gent (Flandern II Stellung). Gruppe Wijtschate used the harbour at Kortrijk, where eight harbour cranes were available, which could handle about 1,000 tonnes of supplies per day. Most of the labour for loading and unloading was provided by PoWs and Belgian civilians.

German troops unloading barges in the inland harbour of Roeselare. The landed material could then be immediately loaded onto rail wagons and transported to the front line. (*Deraeve*)

The inland harbour of Menen, on the River Lys, was a hub for the transport and distribution of building materials during the war. Offloaded stores could be immediately transferred onto rail wagons. (*Vancoillie*)

Several quays were constructed along the banks of the River Lys, enabling stores and supplies to be brought as close to where they were needed as possible. Narrow gauge tracks were built to transport the supplies from there to Pionier Parks, or similar destinations, close to the line. (*Deraeve*)

Motorboats on the River Lys, photographed in 1918. These boats were used to transport men and materiel. (*Deraeve*)

Pionier Parks.

Organisation.

The sheer scale of building material that was constantly being transported into the Army area demanded a sophisticated level of organisation to avoid waste. Fourth Army had several Pionier Park Kompagnien (pioneer park detachments), including Landsturm Pionier Park Kompagnien and Armierungs Park Kompagnien, to build and manage their depots. Apart from these specialised personnel, detached German soldiers, Belgian civilians and PoWs worked in the Pionier Parks.

The different higher command levels (Army, Group and Division) each had their own depots – often several of them. Regulations were issued about minimum and maximum stock levels of different materials that should be stored in the dumps.

The most important of these depots were the divisional Pionier Parks. They were, ideally, located in an easily accessible central site in the relevant divisional sector. Most of the building material was transported to them by using standard gauge trains; although it might be on occasion be by means of narrow gauge trains or by coastal or inland shipping using the waterways. However, a fully functioning standard gauge connection was essential. This posed no problems in Flanders, given the density of the pre-war network. Nevertheless, the existing rail infrastructure was often improved: from single to double track, increased sidings, platforms and switches, all designed to cope with growing traffic. One of the best known examples in

The Pionier Park of XV Armeekorps in Wervik in June 1915. Sections of wattle-work are being brought in by horse drawn wagons and being stored for future demand by the Corps. (*Deraeve*)

The Pionier Park of XV Armeekorps in Wervik in June 1915. German troops are pictured building new storage sheds. (*Deraeve*)

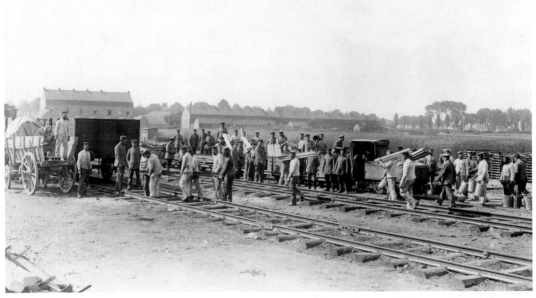

The Pionier Park of XV Armeekorps in Wervik in June 1915. German soldiers, dressed in work clothes (as opposed to their usual uniform), are loading and unloading rails, timber and baskets from and onto standard gauge wagons. A narrow gauge train engine and driver is pictured to the centre right, whilst a standard gauge wagon is on the left. Excellent railroad and road connections were essential for these large Pionier Parks. (*Deraeve*)

A Pionier Park in Houthem (south of Ypres). To the right, supplies of rails, concrete blocks and sheets of corrugated iron can be seen. The goods were brought in by normal gauge trains (the tracks of which are visible in the centre), while they were transported forward, to the battle zone, by the narrow gauge network (on the far left). (*Deraeve*)

The Germans built a huge Pionier Park near Comines church, provided with a spur connection to the standard gauge railway line from Menen to Ypres. German soldiers are unloading screw pickets and barbed wire from the wagons. (*Deraeve*)

Flanders was the Pionier Park at Ledegem, built on the line from Menen to Roeselare. A large depot was built near the church in Comines as well, connected to the line between Menen and Ypres. As the demand for building material in the Army area grew so massively, especially in order to build the bunker lines, the number of large depots increased, not just at divisional but at Gruppe level as well.

Large Pionier Parks were also established near locations where key goods were fabricated. Duck boards, wattle for trenches, Frisian riders, concrete bricks, prepared boards and beams etc. were all manufactured on an almost industrial scale by specialised personnel (Pioniere or Armierungstruppen), often supported by PoWs and Belgian civilians. Koekelare, to the north of the Salient, and Wervik, to the south, were two such army corps Pionier Parks where basic materials were stored, processed to the finished product and thence transported to the divisional Pionier Parks.

From these divisional Pionier Parks the material was transported over the narrow gauge network to forward dumps, usually one per regimental sector. Such forward depots were to be found in places such as Wijtschate, at Veldhoek, west of Geluveld, at Westhoek, near Dadizele, in Zonnebeke, etc. The stocks of material were obviously smaller but still substantial. Technically skilled and specialised military personnel were present to manage and process the goods. These forward Pionier Parks were also the places where the iron rods used in the ferro-concrete of bunkers were cut and bent to the required size. Transportation of building material from these Pionier Parks to the building sites was usually by Förderbahn (narrow gauge wagons moved by manpower or mules), horse drawn vehicles or carried by soldiers.

An advanced Pionier Park in Messines. Plentiful building materials to improve and maintain the trenches were stored here. (*Deraeve*)

A Pionier Park near Poelkapelle. It was used mainly for the storage and distribution of timber and the prefabricated parts of huts (Genter Baracken). (*Schmieschek*)

Some examples: Einsdijk.

A specialist Pionier Park was located in Einsdijk, situated on the Handzamevaart between Esen and Vladslo (near Diksmuide). The Germans made excellent use of the local waterways to transport material and troops by motorboat. They had a fleet of twenty-five of these boats available. To provide concealment, their berths in the harbour/landing area (named Kückshafen) were covered by roofs that extended over the water; the boats sheltered under them against aerial observation and the system extended to the shore, making loading and unloading easier.

Among the most formidable and remarkable feats of German fortification construction on the Yser front was the surface defence line south of the Minoterie in Diksmuide, today to be found across the Yser opposite the Yser Tower. That area was a flooded meadow some 350 metres wide by the end of 1914; it was situated at the limit of the inundations, the result of the Belgian authorities opening the sluices at Nieupoort as a last resort defence in late October 1914. Thousands of sandbags, filled at Einsdijk, were transported by boat and used to build a barricade between the Minoterie (flour mill) and the railway link between Diksmuide and Veurne. Because of frequent shelling and the water, the sandbags were forever having to be replaced, so the Germans decided to build a concrete wall. 1st Ersatz Kompagnie Pionier Bataillon 4 (renamed Pionier Kompagnie 304 on 9 July 1915) was put in charge of the works. Because of the flooding, it was impossible to dig foundations for this wall; the engineers' solution was to ram piles into the ground, even though the Belgian trenches were located only

Right: Pioniere building a wooden platform for the Kück Stellung in Dixmude. (*Pionier Bataillon 4*)

Below: The finished Kück Stellung. At the bottom, the wall, built with concrete blocks, was 2.5 metres thick, but at the top had a depth of only forty centimetres. (*Pionier Bataillon 4*)

Anlage 2. **406.**

Ausstattung eines Gruppen-Pionierparks

an Sprengminen, Nahkampfmitteln und Baustoffen.

(Einheit ist, soweit nichts anderes angegeben, <u>Stückzahl</u>.)

a) Munition.

1. Sprengminen, ganze schwere	200.
2. " mittlere	600.
3. " leichte	10000.
4. Gasminen, leichte	500.
5. Wurfgranaten	6000.
6. Stielhandgranaten	100000.
7. Eierhandgranaten	40000.
8. Sicherheitssprengstoff kg	10000.
9. Zündladungskörper	200.
10. Sprengkapseln 8	200.
11. Glühzünder	200.
12. Guttaperchazündschnur m	200.
13. Blanker Draht m	2000.
14. Guttapercha-Draht m	2000.
15. Glühzündapparate	2.
16. Leitungsprüfer	2.
17. Werkzeugtaschen	4.
18. Leuchtpatronen	60000.
19. Signalpatronen Doppelst.rot	10000.
20. " " grün	10000.
21. " schweb.Kug. gelb	10000.
22. Leuchtpistolen	200.

b) Schanzzeug.

23. Spaten	12000.
24. Spatenstiele	2000.
25. Schaufeln oder entsprechende Zahl Spaten mehr	6000.
26. Kreuzhacken	4000.
27. Kreuzhackenstiele	2000.
28. Aexte	2000.
29. Axtstiele	500.
30. Beile	500.
31. Sägen (Schrot-)	200.
32. " (Hand-)	400.
33. Schlägel	1000.
34. Schlägelstiele	1000.
35. Hämmer	600.
36. Kneifzangen	300.
37. Flachzangen	100.
38. Drahtscheren, nicht isol.	1200.

c) Hindernis-Baustoffe.

39. Schraubpfähle	40000.
40. Winkeleisenpfähle	10000.
41. Hölzerne Hindernispfähle	50000.
42. Spanische Reiter	6000.
43. Stacheldraht t	100.
44. Glatter Draht 5mm t	20.
45. " " 2 u.3mm t	10.
46. Stacheldrahtwalzen	2000.
47. Dachförm.Hindernis m	10000.
48. Drahttigel	5000.
49. Drahtkrampen t	1.

d) Unterstands-Baustoffe.

50. Schurzholz 2 80/120	2000
51. " 3 80/160	2000
52. " 4 120/180	2000
53. Schurzblechrahmen ("Siegfried")	5000
54. Wellblechunterstände ("Heinrich")	500
55. Bretter qm	10000
56. Schalbretter qm	10000
57. Bohlen qm	6000
58. Kantholz lfdm	8000
59. Hurden	6000
60. Maschendraht, leicht, Rollen	200
61. " schwer "	100
62. Eiserne Eisenbahnschwellen	1000

e) Sonstiges.

63. Jnfanterieschilde	200
64. Laufroste	5000
65. Sandsäcke	1000000
66. Richtband km	20
67. Haspeln	40
68. Alarmvorrichtungen:	
a) Torpedopfeifen	300
b) Signalhörner	200
c) große Alarmglocken	200
d) Gongs	200
e) Hupen mit Luftpumpe	100
69. Laufgrabenspiegel	100
70. Karbidlampen	100
71. Karbid kg	200
72. Bandeisen Rollen oder Bund	200
73. Bauklammern	10000
74. Nägel t	15
75. Pappnägel kg	5000
76. Dachpappe qm	50000
77. Schnellbrücken m	500
78. Förderbahngleis m	1000
79. Drehscheiben	4
80. Weichen	4
81. Laufgrabenpumpen	50

Inventory of a Gruppen Pionier Park behind the Flandern IV Stellung (later renamed Flandern II Stellung) during the winter of 1917-1918. (*BayHStA/Abt. IV*)

a few dozen metres away on the other side of the Yser. The rammer going up and down was understandably a popular target for the Belgian infantry, yet the Germans managed to ram no less than 7,000 wooden piles into the ground in an area 350 metres long and five metres wide. The piles were then cut off thirty centimetres above water level and five centimetre thick beams were then positioned on top and nailed onto the piles. This created a platform on to which the wall could be built, using concrete bricks. The bricks were cuboids, with a rib of forty centimetres. They were made from ferro-concrete and had a carrying iron fitted to make transporting them easier. The bricks were all made in Einsdijk. The wall was 2.5 metres wide at the base and the bricks were then laid in stretcher bonds, with concrete poured between the joints. The wall, which was some 2.5 metres high, was only forty centimetres wide at the top, ie one brick. The Germans worked on the wall from February 1915 to March 1916; it was named Kück Stellung. Although the trench wall was no longer occupied after 1916, it survived the war and was a tourist attraction until many years after it ended.

Pionier Parks for the (new) Flandern II Stellung.
New Pionier Parks had to be built in the winter of 1917-1918 solely to have supplies nearby for the construction of the Flandern II Stellung. An order was issued on 17 December 1917 to build two Gruppen Pionier Parks (army corps dumps) in Aalter and Deinze and fourteen Divisional Pionier Parks (divisional dumps) in Dudzele West, Brugge Schirrhof, Steenbrugge, Hertsberge, Kortekeer Ruddervoorde, Wingene East, Wingene West, Dentergem, Markegem, Wakken, Waregem, Vichte East, Vichte West and Heestert. Thirty Genter Baracken, 5,000 metres of rails, ten switches and ten railway turntables were needed for a Gruppen Pionier Park and six normal Genter Baracken, ten half-size Genter Baracken, 2,000 metres of rails, four switches and four railway turntables for a Division's Pionier Park. The building material was delivered from January 1918. For each Pionier Park there was an opening inventory of over eighty items, mainly building material and tools but also ammunition.

Tours Section

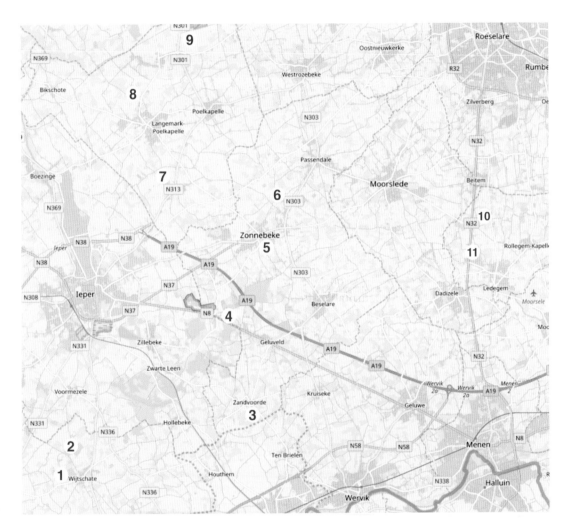

Some bunkers that may be visited today.

Many German Great War sites and evidence of their construction work in the area of the Ypres front have survived, a number of which have been restored and can be visited. This is just a small overview of some of such places that are accessible to the public or, at the very least, to view from a distance; to gain access to some of them you will need to do so via the relevant Tourist Office. The selection has been made to offer the reader a variety of bunker types.

Please note a few basic points:
- Numerous bunkers can be found in fields and meadows on private property. Visiting those should only be done after agreement with the owner or the tenant of the land.
- Just because you can access a bunker does not mean that there are no hazards. Great care should be taken when entering a bunker (if that is permitted) and walking around its immediate surrounds. Appropriate footwear should be worn.
- If touring in a car, please be aware of other road users when looking for a parking space. The roads and tracks which provide the nearest point of access to many of the bunkers mentioned below are often narrow, yet can be busy – frequently with heavy agricultural vehicles. Simple courtesy is all that is required. Be aware that you cannot park on the cycle paths on the side of roads and which are a widespread feature in Belgium.
- Although much of the Salient is given over to pastoral farming, there is also a significant maize crop. If you are seeking good fields of view from these bunkers, some (but by no means all!) of them can be almost hidden by the maize, especially in September/October and into early November.

Wijtschate.

1. A bunker protecting the Dietrich Mineshaft

This bunker is accessible via a footpath from either Wijtschatestraat or Vierstraat. These are busy and rather narrow roads and so, if travelling by car, it would be best to park in the village centre of Wijtschate or by the CWGC Wytschaete Military Cemetery. Please note that the access tracks can be very muddy.

Remains of ten concrete bunkers can be found today in Wijtschatebos (Bois de Wytschaete on British trench maps). The most remarkable among them is a partially destroyed bunker that is combined with a German counter-mine shaft. Not many of these shafts have survived to the present day and the combination of a shaft built with concrete blocks and with a protective bunker makes this example quite unique. This construction was a ferro-concrete monolith but it has been partly demolished, probably soon after the war, in order to salvage the reinforcing bars from the ferro-concrete for sale as scrap metal.

By late 1916 – if not earlier – the Germans were aware that the British were mining extensively under the Wytschaete Salient. In fact the British mines that were subsequently used at the opening of the Battle of Messines on 7 June 1917, including some blown in this Salient, for the most part, had been dug and prepared for firing by the September of 1916.

The Germans started taking counter-measures, a skill that by this date in the war was well established. A whole series of vertical mineshafts, thirty to forty metres deep, were dug as part of these defensive measures. In Wijtschatebos two shafts are known to have been constructed: one shaft was further south, off Nancy Avenue, and codenamed *Daniel*, which has not been preserved; and this one, codenamed *Dietrich*, off Nancy Drive. To avoid enemy observation of the mineshaft and to prevent it from being destroyed by enemy artillery, the Germans built a concrete bunker over it.

Dietrich was built in early 1917, using prefabricated ferro-concrete blocks. The Germans called this type a Mauersenkschacht mit Formsteinen (literally a brick-laid drop shaft with ferro-concrete blocks). The blocks were made in a specialist workshop not far behind the front

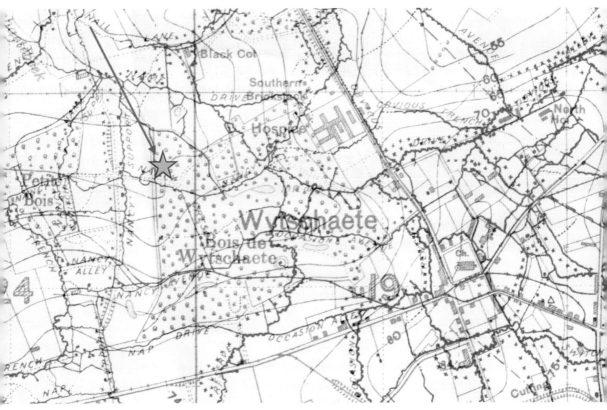

Trench map showing the Bois de Wytschaete area. Dietrich is indicated by a green star (28 SW2 Edition 5A 1 April 1917).

Pedestrian access route to Mineshaft Dietrich.

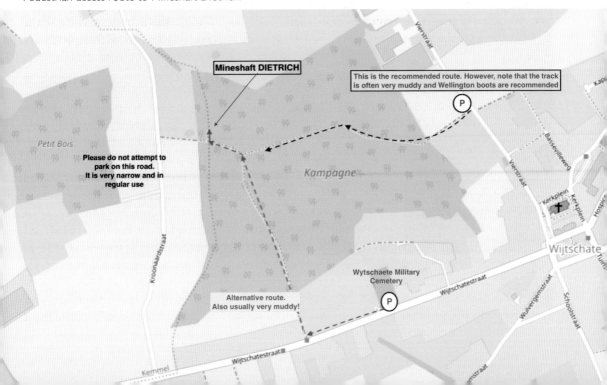

Men of Pionier Mineur Kompagnie 314 making Formsteine for Mauersenkschächte in Bas Warneton. They were then transported to the front line to be used for shafts similar to *Dietrich's*. (*Der Mineur in Flandern*)

Mineshaft *Hugo* in Messines. This shaft was very similar to the *Dietrich* shaft, but it did not have a bunker to protect it. (*Der Mineur in Flandern*)

Mineshaft *Dietrich* and the remains of the protecting bunker today. Whether the bunker was destroyed as a result of artillery fire in 1917-1918 or after the war is unknown. It is located close to the edge of the wood. (*Vancoillie*)

Mineshaft *Dietrich* today. Note the water. Ground water levels are very high in Flanders, even during relatively dry periods. One can only imagine how difficult it must have been to keep these shafts from flooding during the war. (*Vancoillie*)

More bunkers can be found inside Bois de Wytschaete but are not accessible. This one has been sealed up and serves as a bat shelter. (*Vancoillie*)

and transported to Wijtschate using narrow gauge tracks and manpower. The exact depth of the shaft is unknown; some say twenty five metres, others more than forty metres. At the bottom of the shaft there would have been a wood framed tunnel, used to listen to the enemy underground's activity or to dig out towards the enemy's working and to lay a counter-mine, a camouflet. This tunnel is believed not to have been completed.

The Germans were unable to detect or intercept the Petit Bois mines, which were the closest mines to this location. Bois de Wytschaete was captured on 7 June 1917, at the opening of Plumer's Messines offensive, by the 16th (Irish) Division, to which a memorial was erected to the south of the forest, immediately adjacent to Wytschaete Military Cemetery. The bunker itself was probably captured by 6th Royal Irish Rifles, 47 Brigade.

Wijtschate.

2. Bayernwald (Bois Quarante) bunkers.

This site is a must for anyone who wants to see how German trenches and bunkers were built in the Ypres area.

To visit the site you first need to go to the Heuvelland Tourist Office, located in nearby Kemmel (Sint-Laurentiusplein 1); there is a website that gives all the opening hours and

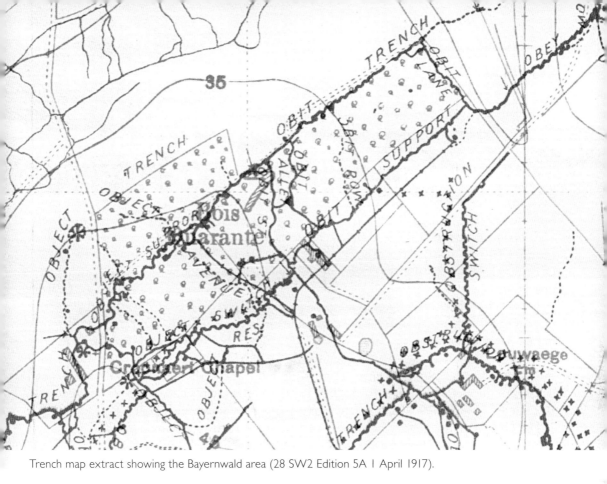

Trench map extract showing the Bayernwald area (28 SW2 Edition 5A 1 April 1917).

Location map of Bayernwald trenches and bunkers.

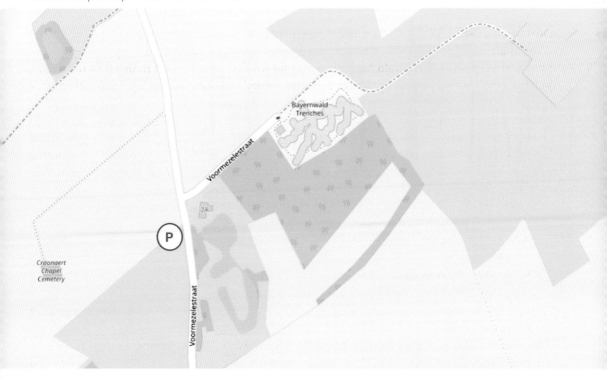

up to date information: www.toerismeheuvelland.be. The office opening hours are usually 09.30 – 1700, with an hour for lunch from midday; the timings vary on Sundays. There you buy a ticket (varying prices, depending if for an individual or a group – in any case, not expensive and well worthwhile) to access the automated entrance gate of Bayernwald (which is open 0900 – 1800). Note that there are very limited periods when the site is closed because of hunting. There is a small car and bus park off the nearby Voormezelestraat. One should park here and then go on foot towards the entrance of the site off a minor road (also called Voormezelestraat) – note that this is a cul de sac and so do not be tempted to drive down here.

At first it was called Beilwald (Hatchet Wood) because of the shape of the wood; it was given the name Bayernwald (Bavarian Wood) after its capture by Bavarian troops during the First Battle of Ypres. The Allies called it Bois Quarante from the contour line on which it sat. Trenches were dug on the inner edge of the wood, on its northern and western edges, which formed the German front line until 7 June 1917. Bayernwald was captured by troops of the 19th (Western) Division on that day and it remained in British hands until late April 1918, when it was retaken by the Germans during the latter stages of the Battle of the Lys. In September 1918, the 6th Bayerische Reserve Division was in the line when it was recaptured by the 34th Division. A Victoria Cross was awarded to Acting Sergeant Louis McGuffie, 1/5th King's Own Scottish Borderers, for taking several bunkers in the area Bois Quarante-Picadilly Farm on 28 September 1918. He was subsequently killed in the same area on 4 October and is buried in Zantvoorde British Cemetery (I.D.12).

The pond near the holiday house was created by detonating the ammunition that was left behind after the war. The Becquart family acquired the wood and built a small country house after the Second World War. André Becquart discovered the German countermine shaft in

General view of the reconstructed *Bayernwald* trenches. They are located exactly where the original trenches were and have been constructed using the same techniques as the Germans used here. (*Vancoillie*)

Above: Four very similar bunkers remain in Bayernwald today. They have been constructed with concrete blocks. One of the bunkers is seriously damaged while the other three are largely intact. The chambers are very small because they had a serious impact on the strength of the bunker. They were also designed as shelters and not as a resistance point. (*Vancoillie*)

Right: Archaeological survey plan of one of the Bayernwald bunkers. (*Bayernwald*)

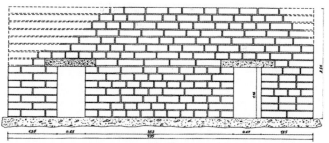

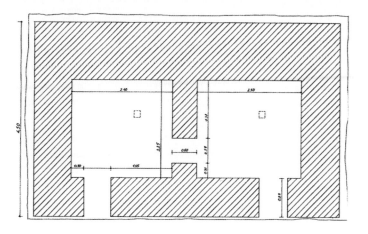

the wood during the course of a hunting party in the early 1970s and decided to turn the site into a tourist attraction. A mine shaft was pumped out as far as possible and new 'trenches' were dug inside the forest that linked the shaft and the bunkers. For some time it was also possible to enter the German tunnel system here, effectively a subway; alas, health and safety considerations soon led to its closure. There was also a small museum in the house. The whole was delightfully amateur and eclectic; a tour (using an eccentrically translated guide sheet) was accompanied by songs from *Oh! What a Lovely War!* played over a speaker system, with the sound of the odd banger going off in a miniature cannon. After André's death – a man much missed by many British visitors to the Salient – in 1986, the site decayed as the family disagreed over the inheritance and the museum was plundered. The house was damaged by a storm and then there was a fire, which sealed the fate of André's highly unusual trench museum.

In 1998 the commune of Heuvelland took action to have the site restored. After some preliminary research and an archaeological survey, the site was renovated and opened to public in 2004. The German countermine shaft and bunkers were cleared, the trenches were excavated and reconstructed on their original locations after archaeological research and, by studying contemporary pictures to achieve accuracy, with materials that were used during the war. There is a shelter explaining the site and the Battle of Messines; whilst several information boards give further comment on the remains, which include several bunkers.

The bunkers were built with concrete blocks, as the position formed part of the German front line; pouring concrete was not an option here so close to the enemy's positions. Most of these block bunkers were dismantled after the war; the metal rods were sold as scrap iron while the blocks were used to provide hard core for roads and to build walls and farmyards. The accommodation space inside the bunkers is very small and the roofs are notably low; this restriction was necessary so that the strength of the construction would not be compromised.

Zandvoorde.

3. Command post

This bunker can be found at the southern end of the village, on the corner of Gaverstraat and Komenstraat. Parking is possible and there is a field path to the bunker, which is open to the public (boots – preferably wellington boots – may be advisable if you want to visit the interior, as there is usually water on the floor that can be too deep for shoes or ankle high walking boots).

This is an excellent example of a command post built in the German rear areas close to the front. It is built on the reverse slope of a hill, thus covering it from allied direct observation and artillery fire. It was used as a battle headquarters for the division holding the Zandvoorde sector and was located along an important supply route, Komenstraat, which leads to Ten Brielen and Wervik.

The bunker has six rooms. The two southernmost rooms probably housed messengers, communication personnel and the telephone exchange. These rooms were separated from the four other rooms, which probably served as secure bases for staff officers from which to conduct operations, allowing them to be close to the front line. The entrances to these rooms were protected by a curved wall, with an extra wall behind that, which ran along the whole length of the bunker. This was to prevent shrapnel from shells that landed behind the bunker penetrating the rooms via the doorways.

Trench map extract showing the Zandvoorde Command Post (28 SEI Edition 7A I November 1917). The bunker was well hidden and did not appear on British trench maps until late 1917.

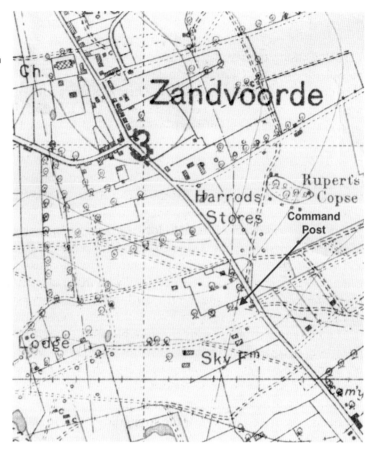

The Zandvoorde Command Post was constructed on the reverse slope of a ridge and protected from aerial observation by earth on top of the bunker. (MMP.1917)

The southernmost entrance to the Zandvoorde Command Post, showing a rare example of a commemorative plaque to the builders of the bunker. (*MMP.1917*)

A German soldier posing at the back of the Zandvoorde Command Post in September 1916. (*MMP.1917*)

Even though the German army officially disapproved of any embellishments and decorations on this type of construction, the builders of this bunker have left their mark. At the southernmost entrance a special mould was incorporated into the formwork, thus creating a commemorative plaque. It reads *Erbaut 3. Komp. Arm. Btl. 27 1916* (built by 3rd Kompagnie Armierungs Bataillon 27 [in] 1916).

This bunker would have been a hive of activity during periods when intensive fighting raged at the front. Runners would arrive and leave with orders and reports from and to the front and the higher echelons; there might have been carrier pigeons and messenger dogs as well and the phones would be ringing incessantly; light signals could be received and sent. *Strippenflicker* (soldiers' slang for those engaged in the extremely dangerous task of repairing broken telephone lines) would have been kept very busy, especially during artillery duels.

Geluveld.

4. Cryer Farm (Medical Bunker)

This is a rare remaining example of a bunker specifically constructed as a medical post. It is located next to a farm at Menenstraat 43 at the western end of Geluveld (Zonnebeke). It can be accessed via a small road near the Gloucestershire Regimental Memorial at Clapham

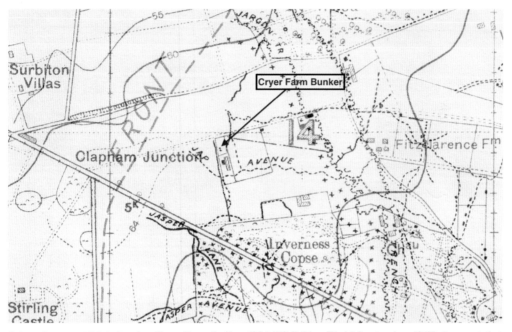

A trench map extract showing Cryer Farm Bunker (28 NE3 Edition 7A 14 September 1917). It was at that date located on the German front line.

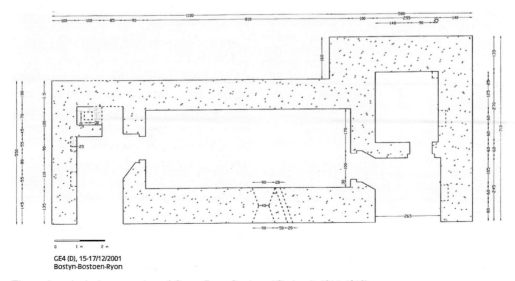

GE4 (D), 15-17/12/2001
Bostyn-Bostoen-Ryon

The archaeological survey plan of Cryer Farm Bunker. (*Gheluvelt 1914-1918*)

A view inside Cryer Farm Bunker, looking towards the central chamber. Note the wide passage, allowing space for a stretcher to pass. A small (dressing?) room is visible on the right. When British troops captured the bunker, they tried to create a new entrance here, but gave up the attempt. (*Michael Sheil*)

Junction. The bunker is located on private property and *access is only possible by appointment* with the Memorial Museum Passchendaele 1917 in Zonnebeke. Please do not try to visit the bunker without an appointment and do not drive onto the farm property or block the driveway.

This bunker was most probably built during the winter of 1916-1917 as a medical post for Reserve Infanterie Regiment 209. It is located near the Albrecht Stellung, between two important communication trenches, Geyerweg (Jargon Drive) and Meissengasse (Jap Avenue), close by the remains of a small farm building. Its function as a medical post is clearly indicated by the extra wide entrances and the unusual doorways towards the central room, which can be only explained by the need to allow passage with a loaded stretcher. The central room is three metres wide and 8.10 metres long, with a side opening to place a stove to heat the room. A small room to one side probably served as the living quarters for the medical personnel or as a bandaging room. The bunker is L-shaped and is in total 16.80 metres long and 7.10 metres wide. Its roof is about 1.30 metres thick.

During the Third Battle of Ypres, as the British line inched westwards, the bunker was located on the front line in August and September 1917. At that point it was used as a strongpoint, held from late August 1917 onwards by Bayerisches Reserve Infanterie Regiment 4. Life in these bunkers was far from comfortable:

> *The space in these concrete bunkers, which were of course targeted by the enemy artillery, was so cramped that the people could only sit crowded together and many had to keep standing. And then there were also the messenger dogs, carrier pigeons etc. that had to fit in as well.*

The 47th (2nd London) Division attacked the strongpoint on 15 September 1917 in what can best be described as a very large raid, a prelude to the major attack along the Menin Road that was launched on 20 September. After a practice (or possibly a deception) barrage in the morning, a second artillery barrage accompanied the attack at 4 pm (5 pm German time) by 1/7th (City of London) London Regiment. They managed to break into the German line and capture the German bunker at the cost of two officers (one killed) and ten other ranks. An immediate German counter-attack was repulsed, as was a second one at 11 pm (German time). The German losses came to forty four men, thirty eight of whom belong to 5th Kompagnie Bayerisches Reserve Infanterie Regiment 4. The British took thirty six prisoners (four of whom were wounded) and captured one machine gun in and around the bunker. Messages of congratulation were received by the division from both the Army and Corps Commanders.

Two more hastily staged German counter-attacks in the early hours of 16 September 1917 failed to reach the bunker as well, although the British officer in command of the raid, Lieutenant BB Cryer, was killed. He has no known grave and is (unusually – 'missing' British dead by this date are usually commemorated at Tyne Cot) commemorated on the Menin Gate. The bunker and the farm ruins were hereafter named after him, becoming Cryer Farm on British trench maps.

A new attempt to recapture the bunker was planned for the early hours of 20 September 1917 by the newly formed Sturmkompagnie of Bayerisches Reserve Infanterie Regiment 4. Only one of the three attack columns reached the front line and moved forward to attack. When the attacking force had almost reached the bunker, the British artillery bombardment in preparation for the Battle of the Menin Road opened up. The Germans were forced back and the bunker remained in British hands until May 1918 (Battle of the Lys). At some point in this period of British occupation the original entrances (towards the east) were closed by Royal Engineers and a new entrance (on the west side) was made by using explosives.

After the war the farm was rebuilt close to the bunker. As the new farm buildings were very close, the bunker could not be demolished by the use of explosives and it was left as it now is. In May 1940, during the German invasion, the bunker was cleared and the water pumped out so that it could be used as a civilian shelter. In 1944, because of its size and ability to accommodate a large number of people, it was once more cleaned out by the commune workers of Geluveld to be used as an official air raid shelter. After the war the bunker was closed again and used as a cesspool by the farmer. In December 2001 it was once more cleared out and made accessible to the public; visits must be made by arrangement with the Zonnebeke tourist office, situated in the grounds of Zonnebeke Chateau.

Zonnebeke.

5. Memorial Museum Passchendaele 1917

The Memorial Museum Passchendaele 1917 is located in the former chateau in the centre of Zonnebeke. The museum has a tour route that winds its way over 600 metres, with numerous exhibits, featuring numerous photographs and objects related to the First World War in this locality. It gives a clear overview of the war, but has a strong focus on the Third Battle of Ypres.

The Memorial Museum Passchendaele 1917 is located in the chateau of Zonnebeke. (MMP.1917)

The Memorial Museum Passchendaele 1917 houses a large collection of artefacts; it pays particular attention to the technical aspects of the Great War. (*MMP.1917*)

It devotes considerable space to military construction by both sides, including the German army's bunker building. Of particular interest to the reader of this book are several displays showing bunker and trench building and a reconstructed (British) deep dug-out. An outside extension to the museum shows several types of both British and German trench and shelter constructions.

More information can be found on www.passchendaele.be.

This is probably the most suitable museum to visit in the Salient if your interest is in the development and fortification of trench systems during the course of the war. The museum, of course, does far more than that, but one might describe this aspect as its speciality. In recent years the museum and its facilities (including parking) have been considerably expanded.

A recent addition to the museum (2013) is the outside reconstructions of trenches and shelters. (*MMP.1917*)

Passendale.

6. Tyne Cot Cemetery

Two German bunkers remain clearly visible on the forward (western) edge of Tyne Cot Cemetery in Passendale. They belong to the first line of the first Flandern Stellung, constructed between late 1916 and the summer of 1917. Although trench maps show a formidable trench in this area, Dab Trench, it was no more than half a metre deep, as recent excavations have shown. This shallow German trench mainly served to attract the attention of enemy artillery fire, while the defending soldiers were sheltering inside the bunkers or in nearby shell holes.

A machine gun post still exists close by, in Hamburg Farm; but it is not possible to visit it. The two bunkers in Tyne Cot belonged to a whole line of similar bunkers, most of which were demolished after the war. During the summer of 1917 a second line of bunkers were built; one of these survives under the Cross of Sacrifice in the cemetery. Two other bunkers remain underground, more or less under the pavilions at both ends of the Memorial to the Missing at the eastern end of the cemetery. The number of bunkers in this small area gives a good idea of what the Germans planned when building the Flandern Stellung in 1916-1917. This bunker line was built on a forward slope and one can appreciate the view towards Ypres from here. For defenders the decision to locate defensive lines on forward or reverse slopes was always a challenge, possibly no more so than here at Ypres, given the gentle, undulating nature of the ground. A solution to the vulnerability of the forward slope position was at least partially

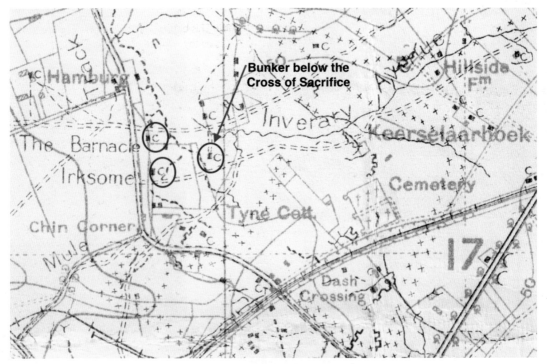

A trench map extract showing the Tyne Cot Cemetery area, to the right of 'The Barnacle' and 'Irksome' (28 NE I Edition 9D 9 August 1918). Note the density of the concrete bunkers.

found by the use of bunkers, which provided shelter for the defending troops but who usually conducted the actual fighting from nearby shell holes.

The two bunkers on Tyne Cot Cemetery and the machine gun post near Hamburg Farm were attacked and captured on 4 October 1917 by the 40th Battalion AIF (Australian Imperial Force). Sergeant Lewis McGee managed to approach one of these bunkers near Hamburg Farm from the rear and killed a machine gun crew on top of it. After this, the Australians managed to eliminate the other bunkers one by one. Sergeant McGee was awarded the Victoria Cross for his bravery; two Military Crosses, one Distinguished Conduct Medal and nine Military Medals were awarded to other men of the battalion for the fighting in this area, during which fifteen machine guns and two Minenwerfer were captured. However, the second line of bunkers remained out of reach (including the one under the Cross of Sacrifice) and the lower line became the British front line. Sergeant McGee was killed on 12 October 1917 and is buried in this cemetery (XX.D.1).

The second line was eventually captured five days later by the 66th (2nd East Lancashire) Division. The bunker under the Cross of Sacrifice, probably a machine gun post, was thereafter used as a medical post and the first burials were made alongside it during the winter of 1917-1918.

Both bunkers in the lower part of the cemetery are typical of the Flandern Stellung of 1916-1917. They are rectangular, approximately eleven metres long and four metres wide. Inside are three rooms that are connected by manholes. There is a small observation slit in the middle of the front side. Machine guns were kept inside until the enemy attacked. At that point the guns were quickly taken out and mounted next to (usually in a handy shell hole) or on top of the bunker.

A German bunker of the original Flandern Stellung, built in 1916-1917. This bunker was nicknamed 'Irksome' after its captured by Australian troops on 4 October 1917. Another bunker is to be found under the Cross of Sacrifice and yet another approximately under one of the pagodas. (Blieck)

A view from the other German bunker of the original Flandern Stellung towards Hamburg Farm, where the Germans had a machine gun post. That bunker was nicknamed 'The Barnacle' after its capture by Australian troops on 4 October 1917. The view from this position is truly astonishing and enables one to clearly understand the value of this defence line. (*Blieck*)

The German bunker that is now under the Cross of Sacrifice in Tyne Cot Cemetery. This bunker was captured in October 1917 and used as an aid post during the winter of 1917-1918. The Germans recaptured this area after the British withdrawal in April-May 1918. (*MMP.1917*)

Sint-Juliaan.

7. Kaserne Herzog Albrecht 2 (An accommodation bunker)

This bunker is located off Peperstraat in Sint-Juliaan (Langemark-Poelkapelle). It is located in the middle of the fields and is not publicly accessible; the state of the building is such that visiting it is definitely not recommended. Visitors can get closer to it when there are no crops on the fields. In summer time the bunker is visible from a footpath along the Steenbeek. Parking is possible in the centre of the village.

The bunker was probably built during 1916 and was twice as big then (approximately forty metres long) as today. Now the bunker is still an impressive 17.40 metres long, 6.60 metres wide and about 2.90 metres high. Inside are four rooms made with sheets of corrugated iron. At the back is a hall from which the rooms could be accessed. Over half of the bunker was torn down after the Second World War because it was in a very bad state.

This bunker was called Kaserne Herzog Albrecht 2 (Duke Albrecht 2 Barracks); a similar bunker was built to the northwest (of which only some concrete pieces can be found today). Each of these bunkers served as living quarters for about two thirds of the company (approximately a hundred men) that was holding the Albrecht Stellung in the 'Hummel' regimental sector. Similar bunkers were constructed in other regimental sectors as well. Near Pond Farm, for example, one section remains of the Kaserne Graf Haeseler (Count Haeseler Barracks – Haeseler was a Prussian field marshal).

Today only a small section of the Kaserne Herzog Albrecht 2 remains. (*Vancoillie*)

The Kaserne Herzog Albrecht 2 in around 1916. It was in use at that time by Reserve Infanterie Regiment 236. (*Vancoillie*)

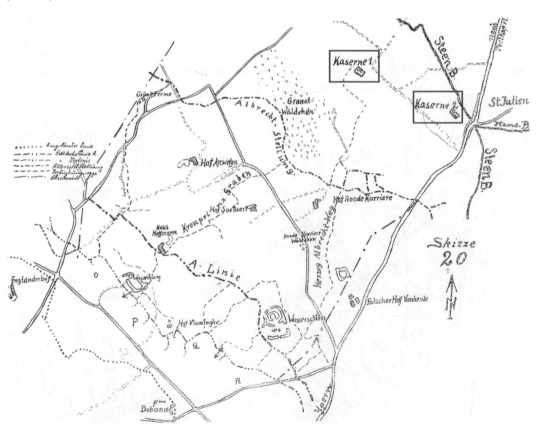

The Regimental Sector of Reserve Infanterie Regiment 28 (185th Infanterie Division) in early 1917. Note the location of both Kasernen west of Sint-Juliaan. (*Reserve Infanterie Regiment 28*)

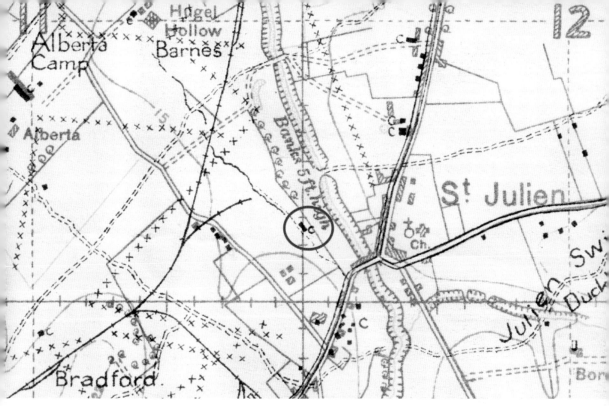

Trench map extract showing the Kaserne Herzog Albrecht 2 (28 NW 2 Edition 6B 30 March 1918).

To the British this bunker was known as Hackney Villa from the summer of 1917 onwards; after it was captured it was used to billet troops. A direct hit on the bunker in August 1917 caused a stack of flares to ignite. The British soldiers in the affected room rushed out into the corridor to escape from the smoke and flames.

Langemark.

8. Machine gun post

This bunker is off Beekstraat, at the northern boundary of the commune of Langemark. In front of the bunker stands a memorial to the 34th Division – a division which suffered very heavily on the first day of the Somme at La Boisselle. Beekstraat is a narrow road that can be quite busy; in addition, the verges may be soft and muddy, so take care when parking here.

In the summer of 1917 the Germans decided that it was necessary to add a second line to the Koekuit Stellung (Wilhelm Stellung) in this area; the bunker formed a part of this development in the defensive system. The first line of the Koekuit Stellung ran a few hundred metres further to the south. The three bunkers in the German cemetery at Langemark were part of this first line. The second line was built as a forward slope defence line just behind a small stream, the Broenbeek. One should not be deceived by the innocuous look of these small streams – even in October 1914 it provided a useful extra obstacle for the British defenders. Given the Salient's fragile drainage systems and the very wet summer of 1917, many of these streams were to become a significant problem in the British offensive.

The bunker was built by the use of poured concrete on a wooden formwork on the inside, while the formwork on the outside was made from wattle-work sections. This is

Entrance towards the 34th Division Memorial, with a machine gun post behind it. (*Vancoillie*)

This machine gun post is one of the few remaining bunkers that was built inside a formwork made with wattle-work, hence the uneven surface. Iron railway sleepers are visible at the corner on the left, indicating this bunker was built in haste and not according to strict regulations. (*Vancoillie*)

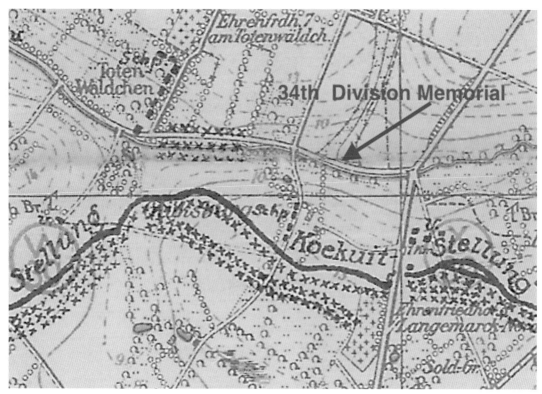

Trench map extract showing the Broenbeek area in August 1917 (Batteriekarte Diksmuide Süd Blatt XII 30 Aug. 1917). The German cemetery existed in 1915 and the bunkers which are visible today belonged to the Koekuit Stellung. At this time there was no indication of the machine gun post north of the Broenbeek.

A close up of one of the bunker openings. (*Vancoillie*)

still clearly visible when viewing the outside surface of the bunker. It was probably built in considerable haste and without too much concern about the quality of the finished product; hardly surprising given the conditions on this part of the front. The different layers of poured concrete can be clearly distinguished. The metal reinforcement was provided by the use of iron railway sleepers, whose use in ferro-concrete construction did not appear in the manual. This is another reason to support the idea that the bunker was built in haste.

The concrete bunker was most probably conceived as a machine gun post, hence its height and the two loopholes in the walls. One opening is directed to the south, overlooking the Broenbeek valley and able to take any attackers with frontal fire, as well as providing coverage of the road heading north towards Madonna; the other opening is towards the east, able to cover the Broenbeek valley with enfilade, or flanking, fire.

The Guards and 29th Divisions tried several times to cross the Broenbeek in August and September 1917. German counter-attacks by Reserve Infanterie Regiment 119 (in August), Infanterie Regiment 121 (in August-September) and Reserve Infanterie Regiment 65 (in September), managed to push the British back. The Guards Division eventually managed to force the Broenbeek crossing on 9 October 1917 and captured this bunker from Infanterie Regiment 417, which at the time was in the process of relieving Bayerisches Infanterie Regiment 6.

The 34th Division took over this sector in due course and the bunker was used as a headquarters for some of its artillery units. After the war a small memorial was erected in front of the bunker in memory of the division's engineer and artillery units. The bunker itself was allegedly used as an advanced dressing station in September 1918 under the command of Robert Lawrence, an older brother of TE Lawrence, of Arabia fame. However, this story is at the best doubtful, as there were no British units in this area in the period September-October 1918.

Langemark-Poelkapelle.

9. Gun turret emplacement

This concrete gun emplacement can be found in the middle of fields. The easiest way to visit this place is to park the car close by the dirt road just before the farm in Houthulstseweg 148, Langemark-Poelkapelle. It is not advisable to drive up the road as it is in a bad state and, perhaps more importantly, is used regularly by agricultural vehicles, which are often very large.

To reach the gun emplacement, walk a few hundred metres to the east until you come to a small wood on the right hand side; the emplacement is on the western side of this wood. This construction is in the process of being classified as a heritage site (February 2017) and so access may be improved in the future.

These straight, long dirt roads were once alleys inside Houthulst Forest. Houthulst Forest, still an impressive woodland feature, was in 1914 approximately three times bigger than its current size of 3.52 square kilometres. It was completely destroyed during the First World War and only partially replanted afterwards. Some two square kilometres is under military control; it is here where most of the unexploded ammunition of the two world wars is gathered and either detonated in controlled explosions (standard ammunition) or dismantled under strict conditions (poison gas).

The Germans had numerous artillery positions, with weapons of all calibres, inside the shelter of the woods. Amongst these there were two heavy gun positions, one for two 24 centimetre naval guns and another one for a 21 centimetre howitzer. This position is most probably a concrete gun emplacement for the two 24 centimetre guns (SK L/40) in a turret (Drh. L. C/98 twin turret). The turret and guns were taken from the armoured cruiser SMS *Fürst Bismarck* in September 1916. After the concrete gun emplacement was built, the turret and guns were transported by rail to Houthulst Forest (a special standard gauge track was built up to the emplacement) and installed. The unit that operated the twin turret was Fußartillerie Batterie 1025. It is unknown how long the battery engaged in active operations; by late July 1917 it came under precision bombardment from the allies' heaviest artillery pieces, as a consequence of which the Germans removed the guns from the turret.

This concrete artillery emplacement measures about 11.30 metres across (outside measurements) and on the inside about 6.90 metres across. Several recesses and niches can be seen inside the circular construction that were necessary for the positioning of the turret. Note that there is always standing water in the emplacement that, unfortunately, makes it impossible to see the lower parts.

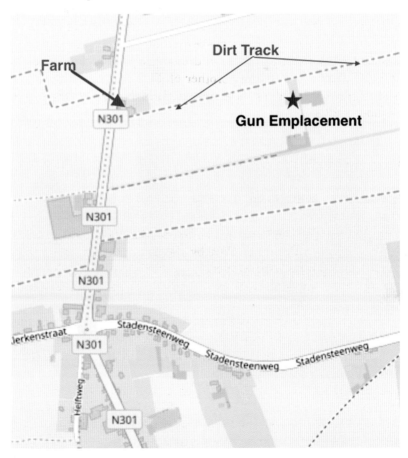

A modern map of the area. The gun turret emplacement is to the west of a stand of woods. Note that the dirt tracks around here were once alleys in Houthulst Forest. (*OpenStreetMap*)

The guns were dismounted from the turret in the summer of 1917; however, the empty turret could not be salvaged. (*Deraeve*)

German soldiers posing by the empty gun turret in the winter of 1917-1918. This photograph gives a better idea of the scale and size of the emplacement. (*Deraeve*)

2. Panzerturm, Houthulster Wald

Today only the concrete gun emplacement remains; and, unfortunately, there is always water in it. (*Vancoillie*)

Ledegem.

10 and 11. Flandern I Stellung

Built during the winter of 1917-1918, several bunkers of the (new) Flandern I Stellung remain in the Ledegem area. They are mostly Einheitsunterstände, the standard bunker design developed at that time. Two very nice examples (10) can be seen alongside Groene Jagerstraat, at the northern end of Ledegem. These two bunkers are not open to the public and there is standing water in them during most of the year, but they are located close to the street and are easy to view from a distance.

A bit further south, there is a small road off the Industrieweg (Sint-Pieterstraat) that provides access to a farm. On the eastern side of the farm, Lord Farm (11) on British trench maps, a large bunker can be visited. It is located on private property, but was opened to the public some years ago.

Construction planning for a new Divisionsgefechtsstand (divisional battle headquarters) in what at that point was part of the Artillerie Schutz Stellung, itself part of the Flandern II Stellung, was prepared on paper on 16 October 1917 by the 3rd Landwehr Pionier Kompagnie

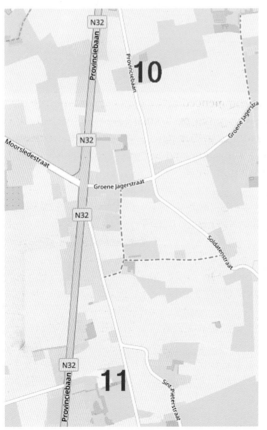

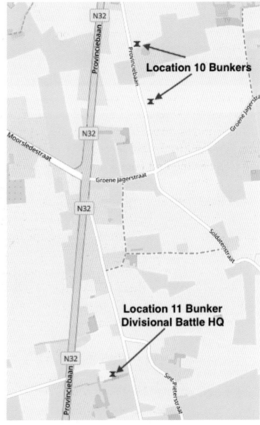

A modern map of the area north of Ledegem, showing the locations of the bunkers of the Flandern I Stellung. (*OpenStreetMap*)

A modern map of the area north of Ledegem, showing the locations of the bunkers of the Flandern I Stellung.

A modern sketch of Lord (sometimes Lord's) Farm and its associated bunker after its capture in autumn 1918 by the 9th (Scottish) Division. The sketch appears at the top of a sign (in Dutch) at the beginning of the access path to the bunker. (*Vancoillie*)

des XIII Armeekorps. Actual work on the ground commenced on 18 October. Camouflage nets were laid to protect the building operation, which required preliminary work – sheds to store cement and drainage ditches were dug. On 23 October the German Pioniere started to excavate the foundations for the bunker. A trench tramway was connected to the site on 25 October. On 27 October the first concrete was poured for the foundations.

On 1 November 1917, the bunker – at that stage still under construction and with the fighting around Passchendaele reaching a peak – was changed into a Regimentsgefechtsstand (regimental battle headquarters). By 7 November the ground surface was as good as ready and so the wooden formwork and elephant shelters were placed that created the rooms of the building. Rebar cages for the walls were in position by 12 November and the process of pouring concrete started for the walls of the bunker. On 27 November 1917, 3rd Landwehr Pionier Kompagnie des XIII Armeekorps was relieved by 3rd Kompagnie Pionier Bataillon 23, which took over the construction work and finished the bunker, probably within a few weeks. From December 1917 onwards the bunker line became a part of the newly named Flandern I Stellung.

In the autumn of 1918 this area lay in the sector of the 9th (Scottish) Division. They managed to pierce the Flandern I Stellung and captured Ledegem on 1 October 1918; but they had to withdraw behind the railway line that ran between Menen and Roeselare because of a lack of support on the flanks. The bunker at Lord Farm served as a British brigade headquarters in October 1918. A renewed general attack on 14 October 1918 managed to shatter the German defences and the allied advance continued towards Kortrijk (Courtrai).

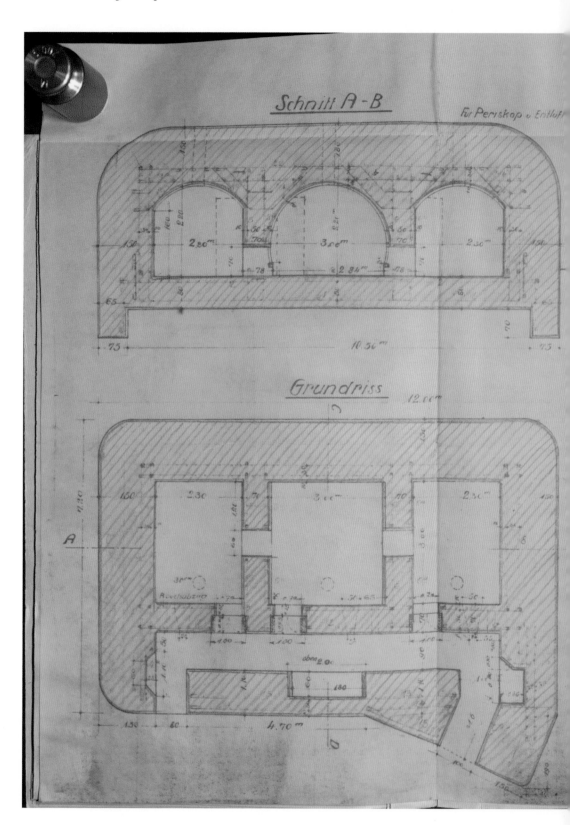

Construction
plan for the
Divisionsgefechtsstand,
dated October 1917.
(*HstAS*)

The rear of the Divisionsgefechtsstand, with two entrances. Note that part of the roof of the bunker seems to be missing, probably done after the war in an attempt to tear it down. (*Vancoillie*)

Interior view of one of the chambers inside the command post. There is always water standing in the bunker, but large concrete slabs have been placed on the floor, so that it is normally possible – with a certain amount of physical dexterity - to visit the bunker wearing normal shoes. (*Vancoillie*)

Stairs at the back of the bunker. In 1917 there would most probably have been a steel cupola on the bunker so it could be used as an observation post. (*Vancoillie*)

The bunker has three rooms, connected by small passages and with a hallway at the rear. An observation cupola was added on the north eastern corner of the building, which was accessible via crampons set in the wall. The bunker measures app. 12 metres by 7.20 metres.

Conclusion

The German army clearly spared no efforts in developing its positions around Ypres – a task made easier by the gains in the Salient as a consequence of the Second Battle of Ypres in April and May 1915 – into a magnificent system of defensive works. In so far as the figures are available, the Germans used considerably more building material in the Ypres Salient than in the other sectors of the Western Front. This highly skilled development of its defence lines ensured that they held the positions there with little difficulty from the end of 1914 until early 1917; though it should be noted that they were never subjected here to a major attack during this period.

The real tests came in and after the summer of 1917. The first of these was the Battle of Messines, 7 – 14 June 1917. The carefully built trenches, barbed wire entanglements and bunker lines were almost completely annihilated within weeks of the opening of this battle and the subsequent Third Ypres on 31 July. The concrete bunkers stood out in a landscape that had many protecting features – woods, farm buildings, houses – destroyed by the mass use of guns of all calibres by the Allies; they were turned into magnets for the enemy gunners, making them death traps for those who were taking shelter inside. It also became quite clear very quickly that many of the bunkers were not built according to the requirements that had been laid down; whilst the German series of defence lines were too close to each other.

This led to disaster for the German defenders on 7 June 1917. The soldiers had to withdraw to a defence line largely composed of shell holes. This should not have come as an enormous surprise, not only because of the fact that both sides now had both many more guns than was the case even in 1915 but that their operators were becoming ever more competent and inventive in their use. This situation had been quite clearly revealed by the end of the 1916 Verdun and Somme offensives.

The Germans drew conclusions from this failure. No sooner was Messines concluded – indeed, even before that, than they started building more concrete bunkers and bunker lines parallel to the front line and perpendicular to the different defence lines. During the Third Battle of Ypres many bunkers of all type were destroyed by well directed artillery fire. Only bunkers that had been built strictly according to the detailed building regulations could withstand the incessant shelling and even direct hits.

Trenches and light shelters were destroyed by the shelling, but barbed wire entanglements survived the bombardments quite well. The bombardments turned the barbed wire fences, laid out almost mathematically and according to the experiences of trench warfare over the course of the war, into an almost impassable jumble of vicious barbs and snaring wire, which improved the defensive advantage for the Germans (though at the same time it restricted cohesive counter attacks). From autumn 1917 the Germans limited themselves to building strong concrete bunkers with barbed wire obstacles in front of and between them. For the rest, they tried to disperse and hide their troops in the empty landscape and the sea of shell holes. Although effective against enemy shelling, this dispersal of men in disconnected holes made command and control very difficult and the supplying of rations and ammunition a quartermaster's nightmare.

The big question, whether the huge German construction effort was a success or a hugely expensive misuse of resources, does not have an easy answer. Many studies of the Third Battle of Ypres consider that the concrete constructions acted as points of resistance that could often only be captured with great difficultly and at the cost of heavy casualties; and when one bunker was captured there always seemed to be another to its rear. The extensive barbed wire entanglements, frequently re-engineered in light of experience elsewhere on the Western Front, were often well concealed and therefore not destroyed – or were only partially destroyed – by shelling, undoubtedly contributing to the strength of the German defence system. It was as well that the nature of the Flanders terrain made the use of tanks, whose most useful contribution (arguably) to a battle at this stage of the war was the ability to flatten belts of barbed wire, very problematic.

German defensive successes on the allied flanks (near Geluveld and the Houthulst Forest) were not so much due to German fortification efforts, but to the lack of sufficient attention by the allies on these strategically important points – ie a failure to realise that they were the key Schwerpunkts of the Salient. On the other hand, since these two locations were vital to the security of the whole German position in the Salient (and possibly beyond, especially to the north), the Germans piled in the necessary resources to ensure that they were retained.

Yet some remarks can be made about the German defensive constructions. The trenches, built, developed and maintained by huge efforts, were largely destroyed even before the actual offensives started. The concrete bunkers, in which troops sheltered, stood out because of the complete destruction of the landscape, becoming easily identifiable targets for the British artillery. Numerous bunkers were not built to the highest standards and were laboriously eliminated one by one, which weakened the German defences severely. The Germans had the advantage that British and French long range heavy artillery lacked the accuracy to score direct hits on the heaviest bunkers built further away from the original front line in the Salient. The functioning bunkers could be surrounded and effectively besieged, especially as German counter-attacks had as much difficulty in making progress as the British attacks in the dreadful muddy and wet conditions that prevailed for much of Third Ypres (with the notable exception of September).

The increasingly difficult economic, food and manpower situation in Germany itself naturally hampered the maintenance, development and expansion of these enormous fortification efforts. Yet the Germans were able to deliver one last gigantic effort at fortifying new lines during the winter of 1917-1918. Using thousands of labourers (not only German military labourers but also prisoners of war and more or less free Belgian civilian labourers), two new bunker lines were constructed in Flanders.

The German strategic and tactical modifications of the elastic defence, adopted in the autumn of 1916, underscored the importance of spreading out the infantry in the 'empty battlefield', while strategic bunker lines were built more according to the strategy of a static defence of the front line, recapturing lost territory at all costs. It was difficult to harmonise the two approaches to defence and, indeed, they remained in conflict right up to the end of the war.

After the series of German Spring Offensives in 1918, most defensive building activities were all but halted, except for road construction to enable better supply of the front line.

And this was at a point when the Allies were copying and implementing some of the German construction ideas!

In the autumn of 1918, the German elastic defence, leaning on almost no new large constructions, was overcome by the allied offensive of September 1918, it would appear, in only one day. However, the Germans managed to hold on for two weeks to the static bunker lines that were built during the winter of 1917-1918. This way of presenting events may be misleading. The condition of the German army and its units in the Ypres Salient in late September 1918 was largely responsible for the failures on the first day of the Allied Final Offensive in Flanders, while the relative success of the defence in the bunker line during the first half of October 1918 can be explained by the logistical difficulties of the Allies, confronted as they were by the destroyed infrastructure of the forward battle zone around Ypres.

One thing is certain. The First World War made the Germans masters of military ferro-concrete construction. The concept of bunker lines was copied after the war on a large scale, for instance in France (the Maginot Line and the fortified sectors along the Belgian-French border), in Belgium (the Koningshooikt – Wavre Line and the 'Bruggenhoofd Gent'), in Finland (the Mannerheim Line), in Czechoslovakia and in several other countries. Even the Germans showed that they had not forgotten their fortification skills, in their case in the shape of the Atlantic Wall. However, in the end, and despite all the concrete bunkers and related construction, evolved as military technology progressed, none of these bunker lines held out and achieved their aim.

Two small bunkers in Oliekotstraat, Dadizele. These were most probably ammunition or storage bunkers of Pionier Park Westhoek. (*Vancoillie*)

A large bunker near Ledegem Church. Its original function is not known. (*Vancoillie*)

And what of the bunkers that have survived to this day? Many that survived the war have been uprooted, demolished and removed since the end of 1918; that is understandable – people have to earn their living and society has to move on. However, what remains is a most eloquent testament to the events that took place here in the extremes of western Belgium; they act as landmarks of great events and of the ingenuity of man when engaged in warfare. They are a symbol of the huge resources that were expended in war. So, barring human interference, their profound strength and looming presence in the landscape will continue to provide a unique testimony to the Great War, certainly outlasting the many monuments that have emerged during the last years in the battle zone of the Ypres Salient.

These bunkers were made to withstand time and enormous forces. It is to be hoped that the relatively few that remain are allowed by human agency – for nothing else could destroy them – to continue to stand and provoke questions and curiosity from the generations to come.

Glossary of some German Terms

Armee Oberkommando   Army Headquarters (Staff).

Armierungs Bataillon   Labour Battalion. These battalions were formed as temporary units to bring the fortresses (in Germany) up to a state of war. They consisted of a varying number of companies and were made up of unarmed men who were considered unfit for active or garrison service. Most labour units were engaged as detached companies under the command of a battalion staff.

Artillerie Schutz Stellung   Artillery protective line. From 1917 onwards positions had two lines: a front zone with different trench lines; and an artillery protective line at some distance from it. This artillery protective line was considered to be out of reach of most of the enemy (lighter) artillery and thus was onsidered a safe distance to place support units.

BTK: Bereitschafts Truppen Kommandeur.   Commander (or his command post) of supporting fighting units. German regiments (comparable to a British brigade) usually had one battalion in the front line, one in the support zone and one resting in reserve. The BTK was commander of all units in the support zone and could make decisions to set up counter attacks, send supports to the front line when requested and request further supports from the reserves. Even if he was outranked by other commanders moving into his zone, he remained the commander on the ground as he was considered to be familiar with the area and knew what had to be done in his zone.

Einheitsunterstand   A standardised bunker for all uses, developed in late 1917.

Etappengebiet   Lines of Communications area.

Feldartillerie Regiment   Field artillery regiment. This basic light artillery regiment had 10.5 and 7.7 cm guns at its disposal. From 1915 on most regiments had nine batteries of four guns (six 7.7 and three 10.5 cm batteries).

Generalkommando   An Army Corps staff

Graben   Trench.

Gruppe   A front line sector commanded by an army corps staff (from 1917 onwards).

Hinterhangstellung   Position situated on a reverse slope.

Infanterie Regiment   Infantry regiment. Basic infantry formation in the German army. It was made up of three battalions (in total twelve rifle companies and a machine gun company in 1914, later twelve rifle companies and three machine gun companies). A regiment numbered some 3,300 officers, NCOs and men in 1914, but this was reduced to about 2,500 (on paper) in 1918. Because of the increasing number of support weapons (light machine guns and later trench mortars) the total possible fire power did not decrease. The difference between active and reserve infantry regiments decreased as the war progressed, although Landwehr and Landsturm units continued to have older men and were more often used in quieter sectors and in defensive roles.

Jäger Bataillon   Light Infantry battalion. These units were, effectively, normal infantry units in 1914, although some were used as scouts (and one battalion was usually attached to a cavalry division, especially in the early months of the war). Later on in the war, some Jäger Bataillone were adapted to the more specialised mountain troops role.

KTK: Kampf Truppen Kommandeur.   Commander (or his command post) of the front line units. German regiments (comparable to a British brigade) usually had one battalion in the front line, one in the support zone and one resting in reserve. The KTK was commander of all units in the front line zone and remained in charge even if units arrived during battle with higher ranking commanders. He was considered to be familiar with all the necessary knowledge about his zone and could request support from the BTK when necessary.

Linie   Line. This was usually one trench line.

Operationsgebiet   Zone of the field army, basically a +/– twenty kilometres wide zone behind the front line, governed and controlled by military formations (divisions and army corps); this zone was later enlarged to +/– forty kilometres.

Pionier   Pioneer, Engineer.

Pionier Bataillon   Each army corps had its own organic Pionier Bataillon, which was expanded into two battalions upon mobilisation. Each of these battalions had three companies (active or reserve). In 1917, each division received a divisional Pionier Bataillon consisting of two Pionier Kompagnien, one Minenwerfer Kompagnie and a Scheinwerferzug (search light section).

Pionier Kompagnie   This was the basic unit of the pioneers/engineers, comparable to a Royal Engineers Field Company in the British army. Its establishment was a theoretical 250 officers and men.

Pionier Regiment   Eight fortress battalions from peacetime were expanded into Pionier Regimente. These regiments consisted of a varying number of companies. These companies and regiments were mainly used as Army troops for more specialised warfare, especially mining. In 1917 the regiments were disbanded and changed into Pioniere Battalione (divisional) or Stopi.

Pionier Park   Pioneer dump.

Stellung   Position. This consisted usually of a series of trench or bunker lines or a combination of both.

Stopi: Stabsoffizier der Pioniere   A small Pioneer/Engineer staff; at least one was attached to each Gruppe (army corps) to oversee all engineering matters. Sometimes more than one Stopi was attached to a Gruppe, in which case this received a very specific task, usually a sector that was to be fortified.

Trichterstellung   Shell hole position.

Unterstand   Shelter. Some examples are minierter Unterstand or Stollen (deep dug out) and betonierter Unterstand (concrete bunker).

Vorderhangstellung   Position situated on a forward slope.

Bibliography

Archival sources

Badisches Generallandesarchiv (Karlsruhe)

GLAK, 456 F6 324, Generalkommando XIV. Armeekorps, 'Kriegstagebuch'.

Bundesarchiv/Militärarchiv (Freiburg im Breisgau)

BA/MA, PH5-II/44, Armeeoberkommando 4, 'Abwehrschlacht in Flandern, Bd. 1 Juni/November 1917'.

BA/MA, PH5-II/443, Armeeoberkommando 4, 'Deutsche Baufirmen und Zivilarbeiter zum Stellungsbau im Bereich der 4. Armee'.

BA/MA, PH5-II/444, Armeeoberkommando 4, 'Bestimmungen und Verordnungen der deutschen Besatzungsbehörden im okkupierten Belgien'.

BA/MA, PH5-II/445, Armeeoberkommando 4, 'Wiederaufbau zerstörter Städte und Dörfer Flanderns'.

BA/MA, PH5-II/446, Armeeoberkommando 4, 'Aufstellung über alliierte Kriegsgefangene im Bereich der 4. Armee'.

BA/MA, PH5-II/447, Armeeoberkommando 4, 'Monatsberichte über Gefangenenlager'.

BA/MA, PH5-II/459, Armeeoberkommando 4, 'Einsatz von Kriegsgefangenen und Zivilarbeitern zum Stellungsbau im Bereich des Armeekommandos 4 (Hermann-Stellung)'.

BA/MA, PH14/273, Pionierbataillon 9, 'Betonbauten und Unterstände'.

BA/MA, PH14/291, Pionier-Bataillon 23, 'Anweisungen und Erfahrungen des Stellungsbaus'.

Bayerisches Hauptstaatsarchiv/Abteilung IV Kriegsarchiv (München)

BayHStA/Abt. IV, Generalkommando III. AK (WK), Bd. 1754, 'Flandern I. u. II. Stellung, Personal'.

BayHStA/Abt. IV, Generalkommando III. AK (WK), Bd. 1758, 'Stopi 150, Rückwärtige Stellungen'.

BayHStA/Abt. IV, Generalkommando III. AK (WK), Bd. 1762, 'Wochenberichte der Bau-Abteilungen und der Baudirektion 4'.

BayHStA/Abt. IV, Generalkommando III. AK (WK), Bd. 2307, 'Flandern I-Stellung'.

BayHStA/Abt. IV, Pioniere Höhere Stäbe (WK), Bd. 743, Stopi 40b, 'Baustabsbefehle Flandern I'.

BayHStA/Abt. IV, Pioniere Höhere Stäbe (WK), Bd. 744, Stopi 40b, 'Baustabsbefehle Flandern II'.

BayHStA/Abt. IV, Pioniere Höhere Stäbe (WK), Bd. 759, Stopi 40b, 'Zivilarbeiter (Arbeitsordnung)'.

BayHStA/Abt. IV, Pioniere Höhere Stäbe (WK), Bd. 760, Stopi 40b, 'Zivilarbeiter Versch.'.

BayHStA/Abt. IV, Pioniere Höhere Stäbe (WK), Bd. 766, Stopi 40b, '3. Ldst. Pion. Komp. XIX.A.K.'.

BayHStA/Abt. IV, Pioniere Höhere Stäbe (WK), Bd. 812, Stopi 40b, 'Stellungsbau I'.

BayHStA/Abt. IV, Pioniere Höhere Stäbe (WK), Bd. 813, Stopi 40b, 'Stellungsbau II'.

BayHStA/Abt. IV, Pioniere Höhere Stäbe (WK), Bd. 814, Stopi 40b, 'Unterstände – Pläne'.

BayHStA/Abt. IV, Pioniere Höhere Stäbe (WK), Bd. 830, Stopi 40b, 'Ausbau der Flandern II-Stellung'.

BayHStA/Abt. IV, Pioniere Höhere Stäbe (WK), Bd. 888, Stopi 40b, 'Geologie Flandern II'.

BayHStA/Abt. IV, Pioniere Höhere Stäbe (WK), Bd. 889, Stopi 40b, 'Geologie Flandern III'.

BayHStA/Abt. IV, Pioniere Höhere Stäbe (WK), Bd. 1067, Stopi 42b, 'Armee- und Gruppenbefehle'.

BayHStA/Abt. IV, Infanteriedivisionen (WK), Bd. 5442, 12. Infanteriedivision, 'Einsatz im westl. Kriegsschauplatz – A.O.K.4'.

BayHStA/Abt. IV, Infanteriedivisionen (WK), Bd. 5449, 12. Infanteriedivision, 'Weisungen für die Kampfführung im Abschnitt "C" des A.O.K.4'.

BayHStA/Abt. IV, Infanteriedivisionen (WK), Bd. 7188, 1. Reservedivision, 'Unterkunft, Allgemeines und Besonderes 1915-1918, Flandern 1917-1918, Feldrekrutendepot 1918, Arbeitsnachweis 1918; Kommandierungen 1917-1918; Truppenschau 1916'.

BayHStA/Abt. IV, Minenwerferformationen (WK) Bd. 58, Bayerische Minenwerfer-Kompagnie Nr. 11, 'Ausbildung'.

BayHStA/Abt. IV, Kriegsgefangeneneinheiten (WK) Bd. 281, Kriegsgefangenenarbeiterbataillon Nr. 29, 'Kriegstagebuch'.

BayHStA/Abt. IV, Kriegsgefangeneneinheiten (WK) Bd. 285, Kriegsgefangenenarbeiterbataillon Nr. 29, 'Kriegstagebuch'.

BayHStA/Abt. IV, Technische Sonderformationen und Wirtschaftsformationen (WK) 1191/2, Stab Bayerisches Armierungs-Bataillon 1, 'Kriegstagebuch'.

Württembergisches Hauptstaatsarchiv (Stuttgart)

HStAS, M 1/11 Bü 361, Kriegsarchiv, 'Kriegsgliederung der 4. Armee'.

HStAS, M 1/11 Bü 362, Kriegsarchiv, 'Kriegsgliederung der 4. Armee'.

HStAS, M 1/11 Bü 363, Kriegsarchiv, 'Kriegsgliederung der 4. Armee'.

HStAS, M 33/2 Bü 499, Generalkommando XIII. Armeekorps, 'Industrie- und Frontbetriebe des Heeres'.

HStAS, M 123 Bü 5, Landsturm-Infanterie-Regiment 39, 'Kriegstagebuch'.

HStAS, M 201 Bü 92, 3. Kompanie Pionier-Bataillon 13, 'Arbeitsnotizen und Berichtsentwürfe des Kompanieführers sowie Pläne, Skizzen, Fotografien und Karten vom Stellungsbau im Abschnitt des Grenadier-Regiments Nr. 123 und Infanterie-Regiments Nr. 127'.

HStAS, M 201 Bü 103, 4. Kompanie Pionier-Bataillon 13, 'Berichte und Skizzen zum Stellungsbau, Pläne von Unterständen, Baracken, Batteriestellungen und Brücken'.

HStAS, M 201 Bü 143, 2. Kompanie Pionier-Bataillon 13, 'Zweitfertigung des Kriegstagebuches mit Kriegsrangliste, Verpflegungs- und Gefechtsstärkennachweisung'.

HStAS, M 201 Bü 145, 2. Kompanie Pionier-Bataillon 13, 'Zweitfertigung des Kriegstagebuches mit Kriegsrangliste, Verpflegungs- und Gefechtsstärkennachweisung'.

HStAS, M 201 Bü 147, 2. Kompanie Pionier-Bataillon 13, 'Zweitfertigung des Kriegstagebuches mit Kriegsrangliste, Verpflegungs- und Gefechtsstärkennachweisung'.

HStAS, M 201 Bü 148, 2. Kompanie Pionier-Bataillon 13, 'Zweitfertigung der Kriegstagebücher mit Kriegsrangliste, Verpflegungs- und Gefechtsstärkennachweisung, Zugehörigkeitslisten'.

HStAS, M 201 Bü 149, 2. Kompanie Pionier-Bataillon 13, 'Zweitfertigung der Kriegstagebücher mit Kriegsranglisten, Verpflegungs- und Gefechtsstärkennachweisungen'.

HStAS, M 201 Bü 150, 2. Kompanie Pionier-Bataillon 13, 'Zweitfertigung des Kriegstagebuches mit Kriegsrangliste, Verpflegungs- und Gefechtsstärkennachweisungen'.

HStAS, M 201 Bü 162, 3. Kompanie Pionier-Bataillon 13, 'Zweitfertigung des Kriegstagebuches mit Kriegsrangliste, Verpflegungs- und Gefechtsstärkenachweisung'.

HStAS, M 203 Bü 92, 3. Landwehr-Pionier-Kompanie, 'Zweitfertigung des Kriegstagebuches mit Kriegsrangliste, Verpflegungs- und Gefechtsstärkenachweisung, Zugehörigkeitsliste'.

HStAS, M 203 Bü 93, 3. Landwehr-Pionier-Kompanie, 'Zweitfertigung des Kriegstagebuches mit Kriegsrangliste, Verpflegungs- und Gefechtsstärkenachweisung, Zugehörigkeitsliste'.

HStAS, M 203 Bü 100, 3. Landwehr-Pionier-Kompanie, 'Zweitfertigung der Anlagen zum Kriegstagebuch vom 3. Oktober bis 31. Dezember 1917'.

HStAS, M 203 Bü 101, 3. Landwehr-Pionier-Kompanie, 'Zweitfertigung der Anlagen zum Kriegstagebuch vom 1. Januar bis 1. Juli 1918'.

HStAS, M 233 Bü 7a, Sanitäts-Kompanie 563, 'Kriegstagebuch'.

HStAS, M 420 Bü 147, 2. Kompagnie Pionier-Bataillon 13, 'Zweitfertigung des Kriegstagebuches mit Kriegsrangliste, Verpflegungs- und Gefechtsstärkennachweisung'.

HStAS, M 420 Bd. 149, Armierungs-Bataillon 131, 'Kriegstagebuch 2. Kompanie'.

HStAS, M 420 Bd. 150, Armierungs-Bataillon 131, 'Kriegstagebuch 2. Kompanie'.

Kriegsministerium [Hrsg.], 'Feldbefestigungs-Vorschrift (F. V.)', Berlin, E. S. Mittler & Sohn, 1893, 84 p.

Published works

Arbeitsgemeinschaft der Münchener Landsturm-Vereinigungen [Hrsg.], 'Festschrift für den 2. Bayer. Landsturmtag in München am 29. und 30. Juni 1929', München, G. Hirth, 1929.

Blondeel P., 'Produceren in oorlogstijd: De Tréfileries Léon Bekaert en Leon Bekaert 1930-1946', Verhandeling aangeboden tot het behalen van de graad van Licentiaat in de Geschiedenis, Universiteit Gent, Academiejaar 2006-2007.

Bostyn F., 'De vergeten oorlog onder de Salient. Bijdrage tot geschiedenis van de Tunnelling Companies in Vlaanderen (1915-1918)', Verhandeling aangeboden tot het behalen van de graad van Licentiaat in de Geschiedenis, Katholieke Universiteit Leuven, 1998.

Bostyn F., Vancoillie J., Barton P., Vandewalle J., 'Bayernwald. Het Croonaertbos in de Eerste Wereldoorlog', Association for Battlefield Archaeology in Flanders Studies 2, Zonnebeke, Association for Battlefield Archaeology in Flanders, 2000.

Buhr W. 'Die Geschichte des I. Westf. Pionier-Bataillons Nr. 7 und seiner Kriegsverbände im Weltkriege 1914/18', Erinnerungsblätter Preußen 369, Oldenburg, Gerhard Stalling, 1938.

Chef des Generalstabes des Feldheeres [Hrsg.], 'Einzelheiten über Stellungsbau. Vom 15. Dezember 1916', Vorschriften für den Stellungskrieg für alle Waffen 1b, Berlin, Reichsdruckerei, 1916.

'Die Industrie im besetzten Frankreich. Bearbeitet im Auftrage des Generalquartiermeisters', R. Oldenbourg, München, 1916.

Cron H., 'Geschichte des Deutschen Heeres im Weltkriege 1914-1918', Osnabrück, Biblio Verlag, 1990.

Cron H., 'Die Organisation des deutschen Heeres im Weltkriege', Forschungen und Darstellungen aus dem Reichsarchiv 5, Berlin, E. S. Mittler & Sohn, 1923.

Dean B., 'Helmets and body armour in modern warfare', Yale, University Press, 1919.

Descamps F., Vancoillie J. en Vandeweyer L., 'Ten oorlog met schop en houweel. Bijdragen over de hulptroepen van de genie van het Belgische, Duitse en Britse leger tijdens de Eerste Wereldoorlog', Ieper, Western Front Association België vzw.

Dziobek O., 'Geschichte des Infanterie-Regiments Lübeck (3. Hanseatisches) Nr. 162', Lübeck, Offizier-Verein ehem. 162er, 1921.

Ehemalige Kameraden des L. I. R. 35 [Hrsg.], 'Märkische Landwehr', 2 Bände, Berlin, Franz Düring, 1925-1928.

Geheugen Collectief, 'Bossen en Natuur in WOI. Onderzoeksrapport i. o. Agentschap voor Natuur en Bos. Antwerpen, Geheugen Collectief, 2014.

General-Inspektion des Ingenieur- und Pionier-Korps und der Festungen (Hrsg.), 'Unsere Pioniere im Weltkriege', Berlin, Kyffhäuser-Verlag, 1920.

General Staff (Intelligence), 'Vocabulary of German Military terms and Abbreviations (Second Edition)', General Headquarters, 1919.

Glück, Wald, 'Das 8. Württembergische Infanterie-Regiment Nr. 126 Großherzog Friedrich von Baden im Weltkrieg 1914-1918', Die württembergischen Regimenter im Weltkrieg 1914-1918 44, Stuttgart, Chr. Belser A.G., 1929.

Gropp H., 'Hanseaten im Kampf. Erlebnisse bei dem Res.-Inf.-Rgt. 76 im Weltkriege 1914/18', Hamburg, Verein ehem. Angeh. Res. 76, 1932.

Hartenstein, 'Das Kurhessische Pionier-Bataillon Nr. 11 im Weltkriege 1914-1918', Aus Deutschlands großer Zeit, Zeulenroda, Bernhard Sporn, 1936.

Held, Berger, Ritter, Obkircher und Habicht, 'Das Königlich Preußische Garde-Pionier-Bataillon und seine Kriegsverbände 1914/18', Potsdam, Carl Fr. Berg, 1932.

Knies L., 'Das württembergische Pionier-Bataillon Nr. 13 im Weltkrieg 1914-1918', Die württembergischen Regimenter im Weltkrieg 1914-1918 41, Stuttgart, Chr. Belser A. G., 1927.

Kriegsministerium [Hrsg.], 'Feldbefestigungs-Vorschrift (F. V.)', Berlin, E. S. Mittler & Sohn, 1893.

Lambrecht E. 'Het onbarmhartige Bos. De gevechten bij het Bos van Houthulst in 1917 (3de Slag bij Ieper)', Wevelgem, Jan Vancoillie, 2014.

Lehmann H. 'Flandern. 2. Lieferung der Bildersammlung des Res.-Jäg.-Batl. 26', Freiberg, Ernst Mauckisch, z.j., z.p.

Lehmann H. 'Flandern. 3. Lieferung der Bildersammlung des Res.-Jäg.-Batl. 26', Freiberg, Ernst Mauckisch, z.j., z.p.

Lehmann K. 'Ein Gang in den Schützengraben zu den Pionieren', München, R. Piper & Co., 1917.

Lilienstein H. 'Drei Jahre Westfront. Gedenkblätter aus dem Weltkrieg', Stuttgart, E. Schreiber GmbH und Greiner & Pfeiffer.

Lucas A., Schmieschek J. 'Fighting the Kaiser's War. The Saxons in Flanders 1914/1918', Barnsley, Pen & Sword Military, 2015.

Ludendorff E., 'Urkunden der Obersten Heeresleitung über ihre Tätigkeit 1916/18', Berlin, E. S. Mittler & Sohn, 1920.

Mayer H., 'Das K. B. 22. Infanterie-Regiment Fürst Wilhelm von Hohenzollern', Erinnerungsblätter Bayern 15, München, Bayerisches Kriegsarchiv, 1923.

Missinne R., 'Gas... een nieuw wapen', Langemark, Robert Missinne, 1995.

N. N., 'Der Mineur in Flandern', Oldenburg, Gerhard Stalling, 1918.

Offizier-Vereinigung des Bataillons [Hrsg.], 'Kgl. Preuß. Magdeburgisches Pionier-Bataillon Nr. 4 1914-1918', Aus Deutschlands großer Zeit 79, Zeulenroda, Bernhard Sporn, 1935.

Oldham P. 'Pill Boxes on the Western Front: A Guide to the Design, Construction and Use of Concrete Pill Boxes 1914-1918', Barnsley, Pen & Sword Military, 2011.

Peters E. 'Das Reserve-Infanterie-Regiment Nr. 28 im Weltkrieg 1914-1918', Erinnerungsblätter Preußen 206, Oldenburg-Berlin, Gerhard Stalling, 1927.

Piedmont C.; Pieper H. en Krall P., 'Geschichte des 5. Rheinischen Infanterie-Regiments Nr. 65 während des Weltkrieges 1914-1918', Erinnerungsblätter Preußen 205, Oldenburg-Berlin, Gerhard Stalling, 1927.

Rämmler B., 'Mobile bauten für die medizinische Versorgung', Technische Universität Berlin, Berlin, 2011.

Riebicke O. 'Was brauchte der Weltkrieg? Tatsachen und Zahlen aus dem deutschen Ringen 1914/18', Berlin, Kyffhäuser-Verlag, 1936, 214 p.

Riemann H., Vogt F. [Hrsg.], 'Das Res.-Feldart.-Regt. Nr. 51 im Weltkriege', Kassel, Gebrüder Müller, 1932.

Rieß A. 'Das Königl. Bayerische Reserve-Infanterie-Regiment Nr. 4', Bamberg, Vereinigung Bayer. Res. Inf. Rgt. Nr. 4, 1934.

Ritter H. 'Geschichte des Schleswig-Holsteinschen Infanterie-Regiments Nr. 163', Hamburg, Leuchtfeuer-Verlag, 1926.

Rohde H. 'Die Eisenbahnen von Oktober 1914 bis zum Kriegsende', Der Weltkrieg 1914-1918 – Die militärischen Operationen zu Lande – Das deutsche Feldeisenbahnwesen 2, Hamburg-Berlin-Bonn, Verlag E. S. Mittler & Sohn, 2010.

Rückbeil G., 'Das 1. Rheinische Pionier-Bataillon Nr. 8 und seine Kriegsverbände im Weltkriege 1914/18', Erinnerungsblätter Preußen 163, Oldenburg-Berlin, Gerhard Stalling, 1926.

Samuels M. 'Command or Control? Command, Training and Tactics in the British and German Armies, 1888-1918', London, Frank Cass, 2003.

Schinnerer F. 'Deutsche Frontbauarbeit im Kriege', Buchgewerbehaus M. Müller & Sohn, München 1920.

Schroeder K. 'Die Etappe', Der Weltkampf um Ehre und Recht Band 7, Leipzig, 1923, pp.198-272.

Schulz, Kißler, Schulze, 'Geschichte des Reserve-Infanterie-Regiments Nr. 209 im Weltkriege 1914-1918', Erinnerungsblätter Preußen 337, Oldenburg-Berlin, Gerhard Stalling, 1930.

Seeßelberg F., 'Der Stellungskrieg 1914 – 1918', Berlin, Mittler & Sohn, 1926.

Seiler R., '10. Rheinisches Infanterie-Regiment Nr. 161 II. Band', Aus Deutschlands großer Zeit 109, Zeulenroda, Bernhard Sporn, 1939.

Stewart, H., 'The New Zealand Division 1916-1919: a Popular History based on Official Records', Auckland-Christchurch-Dunedin-Wellington, Whitcombe and Tombs Limited, 1921.

Stoffleth, 'Geschichte des Reserve-Jäger-Bataillons Nr. 18', Deutsche Tat im Weltkrieg 1914/1918 85, Berlin, Bernard & Graefe, 1937.

Strenge I. 'Spa im Ersten Weltkrieg (1914-1918). Lazarett und Großes Hauptquartier. Deutsche Besatzungspolitik in Belgien', Würzburg, Königshausen & Neumann, 2007.

Tiessen M., 'Königlich Preußisches Reserve-Infanterie-Regiment 213. Geschichte eines Flandernregiments', Glückstadt-Hamburg-New York, J. J. Augustin, 1937.

Tröbst H., Leipold A., 'Das Posensche Pionier-Bataillon Nr. 29 und seine Kriegsformationen Res.-Pion.-Batl. 33, Pion.-Komp. 107, 361 und 401, Pion.-Bel.-Tr. 10 und 29', Berlin, Wilhelm Kolk, 1932.

Unruh K. 'Langemarck. Legende und Wirklichkeit', Koblenz, Bernard & Graefe Verlag, 1986.

Van Acker L., 'Overzicht van de geologie in Vlaanderen', Biekorf. Jaargang 68. Sint-Andries, E. Vercrysse en Zoon, 1967, pp.19-24.

Vancoillie J. 'Bissegem 1914-1918. Tussen Flugplatz en Munitionslager', Wevelgem, Jan Vancoillie, 2016.

Vancoillie J. 'De Duitse militaire begraafplaats Menen Wald. Geschiedenis van de Duitse militaire graven van de Eerste Wereldoorlog in Zuid-West-Vlaanderen', Wevelgem, Jan Vancoillie, 2013.

Vancoillie J. 'Halfweg Menin Road en Ypernstrasse. Gheluvelt 1914-1918', Association for Battlefield Archaeology in Flanders Studies 3, Voormezele, Association for Battlefield Archaeology in Flanders vzw, 2002.

Van Hoonacker E. 'Kortrijk 14-18. Een stad tijdens de Eerste Wereldoorlog', E. Van Hoonacker, Kortrijk, Groeninghe, 1994.

Verdonck A., Vermeiren E., Troubleyn R. 'Zeldzame reminiscenties van de Grooten Oorlog: archivalisch en bouwtechnisch onderzoek van de legerbarakken in Jabbeke (prov. West-Vl.)', Relicta, 8 (2011).

Vermessungs-Abteilung 1 beim A.O.K. 4, 'Batterie-Karte Diksmuide-Süd Blatt IX v. 22.6.1917', German military map, 1917.

Vermessungs-Abteilung 1 beim A.O.K. 4, 'Stellungs-Karte Ypernbogen-Süd Blatt V v. 4. Dezember 1916', German military map, 1916.

von Gemmingen-Guttenberg-Fürfeld, 'Das Grenadier-Regiment Königin Olga (1. Württ.) Nr. 119 im Weltkrieg 1914-1918', Die württembergischen Regimenter im Weltkrieg 1914-1918 39, Stuttgart, Chr. Belser A.G., 1927.

von Loßberg F., 'Meine Tätigkeit im Weltkriege 1914-1918', Berlin, E. S. Mitller & Sohn, 1939.

von Velsen S., 'Das Militäreisenbahnwesen (Eisenbahnen und Schiffahrt)', Der Weltkampf um Ehre und Recht Band 6, Leipzig, 1921.

von Winterfeldt H., 'Die deutsche Verwaltung des Generalgouvernements in Belgien', Der Weltkampf um Ehre und Recht Band 8, Leipzig, o.J., pp. 1-111.

Weber E., Struß H. 'Das Landwehr-Infanterie-Regiment Nr. 77', Erinnerungsblätter Preußen 49, Oldenburg-Berlin, Gerhard Stalling, 1922.

Winter, M. 'Institutionalisierte Hygiene in Deutschland unter den Bedingungen des Krieges 1914-1918 : Personen, Problemstellungen, Ideologien', Neuere Medizin- und Wissenschaftsgeschichte : Quellen und Studien 35, Freiburg im Breisgau, Centaurus-Verlag, 2013.

Wynne G. C. 'If Germany Attacks. The Battle in Depth in the West', London, Faber and Faber Ltd., 1940.

Websites

http://1914-1918.invisionzone.com/forums/
https://inventaris.onroerenderfgoed.be/
http://www.ancestry.de

Index

Note: *The complexity of the lines included in (and the number of) the various* Flandern Stellungen, *as well as their redesignations during the war, makes it practically impossible to index them suitably.*

Albrecht Stellung, ix, 7, 16–18, 21, 23–4, 32, 43, 59, 68, 92, 110, 117, 119, 146, 180–2, 190, 254, 261
Almenhof, 182, 184
ANZAC Strong Post, 105
Ardooie, 137, 139, 141, 222

Basse Ville, 24
Bayern Stellung, 26
Bayernwald, 20
Beitem/Beythem, 132, 152, 198, 203
Bellewaarde/Bellewaerde 6, 169–70
Beselare/Becelaere, xxi, 2, 78–9, 123, 139, 188–9, 192–3
Bikschote/Bixschoote, 59, 117, 145
Bissegem, 139, 198, 206, 222
Boezinge/Boesinghe, 83, 109, 110
    Bois de Wytschaete, 112
Bois Quarante, *see* Bayernwald
Brandenburg Werk, 23, 177, 182
Bremen Redoubt, *see* Brandenburg Werk
British Expeditionary Force,
    Guards Division, 266
    9th (Scottish) Division, 271
    16th (Irish) Division, 244
    29th Division, 266
    34th Division, 246, 263, 264, 266
    47th (2nd London) Division, 254
    66th (2nd East Lancashire) Division, 259
    New Zealand Division, xvii, 31
    1/5th King's Own Scottish Borderers, 246
    6th Royal Irish Rifles, 244

1/7th (City of London) London Regiment, 254
40th Battalion AIF, 259

Camp Marguerre, 86
Clapham Junction/Zandberg, 16, 169, 172
Comines, 97, 220, 233–4
Cryer Farm, 75, 98

Dadizele, x, 25, 113, 132–3, 146, 152, 188–90, 193, 206, 234, 279
Diksmuide/Dixmude, xi, 55, 59, 137, 139, 222, 235
Doppelhöhe 60/Tor Top, 166–7
Drie Grachten, 93

Einheitsunterstand, 73–4, 88, 90, 98, 105, 112–15, 152, 156, 270, 281
Einsdijk, 61, 186, 235–8

Falkenhayn, 15, 116, 175
Franken Stellung, 25–6
Frezenberg, 111, 175, 177, 180, 184, 188–9
Füßlein, Oberstleutnant, 128–9

Garde-Dieu, 24
Geluveld/Gheluvelt, xvi–xviii, xx, xxiii, 9, 18, 23, 33, 65, 108, 123, 128, 145, 159, 171–2, 188–90, 192, 224, 234, 251, 255, 278
Geluwe/Gheluwe, 100, 133, 188–90
Gent/Ghent, 50–1, 142, 192, 207, 214, 228
Gentbrugge, 214
Genter Baracke, 49–52, 58, 214, 235, 238

German Army,
  Army Corps,
    XIII Armeekorps, 18, 186–7
    XV Armeekorps, 167, 170, 185–6, 194, 215, 231–2
    XIX Armeekorps, 3, 59
    IX Reservekorps, 59, 118, 159
    XII Reservekorps, 118, 129
    XXIII Reservekorps, 185–6, 194
    XXVI Reservekorps, 16, 32, 174, 185–6, 194, 200
    XXVII Reservekorps, 194
    III Bayerisches Armeekorps, 118
    Gruppe Gent, 118, 127, 129, 132–3, 137, 139, 204–205, 214, 228
    Gruppe Lille, 29, 133
    Gruppe Nord, 139, 206, 222
    Gruppe Wijtschate, 129, 159, 187, 222, 228
    Gruppe Ypres, 44, 118–19, 123, 128–9, 132–3, 137, 139, 152, 222, 228
    Marinekorps, 59, 139, 185–6, 194, 206, 222
  Divisions,
    15th Infanterie Division, 133
    16th Infanterie Division, 133
    17th Infanterie Division, 44, 145
    25th Infanterie Division, 123, 146
    27th Infanterie Division, 38, 146
    30th Infanterie Division, 159, 186
    38th Infanterie Division, 145
    39th Infanterie Division, 185–6
    119th Infanterie Division, 192
    185th Infanterie Division, 176, 180–1, 183, 185, 262
    195th Infanterie Division, 128, 192
    204th Infanterie Division, 59
    207th Infanterie Division, 59, 189, 192
    233rd Infanterie Division, 44
    17th Reserve Division, 32, 176, 180, 183
    25th Reserve Division, 3
    49th Reserve Division, 145
    51st Reserve Division, 174, 186
    52nd Reserve Division, 185
    1st Bayerische Reserve Division, 159
    6th Bayerische Reserve Division, 192, 245
    19th Landwehr Division, 59
    20th Landwehr Division, 59
    21st Landwehr Division, 117
    4th Ersatz Division, 188–9
    5th Ersatz Division, 186
    2nd Marine Division, 185
    3rd Marine Division, 90
  Brigades,
    1st Landsturm Infanterie Brigade, 119
    11th Landwehr Brigade, 117–18
  Regiments,
    Infanterie Regiment 65, 182
    Infanterie Regiment 105, 171
    Infanterie Regiment 120, 148
    Infanterie Regiment 121, 266
    Grenadier Regiment 123, 147
    Infanterie Regiment 124, 147
    Infanterie Regiment 125, 50
    Infanterie Regiment 126, 159–72
    Infanterie Regiment 132, 171
    Infanterie Regiment 143, 49
    Infanterie Regiment 161, 181–3
    Infanterie Regiment 162, 178, 183
    Infanterie Regiment 163, 176, 178–9, 182
    Infanterie Regiment 172, 28, 171
    Infanterie Regiment 188, 79
    Infanterie Regiment 417, 266
    Bayerisches Infanterie Regiment 6, 266
    Bayerisches Infanterie Regiment 22, 88
    Landwehr Infanterie Regiment 35, 56, 58, 117
    Landwehr Infanterie Regiment 77, 39, 55–6, 157
    Reserve Infanterie Regiment 28, 180, 183, 262
    Reserve Infanterie Regiment 65, 266
    Reserve Infanterie Regiment 76, 177
    Reserve Infanterie Regiment 119, 266
    Reserve Infanterie Regiment 209, 98, 254
    Reserve Infanterie Regiment 235, 19
    Reserve Infanterie Regiment 236, 3, 262
    Reserve Infanterie Regiment 245, 2–3
    Reserve Infanterie Regiment 247, 8
    Bayerisches Reserve Infanterie Regiment 4, 254
    Landsturm Infanterie Regiment 39, 123, 128
  Jäger,
    Reserve Jäger Bataillon, 5, 56, 198
  Armierungstruppen,
    Armierungs Bataillon 27, 186, 188, 250

Armierungs Bataillon 32, 119
Armierungs Bataillon 33, 186–7
Armierungs Bataillon 35, 119, 186
Armierungs Bataillon 48, 186
Armierungs Bataillon 65, 119
Armierungs Bataillon 78, 187
Armierungs Bataillon 86, 119
Armierungs Bataillon 124, 185–6
Armierungs Bataillon 131, 188–93
Bayerisches Armierungs Bataillon 1, 32, 185
Pioniere,
Stopi 40b, 139
Stopi 62, 129, 193
Stopi 154, 139
Pionier Regiment 24, 144, 188–9
Pionier Regiment 25, 144
Kavallerie Pionier Abteilung 3, 3–4
Minenwerfer Kompagnie 27, 44
Pionier Bataillon 4, 235–6
Pionier Bataillon 6, 148
Pionier Bataillon 8, 133, 146
Pionier Bataillon 11, 3–4, 145
Pionier Bataillon 13, 61, 146–51
Pionier Bataillon 15, 146
Pionier Bataillon 22, 171
Pionier Bataillon 23, 132–3, 136, 152, 157, 271
Pionier Bataillon 28, 182
Pionier Bataillon 125, 133
Bayerisches Pionier Bataillon 5, 119
Pionier Kompagnie 237, 192
Pionier Kompagnie 304, 188, 235
Pionier Kompagnie 334, 117
Pionier Kompagnie 336, 119
Bayerische Pionier Kompagnie 16, 119
Bayerische Pionier Kompagnie 17, 119
Reserve Pionier Kompagnie 49, 145
Reserve Pionier Kompagnie 89, 123, 146
Bayerische Reserve Pionier Kompagnie 4, 119
Pionier Mineur Kompagnie 294, 44, 119
Pionier Mineur Kompagnie 322, 44
Pionier Versuchs Kompagnie, 90, 189
3rd Landwehr Pionier Kompagnie des XIII Armeekorps, 152–7, 270–1
3rd Landsturm Pionier Kompagnie des XIX Armeekorps, 145

Other,
Armee Oberkommando 4, 49, 123
Etappen Inspektion 4, 132
Baudirektion 4, 49–50, 225–6
Fuhrpark Kolonne 788, 119
Italiener Kommando I, 196
Italiener Kommando XII, 196
Kriegsgefangenen Arbeiter Bataillon 10, 194
Kriegsgefangenen Arbeiter Bataillon 29, 194–6, 211, 214
Landsturm Infanterie Bataillon Calw, 119
Landsturm Infanterie Bataillon Regensburg (IIIB/14), 128
Landsturm Infanterie Ersatz Bataillon Kassel 2 (XI/6), 194
Bayerische Landsturm Infanterie Ersatz Bataillon Zweibrücken Kaiserslautern (IIB/12), 195
Militär Eisenbahn Direktion 1, 219
Militär Eisenbahn Direktion 3, 197
Militär General Direktion Brüssel, 219
Reserve Feldartillerie Regiment 51, 172–6
Sanitäts Kompagnie 563, 97
Straßenbau Kompagnie 4, 226–7
Straßenbau Kompagnie 23, 226
Glencorse Wood, xxi

Halluin, 137, 192, 212, 214
Hanebeek, 74–5, 80, 177
Herenthage, xxi, 37, 50, 112, 192, 224
Hill 32, 173
Hill 35, 173
Hill 41, 25
   see also Kezelberg
Hill 60, 6, 159–60, 166
Hindenburg, 42, 116, 143, 195, 218
Höhe 28/Plum Farm, 177
Höhe 55 see Zandberg, 169
Höhen Stellung, 24
Holland Stellung, 60, 66, 132, 139
Hollebeke, 85
Hooge, xvi, xxi, 7, 9, 12, 28, 168–72, 186, 224
Hooglede, 132, 200–201, 203
Houthem, 233
Houthulst, xvi, 78, 99, 117, 119, 129, 139, 194

Houthulst Forest, xx, xxii, 35, 48, 56–7, 107, 119, 128, 139, 149–50, 220, 266–7, 278
Hunding Stellung, 116

Inverness Copse, xxi, xxiii, 112

Kalve, 48, 55, 148
Kantintje Cabaret, 7, 9, 18, 172, 192
Kezelberg, 25, 132, 206
Kit and Kat, 104
Klein Zillebeke, 28, 41, 76, 159, 161
Klerken/Clercken, 117
Koekelare, 61, 137, 200, 234
Koelenberg, 128
Kortrijk/Courtrai, 137, 197–8, 200, 214–15, 218, 220, 228, 271
Kruiseke, 48, 112, 128, 162

Langemark, 18, 33, 63, 69, 109, 117, 122, 128, 145, 148, 172, 174, 176, 186, 195, 261, 263, 266
Ledegem, 73, 133, 136, 137, 139, 152–57, 188–9, 194, 205–206, 222, 234, 270–1, 280
Lille, 127, 132, 219, 228
Lord Farm, 152–3, 270–1
Low Farm, 110–11, 180
    see also Ostermorgengut
Ludendorff, 13, 42, 116, 143, 195, 218
Luigem/Luyghem, 99
Lys, xi, xvii, 14, 23–4, 126, 137, 139, 142, 222, 228–30, 245, 254

Maurerhof, 178
Melaene Cabaret, 56
Menin Road, xxii, xxiii, 7, 9, 18, 33, 37, 108, 128, 169, 171–2, 185, 188–9, 224, 254
Mesen/Messines, xvii, xviii, 11, 13, 16, 18, 24, 43, 118, 126–8, 186, 207, 234, 240, 242, 244, 248, 277
Michel Stellung, 116
Molenhoek (near Beselare), 78, 188–9, 192–4
Moorsele/Morseele, 25, 132, 193, 203–204
Moorslede, x, 44, 46, 129, 132, 137, 146, 152, 178, 194, 201, 220–1
Mosselmarkt, 44, 55
Mount Sorrel, 6, 159, 166

Nonne Bosschen, xxi

Oostende/Ostend, 137, 185, 194
Oostnieuwkerke, 55
Oosttaverne, 24, 29, 108
Ostermorgengut, 110–11, 180
Otto Farm, 182
    see also Almenhof
Oudenaarde, 203

Panama Kanal, 176–8
Passendale, ix–x, xvii, xviii, 31, 38–9, 44–5, 48, 55, 88, 117, 119, 122, 128, 132, 135, 137, 146, 148–9, 157, 176–7, 183–4, 201, 258
Pilkem/Pilckem, 16, 60, 145, 177
Poelkapelle, 32, 39, 90, 145, 157, 172, 182, 185–6, 223, 235, 261, 266
Polderhoek (near Geluveld), xxi, 192
Polygon Wood, xx, xxi, 18, 190, 192–3
Pond Farm, 92, 261
Potsdam Redoubt, 23, 43
Preußen Stellung, 25–6

Ravebeek, xvii
Rollegem-Kapelle, 146
Roulers/Roeselare, x, xxii, 25, 43, 61, 94, 117, 132–3, 135–7, 139, 141, 152, 172, 176, 193–4, 196, 198, 200–201, 220–1, 229, 234, 271
Ruisbroek, 214

Sanctuary Wood, xx
Sehnen Stellung, 24
's Graventafel/Grafenstafel, 31, 149
Shrewsbury Forest, xxi, 162, 163
Siegfried Stellung/Hindenburg Line, 47, 92, 116, 209, 210
Sint-Elooi/St Eloi, 24
Sint-Juliaan/St Julien, 32, 92, 111, 174, 177–8, 261–2
Sint-Pieter (near Ledegem), 152, 205, 270
Slypskapelle, 152–3
Spa, 215
Springfield, 178
Staden, 58, 117, 139, 149, 151, 194, 200, 219, 221–2
Stadenberg, 46
Stadendreef, 46

Stampkot, 58, 149–51
Stirling Castle, 38–9

Ten Brielen/Tenbrielen, 48, 126, 146, 194, 248
Terhand, 128, 188–90, 192–4
Thames House, 94–5
Torhout, 137, 194, 200, 211
Trichterstellung, 13
Tyne Cot, 124, 254, 258–60

Veldhoek (near Geluveld), x, 170–2, 188, 190, 192,
    224, 234
Verlorenhoek, 15, 16, 44, 176, 182
Vijfwege (near Dadizele), 190–2
Vijfwegen (near Staden), 117, 145, 221

Wallemolen, 39, 157
Warneton, 24, 106, 242
Wervik/Wervicq, 61, 64–5, 126, 137, 194, 215, 231–2,
    234, 248
Wervicq Sud, 211
Westfälische Bauindustrie A.G., 225–6
Westrozebeke, 45, 84, 117, 119, 123, 137, 145, 148–9,
    172, 178, 194

White Chateau/Château Mahieu, 24
Wijtschate/Wytschaete, xviii, xxi, 3, 13, 24, 29, 62,
    101, 110, 112, 118, 123, 148, 192, 223, 234, 240, 244
Wilhelm Stellung, ix, 7, 17–24, 59, 68, 92, 110, 118–19,
    126, 128, 145, 180–2, 186, 189, 190, 192, 263
Wittenberg Werk, 177, 182
Wotan Stellung, 47, 116, 129, 137
Woumen, 79

Ypres-Comines Canal, 9, 18, 23–4, 32, 43, 126,
    146–7, 185–6
Yser, xi, xvii, 1, 59, 198, 235, 238

Zandvoorde, 41, 48–9, 81–2, 97, 107–108, 126, 159,
    162–3, 166, 248–50
Ziegler bunker, 75, 109–10
Zonnebeke, ix, x, xi, 8, 15, 18–19, 21, 23, 32, 43, 66,
    68, 91, 111, 119, 121, 125, 128, 145, 146, 174,
    176–8, 182–3, 188–90, 234, 251, 254–5
Zonnebeke Redoubt, 23
Zwarteleen, 159–60, 162
Zwevegem, 197, 214